THE NOVEL TODAY

MALCOLM BRADBURY is a leading British novelist, literary critic and television dramatist. Born in 1932, he attended the University College of Leicester, Queen Mary College, London, and Indiana, Yale and Harvard Universities. His first novel, *Eating People Is Wrong*, appeared in 1959, just as he began his academic career teaching at Hull University. He moved to Birmingham University and then in 1966 to the University of East Anglia, Norwich, where he is currently part-time Professor of American Studies and teaches an MA course in Creative Writing.

He has published many works of criticism, including *Possibilities: Essays on the State of the Novel* (1973), *Saul Bellow* (1982), *The Modern American Novel* (1983), *The Modern World: Ten Great Writers* (1988), and *No, Not Bloomsbury* (1988), the first volume of his collected essays. He has edited various volumes including the Penguin *Modernism* (1976), *An Introduction to American Studies* (1981, 1989) and *The Penguin Book of Modern British Short Stories* (1987).

His novels include *Stepping Westward* (1965), *The History Man* (1975), *Rates of Exchange* (1983) and *Cuts* (1987). Some of his television plays are collected in *The After Dinner Game* (1982), and his work for television includes two series, *Anything More Would Be Greedy* (1989) and *The Gravy Train* (1990), as well as adaptations of Tom Sharpe's *Blott on the Landscape* and *Porterhouse Blue* and

Friends.

He is a Fellow of the Royal has honorary degrees from Le

THE NOVEL TODAY

Contemporary Writers on Modern Fiction

Edited by

MALCOLM BRADBURY

New Edition

fp

FONTANA PRESS

First published by Fontana Paperbacks in 1977
This revised edition published by Fontana Press in 1990

Copyright © in the selection Malcolm Bradbury 1977, 1990

Copyright © in the Introduction Malcolm Bradbury 1990

'Against Dryness' copyright © Iris Murdoch 1961; reprinted with permission from *Encounter*, January 1961

'Writing American Fiction' copyright © Philip Roth 1961, 1975; reprinted with permission from *Reading Myself and Others*, Farrar, Straus and Giroux, 1975

'The Novel as Research' copyright © Michel Butor 1970; reprinted with permission from *Inventory: Essays*, Jonathan Cape, 1970; Simon and Schuster, 1968

'Some Notes on Recent American Fiction' copyright © Saul Bellow 1963; reprinted with permission from *Encounter*, 1963

'The Literature of Exhaustion' is reprinted by permission of Lurton Blassingame, the author's agent, copyright © Atlantic Monthly Company 1967

'The Novelist at the Crossroads' copyright © David Lodge 1969; reprinted, abridged, with permission from *The Novelist at the Crossroads*, Routledge, 1971; Cornell, 1971

'The House of Fiction' copyright © *Partisan Review* 1963; reprinted with permission from *Partisan Review*, Vol. xxx, no. 1, Spring 1963

'Notes on an Unfinished Novel' copyright © John Fowles 1969; reprinted with permission from *Afterwords*, ed. by Thomas McCormack, Harper and Row, 1969

'Introduction to *Aren't You Rather Young to be Writing Your Memoirs?*' copyright © the Estate of B. S. Johnson 1973; reprinted with permission from *Aren't You Rather Young to be Writing Your Memoirs?*, Hutchinson, 1973

'Preface to *The Golden Notebook*' copyright © Doris Lessing 1962; reprinted with permission from *The Golden Notebook*, Simon and Schuster, 1972; Michael Joseph, new edition, 1972; Panther Books, 1973

'An Interview with Milan Kundera' copyright © Ian McEwan 1984; reprinted with permission from *Granta* No. 11, 1984

'Cybernetics and Ghosts' reprinted with permission from *The Literature Machine: Essays* trans. Patrick Creagh, © Giulio Einandi editor s.p.a., Torino 1982, English translation © Harcourt Brace Jovanovich Inc. 1982, Secker and Warburg, 1987

The photographs in this book are reproduced by kind permission of the following: Iris Murdoch, Universal Pictorial Press & Agency Ltd (UPPA); Philip Roth, Judy Feiffer; Michel Butor, Etienne Hubert; Saul Bellow, Thomas Victor; David Lodge, Andrew Douglas; John Fowles, UPPA; B. S. Johnson, Mike King; Doris Lessing, UPPA; Italo Calvino, Jerry Bauer; Milan Kundera, Otto Aaron Manheimer.

Printed and bound in Great Britain by William Collins Sons & Co., Glasgow
Fontana Press is an imprint of Fontana Paperbacks, part of the Collins
Publishing Group, 8 Grafton Street, London W1X 3LA

CONTENTS

Introduction to the 1990 Edition

Fiction writing, unlike reportage, eye-witness accounts or scientific descriptions, isn't trying to give information – it *constitutes* reality.
Alain Robbe-Grillet, *From Realism to Reality* (1955)

I began to write fiction on the assumption that the true enemies of the novel were plot, character, setting and theme, and, having once abandoned these familiar ways of thinking about fiction, totality of vision or structure was really all that remained. And structure – verbal and psychological coherence – is still my largest concern as a writer.
John Hawkes, in an interview (1965)

As I have pointed out before, characters are not born like people, of a woman; they are born of a situation, a sentence, a metaphor containing in a nutshell a basic human possibility that the author thinks no one else has discovered or said something essential about.
Milan Kundera, *The Unbearable Lightness of Being* (1984)

I

This is a new and changed edition of a book first published in 1977* – a collection of essays by or interviews with some of the most important contemporary novelists, British, American, European, who have commented seriously and well on both their own work and the situation of the novel today. Reprinted from various sources, the pieces represent, I believe, some of the

* The essays by Philip Stevick and Gerald Graff which appeared in the 1977 edition have been replaced in this edition by the essay by Italo Calvino and Ian McEwan's interview with Milan Kundera.

most interesting opinions we can find on contemporary fiction. They are also concerned not just with the individual creativity of these writers, but the fact that in our age fiction has developed its own distinctive practices, its own climate, its own particular sense of direction. That, I think, has grown much more obvious to readers now than it was when this anthology was first compiled. In the last few years we have increasingly recognized the scale and achievement of contemporary fiction, and the fact that it does have its own clear character, in many ways different from the fiction of the past. The novel now has a flourishing appearance; after a period of appearing little more than commonplace, it has regained much of its stature and its artistic and intellectual interest. Many things have helped. There has been an increase in public discussion, major publishers have concentrated on it, and even the proliferation of literary prizes for fiction has done much to draw attention to contemporary talents. Perhaps, as readers, we are more prepared than a few years ago to acknowledge that we do have our own distinctive fictional tradition – a novel for our own age, the age after the Modern.

Collecting up the pieces for this book, I have assumed that there is always something inherently pleasurable and rewarding about hearing a good writer describe the stimuli, the direction and the nature of his or her creativity. Sometimes such accounts are fundamentally subjective, not surprisingly; fiction has its natural source in subjectivity. But it also depends on larger things – a broader conception of the task of the novel, of the writer's responsibility, the pressures of history on literary form, the need for the novel to discover both the world and the word anew. I find novelists at their most interesting and revealing when they are conscious that the writing of fiction is not only a psychological and aesthetic, but a social and historical, act. The novel has always been a provisional, self-questioning form; and its best practitioners have always seen part of their task as testing out the contemporary nature of the form they use. Novels are complex literary contracts made between the author and a life that becomes imaginatively real and powerful because it has passed through the public fact of a publication and a relation with its reader. They are forms of exploration, enquiring modes of knowledge, and as concepts become written words they become part of the fictional self-discovery of their own times. Like all knowledge, the novel changes with history and its own environment. It depends on its own relation to other discovering languages – those of science, philosophy, history, journalism, travel-writing, autobiography. It is altered by historical events and shifts in ideology and social and gender relations. At the same time it fights its own case for the fictional and discovering imagination amongst the ideas, the politics, the social emphases, the world-views of its times. Styles transform; literary forms reshape and reorder; discovering fictions understand themselves in new ways and use new means. The novel may by now appear a traditional genre, but it is and always has been different in every age.

Indeed the word *novel* means new, and news. When in the seventeenth and eighteenth centuries the novel in Europe became a public literary genre – the 'burgher epic' – it was new indeed. From the start there was a question over its character: was it a predominantly realistic, reportorial genre, a form of biography, history and reportage, or was it essentially a form dedicated to its *own* discovery, a self-sceptical species of art? That double role remains with us, and throughout its recent history the novel has seemed to oscillate in its function. Sometimes it seems a more or less innocent affair, an instrument that expresses our delight in being told a human and familiar story, given important social or historical information, satisfied by the well-resolved plot, the engaging character, the happy ending. Sometimes it seems a radical grammar for exploring experience, consciousness, psychology, the fiction-making process itself. These two functions have always both consorted and contested with each other. In the nineteenth century much of the major fiction inclined toward the realistic, or what Henry James called 'solidity of specification'. In the early twentieth century much of it was predominantly experimental and self-questioning, a development that Henry James was also to celebrate. 'It has arrived, in truth, the novel, late at self-consciousness, but it has done its utmost ever since to make up for lost opportunities,' he wrote in an essay called 'The Future of Fiction', written exactly as the twentieth century came into existence. The self-consciousness James was pointing to marked the growing of a split between the novel as popular form or merchandise, and the novel as art. It also marked the emergence of a new experimental avant-garde, for whom the established traditions of art were over, the forms exhausted, and the age demanded something new. So there seemed to be an Old Novel, moral, realistic and bourgeois, and a New Novel, exploring the mythic and symbolic sources of fiction, its creative nature, and the gap between the word and the thing.

That change, that oscillation, has left us with two different codes for talking about the novel. One, coming from the aesthetics of realism, emphasizes plot and character, setting and theme, denouement and discovery. The other comes from the new symbolist aesthetics of what came to be called the Modern Movement, and it emphasized other terms: myth, symbol, abstraction, angle of vision, point of view, stream of consciousness. The war was fought through several famous duels – between Henry James and H. G. Wells, Virginia Woolf and Arnold Bennett, Marcel Proust and Sainte-Beuve – and it represented a fundamental revolution, a Revolution of the Word, even a Death of the Novel. Certainly the Modern Novel, the New Novel, began to dispense with much of the novel's familiar realism and its dense and habitual sense of character and plot, setting and atmosphere, chronological and historical time. It probed deeper into consciousness, individual and collective, looked outward at a world that seemed less a clear material substance than a place of random time and chaotic history, and it pluralized awareness, multiplied perception, ironized narrative, and looked directly into its own formal nature as art. It became an art of refined practitioners, and many of them – Conrad, Lawrence, Mann, Joyce, Proust, Stein, Svevo, Musil, Woolf, Faulkner, Hemingway, Gide, Kafka – still dominate our sense of the serious novel, our fictionalizing imagination, today.

4

Their work examines itself and discovers itself; their notebooks, diaries and essays, as well as their novels themselves, declare a new historical, aesthetic and creative intention. The novel, once thought of as a lower form, took on the character of a major literary genre, a true companion to poetry and drama.

With the modern novel there therefore came modern criticism. Henry James saw the great reappraisal as essentially an affair of practitioners, of novelists exploring and reflecting on the imaginary and imaginative worlds they sought to compose. But the growing critical movement, developing alongside the systematic study of literature, took to the study of the novel; and in time it came to seem that it was not what novelists said about it but what the critics said that constituted the only worthwhile or reliable interpretation. The critics saw a new art of estrangement and polyphony, explored what Mark Schorer called 'technique as discovery', and acknowledged the novel as a serious form of human investigation, the 'bright book of life'. They constructed the Great Traditions, wove the lineages and inheritances, created complex theories of narratology, examined the nature of the text and the language of fiction. In time, they then deconstructed what they had constructed. In the process a speculative gap often began to appear between what the critics were perceiving and what contemporary novelists were actually doing; and the voice of novelists as makers and finders in their own medium began to grow smaller. It is therefore worth making the point that what modern critics and what novelists are there to do is different, though not unconnected. The critic's task is indeed to explore the history of genres, the nature of imaginative discourse, the conditions of artistic existence; it was also, once, to pursue standards of judgement, measures of seriousness, standards of taste. The novelist's business at best is to make himself or herself an exemplary creative citizen of a world which is still occurring and which needs to be named into existence, to invent the possibilities of an imaginary book in a universe that needs to find names for things. He or she works inside a convention that always has to be de-conventionalized in order to generate a new work authentic to the author and the contemporary occasion.

That is why, in an age remarkably dominated by criticism and literary theory, but not, alas, by a general aesthetic debate, it seems important to allow the author's voice to be heard in a book like this one. Selecting the pieces here, I have tried to think of them as important contributions to the practitioners' debate that, at best, should always surround the making of an art-form. Such debate, of course, goes on inside the novel, in the pages of the works we read, as well as outside and around it. There are writers who prefer their books to be their own commentary, and there are writers who sometimes seem better at commentary than they are as writers. Nonetheless, somewhat muted by the prevalence of critical theory, there has been an important contemporary debate taking place among writers themselves. It has perhaps been most visible in France, where the novel is considered as a philosophical form, and in the United States, where writers have often had academic associations, and where in the 1960s and 1970s novelists like John Barth, William H. Gass and Raymond Federman did attempt some reconciliation between dominant critical ideas and their sense of contemporary literary practice. In France we heard of the *nouveau roman*, and in the United States of 'the literature of exhaustion', 'metafiction' and 'surfiction'. What these writers were very properly reaching for was the notion that we were living in a distinctive age of style, a time that the French writer Nathalie Sarraute called 'the era of suspicion' and American writers sometimes called 'post-modernism'. Whether the terms are useful can still be argued about, as we shall see. The important thing, one I have kept in mind in compiling this anthology, is that in the debate of any given era certain fundamental themes and directions do begin to emerge out of the continued variety, and that the novel in a particular period does begin to take on a distinctive historical character which audiences often take time to grasp.

II

The era of contemporary writing is still called the post-war era, though almost fifty years have now passed since the end of World War II and we are now approaching the end of the twentieth century or the second millenium. The forty years before that war largely made up the period in which the modern literary revolution was conducted, and it went through many movements, many phases, many reverses and upsets, as well as coming from many sources and many different nationalities. With the Second World War, that era and its literary revolution seemed to be over, and after it a shattered world had to reshape itself. Because it seemed over, the Modern Movement now began to acquire a certain clarity and shape, and the several generations of major novelists whose work had developed then took on a central position and a power over our imaginations that still continues. The post-war period has not assumed the same clarity, even though, I believe, it will prove to have a similar scale of achievement. This is partly because we consider that we still live in it, and it has the disorder of the contemporary, partly because it is not distinguished by a sense of radical revolution, and partly because its achievement has been generally more various.

So it is hard to take a general view of an age that contains the wide variety of directions we find in it. It reaches, for example, from the existentialist minimalism of Samuel Beckett and the fictions of Jorge Luis Borges, preoccupied with the status of imaginary acts and the relation between the orders of the mind and those of the universe, to the fragile, imagined worlds of Vladimir Nabokov, unrooted from conventional reality, rich in fictionality, shimmering with a potential symbolism. It spreads from the tight, object-centred, anti-anthropomorphic economy of French *nouveaux romanciers* like Michel Butor, Alain Robbe-Grillet and Nathalie Sarraute to the often contingent but always romantically vivid and highly staged world of Iris Murdoch, and to the flamboyance of Patrick White or the surreal expressionism of Günter Grass. It ranges from the attempts of John Barth to recover a literature of replenishment from an era of literary exhaustion, by modernizing the narrative stock bequeathed us by great narratives like *The 1001 Nights* or Greek legend, to the cybernetic novels of Thomas Pynchon or William Gaddis, where the characters become comic units swamped in a technological world coded with arbitrary plots. It includes the hard ironic black comedy of Muriel Spark and the romantic existentialism of John Fowles and the galactic fantasy of Doris Lessing. It takes in the combinatorial games of Italo Calvino and the rich storytelling invention and 'magic realism' of writers like Gabriel Garcia Marquez and Salman Rushdie; the black feminist novel of Toni Morrison and the feminist fantasy of Angela Carter.

Indeed the contemporary novel is now a very broad community indeed, one which includes amongst its important citizens Max Frisch and Thomas Bernhard, Christa Wolf, Peter Handke and Patrick Süskind, Saul Bellow, Philip Roth, Norman Mailer and John Updike, Eudora Welty, William Burroughs and Richard Brautigan, Muriel Spark, Ian McEwan and B. S. Johnson, Claude Simon, Philippe Sollers, Michel Tournier, Milan Kundera, Vladimir Voinovich and Georges Perec – the list can go on and on. As our international sightlines widen, as our sense of each new generation deepens, we are constantly finding significant and central names to add to it, and that increases our sense of variety and plenitude.

Our modern writing comes out of a world that in some postwar nations saw a climate of victory, in others defeat, in others a bitter legacy of occupation. It also comes from a world divided into two camps and from a time when political fortunes and allegiances among writers have been varied, political pressures and punishments different. It comes too from a world that has grown larger, and many of our most interesting writers come from post-colonial nations, from countries like Canada and Australia, and from Africa and South America. It arises too from a changed world of gender relations which has seen the rise of a new and international tradition of feminist writing that has challenged the myths and prototypes of the fictional tradition. It is inevitably hard to identify broad trends, though I think there are a few markers that might give us some sense of the directions and eddies that have shaped the general pattern of contemporary novel writing.

So in the 1950s it appeared that the movement of Modernism was over, and that the novel was now returning toward a more traditional and realistic view of fiction, pressed perhaps by the immensity of recent history and the strong sense of social change. In France we saw the existentialist novel; in Britain an attempt to return to the line of eighteenth- and nineteenth-century fiction; in Germany the work of writers like Heinrich Böll who were attempting to give a more honest record of recent events; in America the moral realism of Jewish-American fiction.

In the 1960s, when the powerful impact of writers like Beckett, Borges and Nabokov, who had extended many of the experimental possibilities of Modernism, became clear, matters looked different. The movement now seemed to be away from realism and toward what came to be called 'metafiction' – a kind of novel that emphasized its own fictionality and its self-begetting character. There was the impact of the French *nouveau roman* as it had developed during the 1950s, emphasizing the lexical nature of the text and foregrounding certain elements in it, states of mind, objects of description; there was the impact of the Nabokovian view of the fictional process as a parody of form, a game-like construct in which the very relationship of author to text, character to language, book to reader becomes volatile, so that the novel becomes an instrument whereby any one of its elements can be teased, given or not given significance, created or de-created. Reality, as Nabokov said, was now 'in quotes', and this applied to all forms of writing – even history-writing, journalism or biography.

By the 1970s there was a sophisticated reversion back to a concern with the onerous pressure of history and the real, and a reconciliation was found in 'magic realism', which had its chief origins in South American fiction and interwove the legendary and the historical in a way that began to appeal to writers generally. By the 1980s there was much talk of 'dirty realism', a self-conscious, hyper-detailed form of writing especially associated with American writers like Raymond Carver and Richard Ford.

This all suggests the continuing importance of that oscillation I mentioned at the beginning between two views of the novel, one as a report on history and the social and moral world, the other of it as a self-conscious and self-discovering fiction. As Iris Murdoch says in her important essay of 1961, 'Against Dryness', reprinted here, the novel has repeatedly been drawn between the 'journalistic' impulse, which tends to make it contingent and formless, and the 'crystalline', which tends to lead it toward the 'dry' consolations of form, and make it into a small quasi-allegorical object. These terms do roughly equate with the spirit of nineteenth-century realism and the spirit of twentieth-century modernism, and Murdoch suggests that today writers lie in the shadow of both, attempting in a changed world, with a different imagination of the self, to do something new. It is a theme often referred to in these essays, for instance by David Lodge in his piece 'The Novelist at the Crossroads', where he considers the challenge to realism and the growing stress on the 'fictiveness' of fiction, and the relation between fictional structures and those we meet in journalism, autobiography and history-writing.

It is worth remarking that, of course, realism can be a form of radical experimentalism, as it was in the nineteenth century in the fiction of Flaubert and Dickens, George Eliot and the early Henry James. Similarly, experimental novels are concerned with exploring and discovering, if not directly depicting, a reality, even if it is Nabokov's reality 'in quotes'. 'I presume that the movement of fiction should always be in the direction of what we sense as real,' observes one 'post-modern' American writer, Ronald Sukenick, who calls one of his books, with appropriate paradox, *The Death of the Novel And Other Stories* (1969). 'Its forms are expendable. The novelist accommodates the ongoing flow of experience, smashing anything that impedes him in his sense of it, even if it happens to be the novel.'

In the previous edition of this book, I made much of the

emphasis on 'fictionality'. The argument seemed particularly necessary then because, in Britain at least, there did seem to be a tradition of obstinate and often provincialized realism which limited the invention of the novel and discouraged British readers from taking fair account of major developments that were clearly taking place elsewhere. In fact the break was coming already, in the work of writers like Muriel Spark, Iris Murdoch, Anthony Burgess, Doris Lessing, Angus Wilson and John Fowles, many of them represented here. And by that time we were already seeing the emergence of a striking new generation of writers in Britain – as various as Angela Carter, Ian McEwan, Martin Amis, Julian Barnes, Bruce Chatwyn, Graham Swift and Salman Rushdie – who had broken away from the provincializing spirit of much post-war British fiction. That general widening of horizons has led to a much more expansive and interesting discussion of the novel, and a much wider awareness of its general international character. Today many novelists seem impatient with the inherited codes both of realism and modernism. 'The characters in my novels are my own unrealized possibilities,' writes Milan Kundera in *The Unbearable Lightness of Being* (1984). 'That is why I am equally fond of them all and equally horrified by them. Each one has crossed a border that I myself have circumvented. It is that crossed border (the border beyond which my own "I" ends) which attracts me most. For beyond that border begins the secret the novel asks about. The novel is not the author's confession; it is an investigation of human life in the trap the world has become.'

Perhaps the common theme of the essays I have chosen for this book is that they are in their different ways about reaching for those unrealized possibilities of investigating human life in the trap the world has become. Kundera explains that his own novels are not born, like a child, out of life, but out of 'a situation, a sentence, a metaphor containing in a nutshell a basic human possibility that the author thinks no one else has discovered or said something essential about'. His books, then, are born out of experience and language, and they are endeavours to create a portrait of a reality that is human and has not been finalized, in a history that is not – as it might be for ideologues or politicians – a finished picture. They are both fictional and true, fantastic and realistic, and they relate to the many fictions that surround us while becoming a discovering fiction of their own, perhaps more elusive and teasing, made, as he says, of laughter and forgetting. It is a creative, elusive view of the novel, and it perhaps explains why it seems no longer easy to fix on some distinctive contemporary movement or tendency, or treat contemporary writers with a firm critical finality. Perhaps that is why it is better not to seek a critical finality, but to listen to the writers themselves and hear what they have to say.

IRIS MURDOCH

Against Dryness

A Polemical Sketch

(1961)

The complaints which I wish to make are concerned primarily with prose, not with poetry, and primarily with novels, not with drama; and they are brief, simplified, abstract, and possibly insular. They are not to be construed as implying any precise picture of 'the function of the writer'. It is the function of the writer to write the best book he knows how to write. These remarks have to do with the background to present-day literature, in Liberal democracies in general and Welfare States in particular, in a sense in which this must be the concern of any serious critic.

We live in a scientific and anti-metaphysical age in which the dogmas, images, and precepts of religion have lost much of their power. We have not recovered from two wars and the experience of Hitler. We are also the heirs of the Enlightenment, Romanticism, and the Liberal tradition. These are the elements of our dilemma: whose chief feature, in my view, is that we have been left with far too shallow and flimsy an idea of human personality. I shall explain this.

Philosophy, like the newspapers, is both the guide and the mirror of its age. Let us look quickly at Anglo-Saxon philosophy and at French philosophy and see what picture of human personality we can gain from these two depositories of wisdom. Upon Anglo-Saxon philosophy the two most profound influences have been Hume and Kant: and it is not difficult to see in the current philosophical conception of the person the work of these two great thinkers. This conception consists in the joining of a materialistic behaviourism with a dramatic view of the individual as a solitary will. These subtly give support to each other. From Hume through Bertrand Russell, with friendly help from mathematical logic and science, we derive the idea that reality is finally a quantity of material atoms and that significant discourse must relate itself directly or indirectly to reality so conceived. This position was most picturesquely summed up in Wittgenstein's *Tractatus*. Recent philosophy, especially the later work of Wittgenstein and the work of Gilbert Ryle derivative therefrom, alters this a little. The atomic Humian picture is abandoned in favour of a type of conceptual analysis (in many ways admirable) which emphasizes the structural dependence of concepts upon the public language in which they are framed. This analysis has important results in the philosophy of mind, where it issues in modified behaviourism. Roughly: my inner life, for me just as for others, is identifiable as existing only through the application to it of public concepts, concepts which can only be constructed on the basis of overt behaviour.

This is one side of the picture, the Humian and post-Humian side. On the other side, we derive from Kant, and also Hobbes and Bentham through John Stuart Mill, a picture of the individual as a free rational will. With the removal of Kant's metaphysical background this individual is seen as alone. (He is in a certain sense alone on Kant's view also, that is: not confronted with real dissimilar others.) With the addition of some utilitarian optimism he is seen as eminently educable. With the addition of some modern psychology he is seen as capable of self-knowledge by methods agreeable to science and common sense. So we have the modern man, as he appears in many recent works on ethics and I believe also to a large extent in the popular consciousness.

We meet, for instance, a refined picture of this man in Stuart Hampshire's book *Thought and Action*. He is rational and totally free except in so far as, in the most ordinary law-court and commonsensical sense, his degree of self-awareness may vary. He is, morally speaking, monarch of all he surveys and totally responsible for his actions. Nothing transcends him. His moral language is a practical pointer, the instrument of his choices, the indication of his preferences. His inner life is resolved into his acts and choices, and his beliefs, which are also acts, since a belief can only be identified through its expression. His moral arguments are references to empirical facts backed up by decisions. The only moral word which he requires is 'good' (or 'right'), the word which expresses decision. His rationality expresses itself in awareness of the facts, whether about the world or about himself. The virtue which is fundamental to him is sincerity.

If we turn to French philosophy we may see, at least in that section of it which has most caught the popular imagination. I mean in the work of Jean-Paul Sartre, essentially the same picture. It is interesting how extremely Kantian this picture is, for all Sartre's indebtedness to Hegelian sources. Again, the individual is pictured as solitary and totally free. There is no transcendent reality, there are no degrees of freedom. On the one hand there is the mass of psychological desires and social habits and prejudices, on the other hand there is the will. Certain dramas, more Hegelian in character, are of course enacted within the soul; but the isolation of the will remains. Hence *angoisse*. Hence, too, the special anti-bourgeois flavour of Sartre's philosophy which makes it appeal to many intellectuals: the ordinary traditional picture of personality and the virtues lies under suspicion of *mauvaise foi*. Again the only real virtue is sincerity. It is, I think, no accident that, however much philosophical and other criticism Sartre may receive, this powerful picture has caught our imagination. The Marxist critics may plausibly claim that it represents the essence of the Liberal theory of personality.

It will be pointed out that other phenomenological theories (leaving aside Marxism) have attempted to do what Sartre has failed to do, and that there are notable philosophers who have offered a different picture of the soul. Yes; yet from my own knowledge of the scene I would doubt whether any (non-Marxist) account of human personality has yet emerged from phenomenology which is fundamentally unlike the one which I have described and can vie with it in imaginative power. It may be said that philosophy cannot in fact produce such an account. I am not sure about this, nor is this large question my concern here. I express merely my belief that, for the Liberal world, philosophy is not in fact at present able to offer us any other complete and powerful picture of the soul. I return now to England and the Anglo-Saxon tradition.

The Welfare State has come about as a result, largely, of socialist thinking and socialist endeavour. It has seemed to bring a certain struggle to an end; and with that ending has come a lassitude about fundamentals. If we compare the language of the original Labour Party constitution with that of its recent successor we see an impoverishment of thinking and language which is typical. The Welfare State is the reward of 'empiricism in politics'. It has represented to us a set of thoroughly desirable but limited ends, which could be conceived *in non-theoretical terms*; and in pursuing it, in allowing the idea of it to dominate the more naturally theoretical wing of our political scene, we have to a large extent lost our theories. Our central conception is still a debilitated form of Mill's equation: happiness equals freedom equals personality. There should have been a revolt against utilitarianism; but for many reasons it has not taken place. In 1905 John Maynard Keynes and his friends welcomed the philosophy of G. E. Moore because Moore reinstated the concept of experience, Moore directed attention away from the mechanics of action and towards the inner life. But Moore's 'experience' was too shallow a concept; and a scientific age with simple, attainable, empirical aims has preferred a more behaviouristic philosophy.

What have we lost here? And what have we perhaps never had? We have suffered a general loss of concepts, the loss of a moral and political vocabulary. We no longer use a spread-out substantial picture of the manifold virtues of man and society. We no longer see man against a background of values, of realities, which transcend him. We picture man as a brave naked will surrounded by an easily comprehended empirical world.

For the hard idea of truth we have substituted a facile idea of sincerity. What we have never had, of course, is a satisfactory Liberal theory of personality, a theory of man as free and separate and related to a rich and complicated world from which, as a moral being, he has much to learn. We have bought the Liberal theory as it stands, because we have wished to encourage people to think of themselves as free, at the cost of surrendering the background.

We have never solved the problems about human personality posed by the Enlightenment. Between the various concepts available to us the real question has escaped: and now, in a curious way, our present situation is analogous to an eighteenth-century one. We retain a rationalistic optimism about the beneficent results of education, or rather, technology. We combine this with a romantic conception of 'the human condition', a picture of the individual as stripped and solitary: a conception which has, since Hitler, gained a peculiar intensity.

The eighteenth century was an era of rationalistic allegories and moral tales. The nineteenth century (roughly) was the great era of the novel; and the novel throve upon a dynamic merging of the idea of person with the idea of class. Because nineteenth-century society was dynamic and interesting and because (to use a Marxist notion) the type and the individual could there be seen as merged, the solution of the eighteenth-century problem could be put off. It has been put off till now. Now that the structure of society is less interesting and less alive than it was in the nineteenth century, and now that Welfare economics have removed certain incentives to thinking, and now that the values of science are so much taken for granted, we confront in a particularly dark and confusing form a dilemma which has been with us implicitly since the Enlightenment, or since the beginning, wherever exactly one wishes to place it, of the modern Liberal world.

If we consider twentieth-century literature as compared with nineteenth-century literature, we notice certain significant contrasts. I said that, in a way, we were back in the eighteenth century, the era of rationalistic allegories and moral tales, the era when the idea of human nature was unitary and single. The nineteenth-century novel (I use these terms boldly and roughly: of course there were exceptions) was not concerned with 'the human condition', it was concerned with real various individuals struggling in society. The twentieth-century novel is usually either crystalline or journalistic; that is, it is either a small quasi-allegorical object portraying the human condition and not containing 'characters' in the nineteenth-century sense, or else it is a large shapeless quasi-documentary object, the degenerate descendant of the nineteenth-century novel, telling, with pale conventional characters, some straightforward story enlivened with empirical facts. Neither of these kinds of literature engages with the problem that I mentioned above.

It may readily be noted that if our prose fiction is either crystalline or journalistic, the crystalline works are usually the better ones. They are what the more serious writers want to create. We may recall the ideal of 'dryness' which we associate with the symbolist movement, with writers such as T. E. Hulme and T. S. Eliot, with Paul Valéry, with Wittgenstein. This 'dryness' (smallness, clearness, self-containedness) is a nemesis of Romanticism. Indeed it *is* Romanticism in a later phase. The pure, clean, self-contained 'symbol', the exemplar incidentally of what Kant, ancestor of both Liberalism and Romanticism, required art to be, is the analogue of the lonely self-contained individual. It is what is left of the other-worldliness of Romanticism when the 'messy' humanitarian and revolutionary elements have spent their force. The temptation of art, a temptation to which every work of art yields except the greatest ones, is to console. The modern writer, frightened of technology and (in England) abandoned by philosophy and (in France) presented with simplified dramatic theories, attempts to console us by myths or by stories.

On the whole: his truth is sincerity and his imagination is fantasy. Fantasy operates either with shapeless day dreams (the journalistic story) or with small myths, toys, crystals. Each in his own way produces a sort of 'dream necessity'. Neither grapples with reality: hence 'fantasy', not 'imagination'.

The proper home of the symbol, in the 'symbolist' sense, is

poetry. Even there it may play an equivocal role since there is something in symbolism which is inimical to words, out of which, we have been reminded, poems are constructed. Certainly the invasion of other areas by what I may call, for short, 'symbolist ideals', has helped to bring about a decline of prose. Eloquence is out of fashion; even 'style', except in a very austere sense of this term, is out of fashion.

T. S. Eliot and Jean-Paul Sartre, dissimilar enough as thinkers, both tend to undervalue prose and to deny it any *imaginative* function. Poetry is the creation of linguistic quasi-things; prose is for explanation and exposition, it is essentially didactic, documentary, informative. Prose is ideally transparent; it is only *faute de mieux* written in words. The influential modern stylist is Hemingway. It would be almost inconceivable now to write like Landor. Most modern English novels indeed are not *written*. One feels they could slip into some other medium without much loss. It takes a foreigner like Nabokov or an Irishman like Beckett to animate prose language into an imaginative stuff in its own right.

Tolstoy who said that art was an expression of the religious perception of the age was nearer the truth than Kant who saw it as the imagination in a frolic with the understanding. The connection between art and the moral life has languished because we are losing our sense of form and structure in the moral world itself. Linguistic and existentialist behaviourism, our Romantic philosophy, has reduced our vocabulary and simplified and impoverished our view of the inner life. It is natural that a Liberal democratic society will not be concerned with techniques of improvement, will deny that virtue is knowledge, will emphasize choice at the expense of vision; and a Welfare State will weaken the incentives to investigate the bases of a Liberal democratic society. For political purposes we have been encouraged to think of ourselves as totally free and responsible, knowing everything we need to know for the important purposes of life. But this is one of the things of which Hume said that it may be true in politics but false in fact; and is it really true in politics? We need a post-Kantian unromantic Liberalism with a different image of freedom.

The technique of becoming free is more difficult than John Stuart Mill imagined. We need more concepts than our philosophies have furnished us with. We need to be enabled to think in terms of degrees of freedom, and to picture, in a non-metaphysical, non-totalitarian, and non-religious sense, the transcendence of reality. A simple-minded faith in science, together with the assumption that we are all rational and totally free, engenders a dangerous lack of curiosity about the real world, a failure to appreciate the difficulties of knowing it. We need to return from the self-centred concept of sincerity to the other-centred concept of truth. We are not isolated free choosers, monarchs of all we survey, but benighted creatures sunk in a reality whose nature we are constantly and overwhelmingly tempted to deform by fantasy. Our current picture of freedom encourages a dream-like facility; whereas what we require is a renewed sense of the difficulty and complexity of the moral life and the opacity of persons. We need more concepts in terms of which to picture the substance of our being; it is through an enriching and deepening of concepts that moral progress takes place. Simone Weil said that morality was a matter of attention, not of will. We need a new vocabulary of attention.

It is here that literature is so important, especially since it has taken over some of the tasks formerly performed by philosophy. Through literature we can re-discover a sense of the density of our lives. Literature can arm us against consolation and fantasy and can help us to recover from the ailments of Romanticism. If it can be said to have a task, that surely is its task. But if it is to perform it, prose must recover its former glory, eloquence and discourse must return. I would connect eloquence with the attempt to speak the truth. I think here of the work of Albert Camus. All his novels were *written*; but the last one, though less striking and successful than the first two, seems to me to have been a more serious attempt upon the truth: and illustrates what I mean by eloquence.

It is curious that modern literature, which is so much concerned with violence, contains so few convincing pictures of evil.

Our inability to imagine evil is a consequence of the facile, dramatic and, in spite of Hitler, optimistic picture of ourselves with which we work. Our difficulty about form, about images – our tendency to produce works which are either crystalline or journalistic – is a symptom of our situation. Form itself can be a temptation, making the work of art into a small myth which is a self-contained and indeed self-satisfied individual. We need to turn our attention away from the consoling dream necessity of Romanticism, away from the dry symbol, the bogus individual, the false whole, towards the real impenetrable human person. That this person is substantial, impenetrable, individual, indefinable, and valuable is after all the fundamental tenet of Liberalism.

It is here, however much one may criticize the emptiness of the Liberal idea of freedom, however much one may talk in terms of restoring a lost unity, that one is forever at odds with Marxism. Reality is not a given whole. An understanding of this, a respect for the contingent, is essential to imagination as opposed to fantasy. Our sense of form, which is an aspect of our desire for consolation, can be a danger to our sense of reality as a rich receding background. Against the consolations of form, the clean crystalline work, the simplified fantasy-myth, we must pit the destructive power of the now so unfashionable naturalistic idea of character.

Real people are destructive of myth, contingency is destructive of fantasy and opens the way for imagination. Think of the Russians, those great masters of the contingent. Too much contingency of course may turn art into journalism. But since reality is incomplete, art must not be too much afraid of incompleteness. Literature must always represent a battle between real people and images; and what it requires now is a much stronger and more complex conception of the former.

In morals and politics we have stripped ourselves of concepts. Literature, in curing its own ills, can give us a new vocabulary of experience, and a truer picture of freedom. With this, renewing our sense of distance, we may remind ourselves that art too lives in a region where all human endeavour is failure. Perhaps only Shakespeare manages to create at the highest level both images and people; and even *Hamlet* looks second-rate compared with *Lear*. Only the very greatest art invigorates without consoling, and defeats our attempts, in W. H. Auden's words, to use it as magic.

PHILIP ROTH

Writing American Fiction

(1961)

Several winters back, while I was living in Chicago, the city was shocked and mystified by the death of two teenage girls. So far as I know, the populace is mystified still: as for the shock, Chicago is Chicago, and one week's dismemberment fades into the next's. The victims this particular year were sisters. They went off one December night to see an Elvis Presley movie, for the sixth or seventh time we are told, and never came home. Ten days passed, and fifteen and twenty, and then the whole bleak city, every street and alley, was being searched for the missing Grimes girls, Pattie and Babs. A girlfriend had seen them at the movie, a group of boys had caught a glimpse of them afterwards getting into a black Buick, another group said a green Chevy, and so on and so forth, until one day the snow melted and the unclothed bodies of the two girls were discovered in a roadside ditch in a forest preserve west of Chicago. The coroner said he didn't know the cause of death, and then the newspapers took over. One paper ran a drawing of the girls on the back page, in bobby socks and Levi's and babushkas: Pattie and Babs a foot tall, and in four colours, like Dixie Dugan on Sundays. The mother of the two girls wept herself right into the arms of a local newspaper lady, who apparently set up her typewriter on the Grimeses' front porch and turned out a column a day, telling us that these had been good girls, hard-working girls, average girls, church-going girls, et cetera. Late in the evening one could watch television interviews featuring schoolmates and friends of the Grimes sisters: the teenage girls look around, dying to giggle, the boys stiffen in their leather jackets. 'Yeah, I knew Babs, yeah, she was all right, yeah, she was popular . . .' On and on, until at last comes a confession. A skid-row bum of thirty-five or so, a dishwasher, a prowler, a no-good named Benny Bedwell, admits to killing both girls, after he and a pal cohabited with them for several weeks in various flea-bitten hotels. Hearing the news, the weeping mother tells the newspaper lady that the man is a liar – her girls, she insists now, were murdered the night they went off to the movie. The coroner continues to maintain (with rumblings from the press) that the girls show no signs of having had sexual intercourse. Meanwhile, everybody in Chicago is buying four papers a day, and Benny Bedwell, having supplied the police with an hour-by-hour chronicle of his adventure, is tossed in jail. Two nuns, teachers of the girls at the school they attended, are sought out by the newspapermen. They are surrounded and questioned, and finally one of the sisters explains all. 'They were not exceptional girls,' the sister says, 'they had no hobbies.' About this time, some good-natured soul digs up Mrs Bedwell, Benny's mother, and a meeting is arranged between this old woman and the mother of the slain teenagers. Their picture is taken together, two overweight, overworked American ladies, quite befuddled but sitting up straight for the photographers. Mrs Bedwell apologizes for her Benny. She says, 'I never thought any boy of mine would do a thing like that.' Two weeks later, maybe three, her boy is out on bail, sporting several lawyers and a new one-button-roll suit. He is driven in a pink Cadillac to an out-of-town motel where he holds a press conference. Yes, he is the victim of police brutality. No, he is not a murderer; a degenerate maybe, but even that is changing. He is going to become a carpenter (a carpenter!) for the Salvation Army, his lawyers say. Immediately, Benny is asked to sing (he plays the guitar) in a Chicago night spot for two thousand dollars a week, or is it ten thousand? I forget. What I remember is that suddenly, into the mind of the onlooker, or newspaper reader, comes The Question: is this all public relations? But of course not – two girls are dead. Still, a song begins to catch on in Chicago, 'The Benny Bedwell Blues'. Another newspaper launches a weekly contest:

PHILIP ROTH

'How Do You Think the Grimes Girls Were Murdered?' and a
prize is given for the best answer (in the opinion of the judges).
And now the money begins to flow; donations, hundreds of
them, start pouring in to Mrs Grimes from all over the city and
the state. For what? From whom? Most contributions are
anonymous. Just the dollars, thousands and thousands of them
– the *Sun-Times* keeps us informed of the grand total. Ten
thousand, twelve thousand, fifteen thousand. Mrs Grimes sets
about refinishing and redecorating her house. A stranger steps
forward, by the name of Shultz or Schwartz – I don't really
remember – but he is in the appliance business and he presents
Mrs Grimes with a whole new kitchen. Mrs Grimes, beside
herself with appreciation and joy, turns to her surviving daugh-
ter and says, 'Imagine me in that kitchen!' Finally, the poor
woman goes out and buys two parakeets (or maybe another Mr
Shultz presents them as a gift); one parakeet she calls Babs, the
other Pattie. At just about this point, Benny Bedwell, doubtless
having barely learned to hammer a nail in straight, is extradited
to Florida on the charge of having raped a twelve-year-old girl
there. Shortly thereafter I left Chicago myself, and so far as I
know, though Mrs Grimes hasn't her two girls, she has a brand-
new dishwasher and two small birds.

And what is the moral of the story? Simply this: that the
American writer in the middle of the twentieth century has his
hands full in trying to understand, describe, and then make
credible much of American reality. It stupefies, it sickens, it
infuriates, and finally it is even a kind of embarrassment to one's
own meagre imagination. The actuality is continually outdoing
our talents, and the culture tosses up figures almost daily that
are the envy of any novelist. Who, for example, could have
invented Charles Van Doren? Roy Cohn and David Schine?
Sherman Adams and Bernard Goldfine? Dwight David
Eisenhower?

Several months back, most of the country heard one of the
candidates for the Presidency of the United States say something
like, 'Now if you feel that Senator Kennedy is right, then I
sincerely believe you should vote for Senator Kennedy, and if

you feel that I am right, I humbly submit that you vote for me. Now, I feel, and this is certainly a personal opinion, that I am right . . .' and so on. Though it did not appear this way to some thirty-four million voters, it still seems to me a little easy to ridicule Mr Nixon, and it is not for that reason that I have bothered to paraphrase his words here. If one was at first amused by him, one was ultimately astonished. Perhaps as a satiric literary creation, he might have seemed 'believable', but I myself found that on the TV screen, as a real public figure, a political fact, my mind balked at taking him in. Whatever else the television debates produced in me, I should point out, as a literary curiosity, they also produced professional envy. All the machinations over make-up and rebuttal time, all the business over whether Mr Nixon should look at Mr Kennedy when he replied, or should look away – all of it was so beside the point, so fantastic, so weird and astonishing, that I found myself beginning to wish I had invented it. But then, of course, one need not have been a fiction writer to wish that *someone* had invented it, and that it was not real and with us.

The daily newspapers, then, fill us with wonder and awe (is it possible? is it happening?), also with sickness and despair. The fixes, the scandals, the insanity, the idiocy, the piety, the lies, the noise . . . Recently, in *Commentary*, Benjamin DeMott wrote that the 'deeply lodged suspicion of the times [is] namely, that events and individuals are unreal, and that power to alter the course of the age, of my life and your life, is actually vested nowhere'. There seems to be, said DeMott, a kind of 'universal descent into unreality'. The other night – to give a benign example of the descent – my wife turned on the radio and heard the announcer offering a series of cash prizes for the three best television plays of five minutes' duration, written by children. It is difficult at such moments to find one's way around the kitchen. Certainly few days go by when incidents far less benign fail to remind us of what DeMott is talking about. When Edmund Wilson says that after reading *Life* magazine he feels he does not belong to the country depicted there, that he does not live in this country, I understand what he means.

However, for a writer of fiction to feel that he does not really live in his own country – as represented by *Life* or by what he experiences when he steps out the front door – must seem a serious occupational impediment. For what will his subject be? His landscape? One would think that we might get a high proportion of historical novels on contemporary satire – or perhaps just nothing. No books. Yet almost weekly one finds on the best-seller list another novel which is set in Mamaroneck or New York City or Washington, with characters moving through a world of dishwashers and TV sets and advertising agencies and senatorial investigations. It all *looks* as though the writers are turning out books about our world. There is *Cash McCall* and *The Man in the Grey Flannel Suit* and *Marjorie Morningstar* and *The Enemy Camp* and *Advise and Consent*, and so on. But what is noteworthy is that these books aren't very good. Not that the writers aren't sufficiently horrified with the landscape to suit me – quite the contrary. They are generally full of concern for the world about them; finally, however, they just don't imagine the corruption and vulgarity and treachery of American public life any more profoundly than they imagine human character – that is, the country's private life. All issues are generally solvable, suggesting that they are not so much awe-struck or horror-struck as they are provoked by some topical controversy. 'Controversial' is a common word in the critical language of this literature, as it is, say, in the language of the TV producer.

It is hardly news that in best-sellerdom we frequently find the hero coming to terms and settling down in Scarsdale, or wherever, knowing himself. And on Broadway, in the third act, someone says, 'Look, why don't you just love each other?' and the protagonist, throwing his hand to his forehead, cries, 'God, why didn't *I* think of that!' and before the bulldozing action of love, all else collapses – verisimilitude, truth, and interest. It is like 'Dover Beach' ending happily for Matthew Arnold, and for us, because the poet is standing at the window with a woman who understands him. If the literary investigation of our era were to become solely the property of Wouk, Weidman, Sloan

Wilson, Cameron Hawley, and Broadway's *amor-vincit-omnia* boys it would be unfortunate indeed – like leaving sex to the pornographers, where again there is more to what is happening than first meets the eye.

But the times have not yet been given over completely to lesser minds and talents. There is Norman Mailer. And he is an interesting example of a writer in whom our era has provoked such a magnificent disgust that dealing with it in fiction has almost come to seem, for him, beside the point. He has become an actor in the cultural drama, the difficulty of which is that it leaves one with less time to be a writer. For instance, to defy the civil-defence authorities and their H-bomb drills, you have to take off a morning from the typewriter and go down and stand outside of City Hall; then, if you're lucky and they toss you in jail, you have to give up an evening at home and your next morning's work as well. To defy Mike Wallace, or challenge his principle-less aggression, or simply use him or straighten him out, you must first be a guest on his programme – there's one night shot. Then you may well spend the next two weeks (I am speaking from memory) disliking yourself for having gone, and then two more writing an article attempting to explain why you did it and what it was like. 'It's the age of the slob,' says a character in William Styron's new novel. 'If we don't watch out they're going to drag us under . . .' And the dragging under can take many forms. We get, from Mailer, for instance, a book like *Advertisements for Myself*, a chronicle for the most part of why I did it and what it was like – and who I have it in for: his life as a substitute for his fiction. An infuriating, self-indulgent, boisterous, mean book, not much worse than most advertising we have to put up with – but, taken as a whole, curiously moving in its revelation of despair, so great that the man who bears it, or is borne by it, seems for the time being to have given up on making an imaginative assault upon the American experience, and has become instead the champion of a kind of public revenge. However, what one champions one day may make one its victim the next; once having written *Advertisements for Myself*, I don't see that you can write it again. Mailer probably now finds himself in the unenviable position of having to put up or shut up. Who knows – maybe it's where he wanted to be. My own feeling is that times are tough for a fiction writer when he takes to writing letters to his newspaper rather than those complicated, disguised letters to himself, which are stories.

The last is not intended to be a sententious, or a condescending remark, or even a generous one. However, one suspects Mailer's style or his motives, one sympathizes with the impulse that leads him to want to be a critic, a reporter, a sociologist, a journalist, or even the Mayor of New York. For what is particularly tough about the times is writing about them, as a serious novelist or storyteller. Much has been made, much of it by the writers themselves, of the fact that the American writer has no status, no respect, and no audience. I am pointing here to a loss more central to the task itself, the loss of a subject; or, to put it another way, a voluntary withdrawal of interest by the fiction writer from some of the grander social and political phenomena of our times.

Of course there have been writers who have tried to meet these phenomena head-on. It seems to me I have read several books or stories in the past few years in which one character or another starts to talk about 'The Bomb', and the conversation usually leaves me feeling less than convinced, and in some extreme instances, with a certain amount of sympathy for fallout; it is like people in college novels having long talks about what kind of generation they are. But what then? What can the writer do with so much of the American reality as it is? Is the only other possibility to be Gregory Corso and thumb your nose at the whole thing? The attitude of the Beats (if such a phrase has meaning) is not entirely without appeal. The whole thing is a joke. America, ha-ha. But that doesn't put very much distance between Beatdom and its sworn enemy, best-sellerdom – not much more than what it takes to get from one side of a nickel to the other: for is America, ha-ha, really any more than America, hoo-ray, stood upon its head?

Now it is possible that I am exaggerating the serious writer's response to our cultural predicament and his inability or unwillingness to deal with it imaginatively. There seems to me little, in the end, to prove an assertion about the psychology of a nation's writers, outside, that is, of their books themselves. In this case, unfortunately, the bulk of the evidence is not books that *have* been written but the ones that have been left unfinished, and those that have not even been considered worth the attempt. Which is not to say that there have not been certain literary signs, however, certain obsessions and innovations, to be found in the novels of our best writers, supporting the notion that the social world has ceased to be as suitable or as manageable a subject as it once may have been.

Let me begin with some words about the man who, by reputation at least, is *the* writer of the age. The response of college students to the work of J. D. Salinger indicates that perhaps he, more than anyone else, has not turned his back on the times but, instead, has managed to put his finger on whatever struggle of significance is going on today between self and culture. *The Catcher in the Rye* and the recent stories in *The New Yorker* having to do with the Glass family surely take place in the immediate here and now. But what about the self, what about the hero? The question is of particular interest here, for in Salinger, more than in most of his contemporaries, the figure of the writer has lately come to be placed directly in the reader's line of vision, so that there is a connection, finally, between the attitudes of the narrator as, say, brother to Seymour Glass, and as a man who writes by profession.

And what of Salinger's heroes? Well, Holden Caulfield, we discover, winds up in an expensive sanitarium. And Seymour Glass commits suicide finally, but prior to that he is the apple of his brother's eye – and why? He has learned to live in this world – but how? By not living in it. By kissing the soles of little girls' feet and throwing rocks at the head of his sweetheart. He is a saint, clearly. But since madness is undesirable and sainthood, for most of us, out of the question, the problem of how to live *in* this world is by no means answered; unless the answer is that one cannot. The only advice we seem to get from Salinger is to be charming on the way to the loony bin. Of course, Salinger is under no obligation to supply advice of any sort to writers or readers – still, I happen to find myself growing more and more curious about this professional writer, Buddy Glass, and how *he* manages to coast through life in the arms of sanity.

There is in Salinger the suggestion that mysticism is a possible road to salvation; at least some of his characters respond well to an intensified, emotional religious belief. Now my own reading in Zen is minuscule, but as I understand it from Salinger, the deeper we go into this world, the further we can get away from it. If you contemplate a potato long enough, it stops being a potato in the usual sense; unfortunately, however, it is the usual sense that we have to deal with from day to day. For all his loving handling of the world's objects there seems to me, in Salinger's Glass family stories as in *The Catcher*, a spurning of life as it is lived in the immediate world – this place and time is viewed as unworthy of those few precious people who have been set down in it only to be maddened and destroyed.

A spurning of our world – though of a different order – occurs in the work of another of our most gifted writers, Bernard Malamud. Even when Malamud writes a book about baseball, *The Natural*, it is not baseball as it is played in Yankee Stadium but a wild, wacky game, where a player who is instructed to knock the cover off the ball promptly steps up to the plate and does just that: the batter swings and the inner core of the ball goes looping out to centre field, where the confused fielder commences to tangle himself in the unwinding sphere; then the shortstop runs out and, with his teeth, bites the centre fielder and the ball free from one another. Though *The Natural* is not Malamud's most successful book, it is at any rate our introduction to his world, which is by no means a replica of our own. There are really things called baseball players, of course, and really things called Jews, but there much of the similarity ends. The Jews of *The Magic Barrel* and the Jews of *The Assistant* are not the Jews of New York City or Chicago. They are Malamud's invention, a metaphor of sorts to stand for certain possibilities and promises, and I am further inclined to believe this when I read the statement attributed to Malamud which goes, 'All men are Jews.' In fact, we know this is not so; even the men who are Jews aren't sure they're Jews. But Malamud, as a writer of fiction, has not shown specific interest in the anxieties and dilemmas and corruptions of the contemporary American Jew, the Jew we think of as characteristic of our times. Rather, his people live in a timeless depression and a placeless Lower East Side; their society is not affluent, their predicament is not cultural. I am not saying – one cannot, of Malamud – that he has spurned life or an examination of its difficulties. What it is to be human, and to be humane, is his deepest concern. What I do mean to point out is that he does not find – or has not yet found – the *contemporary* scene a proper or sufficient backdrop for his tales of heartlessness and heartache, of suffering and regeneration.

Now, Malamud and Salinger cannot, of course, be considered to speak for all American writers, and yet their fictional response to the world about them – what they choose to emphasize or to ignore – is of interest to me simply because they are two of the best. Of course there are plenty of other writers around, capable ones too, who do not travel the same roads; however, even among these others, I wonder if we may not be witnessing a response to the times, less apparently dramatized perhaps than the social detachment in Salinger and Malamud, but there in the body of the work nonetheless.

Let us take up the matter of prose style. Why is everybody so bouncy all of a sudden? Those who have been reading Saul Bellow, Herbert Gold, Arthur Granit, Thomas Berger, and Grace Paley will know to what I am referring. Writing recently in *The Hudson Review*, Harvey Swados said that he saw developing 'a nervous muscular prose perfectly suited to the exigencies of an age which seems at once appalling and ridiculous. These are metropolitan writers, most of them are Jewish, and they are specialists in a kind of prose-poetry that often depends for its effectiveness as much on how it is ordered, or how it looks on the printed page, as it does on what it is expressing. This is risky writing . . .' Swados added, and perhaps it is in its very riskiness that we can discover some kind of explanation for it. I'd like to compare two short descriptive passages, one from Bellow's *The Adventures of Augie March*, the other from Gold's new novel, *Therefore Be Bold*, in the hope that the differences revealed will be educational.

As numerous readers have already pointed out, the language of *Augie March* combines literary complexity with conversational ease, joins the idiom of the academy with the idiom of the streets (not all streets – certain streets); the style is special, private, energetic, and though it can at times be unwieldy, it generally serves Bellow brilliantly. Here, for instance, is a description of Grandma Lausch:

> With the [cigarette] holder in her dark little gums between which all her guile, malice, and command issued, she had her best inspirations of strategy. She was as wrinkled as an old paper bag, an autocrat, hard-shelled and jesuitical, a pouncy old hawk of a Bolshevik, her small ribboned grey feet immobile on the shoekit and stool Simon had made in the manual-training class, dingy old wool Winnie [the dog] whose bad smell filled the flat on the cushion beside her. If wit and discontent don't necessarily go together, it wasn't from the old woman that I learned it.

Herbert Gold's language has also been distinctly special, private, energetic. One notices in the following passage from *Therefore Be Bold* that here too the writer begins by recognizing a physical similarity between the character to be described and some unlikely object, and from there, as in Bellow's Grandma Lausch passage, attempts to wind up, via the body, making a discovery about the soul. The character described is named Chuck Hastings.

> In some respects he resembled a mummy – the shrivelled yellow skin, the hands and head too large for a wasted body, the bottomless eye sockets of thought beyond the Nile. But his agile Adam's apple and point-making finger

made him less the Styx-swimmer dog-paddling toward Coptic limbos than a high-school intellectual intimidating the navel-eyed little girls.

First, the grammar itself has me baffled: '. . . bottomless eye sockets of thought beyond the Nile'. Is the thought beyond the Nile, or the eye sockets? What does it mean to be beyond the Nile anyway? These grammatical difficulties have little in common with the ironic inversion with which Bellow's description begins: 'With the holder in her dark little gums between which all her guile, malice, and command issued . . .' Bellow goes on to describe Grandma Lausch as an 'autocrat', 'hard-shelled', 'jesuitical', 'a pouncy old hawk of a Bolshevik' – imaginative certainly, but tough-minded, *exact*, not primarily exhibitionistic. Of Gold's Chuck Hastings, however, we learn, 'His agile Adam's apple and point-making finger made him less the Styx-swimmer dog-paddling toward Coptic limbos', etc. . . . Language in the service of the narrative, or literary regression in the service of the ego? In a recent review of *Therefore Be Bold*, Granville Hicks quoted this very paragraph in praise of Gold's style. 'This is high-pitched,' Mr Hicks admitted, 'but the point is that Gold keeps it up and keeps it up.' I take it the sexual pun is not deliberate; nevertheless, it might serve as a reminder that showmanship and passion are not one and the same. What we have here is not stamina or vitality but reality taking a back seat to personality – and not the personality of the imagined character, but of the writer who is doing the imagining. Bellow's description seems to arise out of a writer's firm grasp of his character: Grandma Lausch *is*. Behind the description of Chuck Hastings there seems to me something else that is being said: Herbert Gold is. Look at me, I'm writing.

Now, I am not trying to sell selflessness here. Rather, I am suggesting that this nervous muscular prose that Swados talks about may perhaps have something to do with the unfriendly relations that exist between the writer and the culture. The prose suits the age, Swados suggests, and I wonder if it does not suit it, in part, because it rejects it. The writer thrusts before our eyes

– it is in the very ordering of his sentences – *personality*, in all its separateness and specialness. Of course, the mystery of personality may be nothing less than a writer's ultimate concern; and certainly when the muscular prose is revealing of character and evocative of an environment – as in *Augie March* – it can be wonderfully effective; at its worst, however, as a form of literary onanism, it seriously curtails the fictional possibilities, and may perhaps be thought of as a symptom of the writer's loss of the community – or what is *outside* himself – as subject.

True, the bouncy style can be understood in other ways as well. It is not surprising that most of the practitioners Swados points to are Jewish. When writers who do not feel much of a connection to Lord Chesterfield begin to realize that they are under no real obligation to try and write like that distinguished old stylist, they are likely enough to go out and be bouncy. Also, there is the matter of the spoken language which these writers have heard, as our statesmen might put it, in the schools, the homes, the churches and the synagogues of the nation. I would even say that when the bouncy style is not an attempt to dazzle the reader, or one's self, but to incorporate into American literary prose the rhythms, nuances, and emphases of urban and immigrant speech, the result can sometimes be a language of new and rich emotional subtleties, with a kind of back-handed charm and irony all its own, as in Grace Paley's book of stories *The Little Disturbances of Man*.

But whether the practitioner is Gold, Bellow, or Paley, there is a further point to make about the bounciness: it is an expression of pleasure. However, a question: If the world is as crooked and unreal as it feels to me it is becoming, day by day; if one feels less and less power in the face of this unreality; if the inevitable end is destruction, if not of all life, then of much that is valuable and civilized in life – then why in God's name is the writer pleased? Why don't all our fictional heroes wind up in institutions, like Holden Caulfield, or suicides, like Seymour Glass? Why is it that so many of them – not just in books by Wouk and Weidman but in Bellow, Gold, Styron, and others – wind up affirming life? For surely the air is thick these days with affirmation, and though we shall doubtless get our annual editorial this year from *Life* calling for affirmative novels, the fact is that more and more books by serious writers seem to end on a note of celebration. Not just the tone is bouncy, the moral is bouncy too. In *The Optimist*, another of Gold's novels, the hero, having taken his lumps, cries out in the book's last line, 'More. More. More! More! More!' Curtis Harnack's novel, *The Work of an Ancient Hand*, ends with the hero filled with 'rapture and hope' and saying aloud, 'I believe in God.' And Saul Bellow's *Henderson the Rain King* is a book given over to celebrating the regeneration of the heart, blood, and general health of its hero. Yet it is of some importance, I think, that the regeneration of Henderson takes place in a world that is thoroughly and wholly imagined, *but that does not really exist.* It is not the tumultuous Africa of the newspapers and the United Nations discussions that Eugene Henderson visits. There is nothing here of nationalism or riots or apartheid. But why should there be? There is the world, and there is also the self. And the self, when the writer turns upon it all his attention and talent, is revealed to be a most remarkable thing. First off, it exists, it's real. *I am*, the self cries out, and then, taking a nice long look, it adds, *and I am beautiful.*

At the conclusion to Bellow's book, his hero, Eugene Henderson, a big, sloppy millionaire, is returning to America, coming home from a trip to Africa, where he has been plague fighter, lion tamer, and rainmaker; he is bringing back with him a real lion. Aboard the plane he befriends a small Persian boy, whose language he cannot understand. Still, when the plane lands at Newfoundland, Henderson takes the child in his arms and goes out onto the field. And then:

> Laps and laps I galloped around the shining and riveted body of the plane, behind the fuel trucks. Dark faces were looking from within. The great, beautiful propellers were still, all four of them. I guess I felt it was my turn to move, and so went running – leaping, leaping, pounding, and tingling over the pure white lining of the grey Arctic silence.

And so we leave Henderson, a very happy man. Where? In the Arctic. This picture has stayed with me since I read the book a year ago: of a man who finds energy and joy in an imagined Africa, and celebrates it on an unpeopled, icebound vastness.

Earlier I quoted from Styron's new novel, *Set This House on Fire*. Now Styron's book, like Bellow's, also tells of the regeneration of an American who leaves his own country and goes abroad for a while to live. But where Henderson's world is wildly removed from our own, Kinsolving, Styron's hero, inhabits a place we immediately recognize. The book is thick with detail that twenty years from now will probably require extensive footnotes to be thoroughly understood. The hero is an American painter who has taken his family to live in a small town on the Amalfi coast. Cass Kinsolving detests America, and himself. Throughout most of the book he is taunted, tempted, and disgraced by Mason Flagg, a fellow countryman, who is rich, boyish, naïve, licentious, indecent, cruel, and stupid. Kinsolving, by way of his attachment to Flagg, spends most of the book choosing between living and dying, and at one point, in a tone that is characteristic, says this about his expatriation:

> ... the man I had come to Europe to escape [why he's] the man in all the car advertisements, you know, the young guy waving there — he looks so beautiful and educated and everything, and he's got it *made*, Penn State and a blonde there, and a smile as big as a billboard. And he's going places. I mean electronics. Politics. What they call communication. Advertising. Saleshood. Outer space. God only knows. And he's as ignorant as an Albanian peasant.

However, despite all his disgust with what American public life can do to a man's private life, Kinsolving, like Henderson, comes back to America at the end, having opted for existence. But the America that we find him in seems to me to be the America of his childhood, and (if only in a metaphoric way) of everyone's childhood: he tells his story while he fishes from a boat in a Carolina stream. The affirmation at the conclusion is not as go-getting as Gold's 'More! More!' or as sublime as Harnack's 'I believe in God', or as joyous as Henderson's romp on the Newfoundland airfield. 'I wish I could tell you that I had found some belief, some rock . . .' Kinsolving says, 'but to be truthful, you see, I can only tell you this: that as for being and nothingness, the only thing I did know was that to choose between them was simply to choose being . . .' Being. Living. Not where one lives or with whom one lives – but *that* one lives.

And what does all of this add up to? It would, of course, drastically oversimplify the art of fiction to suggest that Saul Bellow's book or Herbert Gold's prose style arise ineluctably out of our distressing cultural and political predicament. Nonetheless, that the communal predicament *is* distressing weighs upon the writer no less, and perhaps even more, than upon his neighbour – for to the writer the community is, properly, both subject and audience. And it may be that when this situation produces not only feelings of disgust, rage, and melancholy, but impotence too, the writer is apt to lose heart and turn finally to other matters, to the construction of wholly imaginary worlds, and to a celebration of the self, which may, in a variety of ways, become his subject, as well as the impetus that establishes the perimeters of his technique. What I have tried to point out is that the vision of self as inviolable, powerful, and nervy, self-imagined as the only seemingly real thing in an unreal-seeming environment, has given some of our writers joy, solace, and muscle. Certainly to have come through a serious personal struggle intact, simply to have survived, is nothing to be made light of, and it is for just this reason that Styron's hero manages to engage our sympathies right down to the end. Still, when the survivor cannot choose but be ascetic, when the self can only be celebrated as it is excluded from society, or as it is exercised and admired in a fantastic one, we then do not have much reason to be cheery. Finally, for me there is something unconvincing about a regenerated Henderson up on the pure white lining of the world dancing around that shining airplane. Consequently, it is not with this scene that I should like to conclude, but instead with the image of his hero that Ralph Ellison presents at the end of *Invisible Man*. For here too the hero is left with the simple stark fact of himself. He is as alone as a man can be. Not that he hasn't gone out into the world; he has gone out into it, and out into it, and out into it – but at the end he chooses to go underground, to live there and to wait. And it does not seem to him a cause for celebration either.

MICHEL BUTOR

The Novel as Research
(1968)

I

The novel is a particular form of narrative.

And narrative is a phenomenon which extends considerably beyond the scope of literature; it is one of the essential constituents of our understanding of reality. From the time we begin to understand language until our death, we are perpetually surrounded by narratives, first of all in our family, then at school, then through our encounters with people and reading.

Other people, for us, are not only what we have seen of them with our own eyes, but also what they have told us about themselves, or what others have told us about them. They are not only the people we have seen, but also all those we have been told about by others.

This is true not only of human beings, but of things themselves, and of places, for example, where we have never been but which have been described to us.

This narrative in which we are steeped takes the most varied forms, from family tradition, or the news we exchange at dinner about what we have done during the day, to journalistic reports or historical works. Each of these forms links us to a particular segment of reality.

All these veracious narratives have one characteristic in common: they are always, in principle, verifiable. I should be able to check what someone has told me by information from another source, and so on indefinitely; otherwise, I am dealing with a mistake or a fiction.

Among all these narratives by which a large share of our daily world is constituted, there may be some which are deliberately invented. If, in order to avoid any misunderstanding, we assign to the events which are recounted to us certain characteristics which immediately distinguish them from those we usually see with our own eyes, we are dealing with a literature of fantasy, myths, tales, and so on. The novelist, on the other hand, presents us with events that resemble everyday events; he wants to give them as much as possible the appearance of reality, and this can even go to the point of staging a hoax (Defoe).

But what the novelist tells us is not verifiable, and, as a consequence, what he says about it must suffice to give it that appearance of reality. If I meet a friend and he gives me some surprising piece of news, in order to convince me of its truth he can always resort to telling me that such and such people were also witnesses, that all I have to do is check the story with them. On the other hand, from the moment a writer puts the word *novel* on the cover of his book, he declares that it is useless to seek this kind of confirmation. It is only by what he tells us about his characters, and by this alone, that they can convince us, can live, even if they have actually existed in reality.

Suppose we were to discover a letter writer of the nineteenth century telling his correspondent that he knew Père Goriot very well, that he was nothing at all like the man Balzac has described, and that on such and such a page there are even enormous errors of fact; this would obviously have no importance for us: Père Goriot is what Balzac tells us about him (and what we can go on to say about him after that); I may consider Balzac mistaken in his judgements of his own creation, I may even decide that the character eludes him, but to justify my position I shall have to rely on the very sentences of Balzac's text; I cannot invoke any other witness.

Even though veracious narrative always has the support, the last resort, of external evidence, the novel must suffice to create what it tells us. That is why it is the phenomenological realm par excellence, the best possible place to study how reality appears to us, or might appear; that is why the novel is the laboratory of narrative.

II

Work on the form of novel, therefore, assumes a major importance.

For veracious narratives, by becoming public and historic, are gradually stabilized, classified and grouped according to certain principles (in fact the principles of what is today known as the traditional novel, the novel which raises no questions). Our primitive understanding is replaced by another, much more impoverished one which systematically rejects certain aspects; it gradually disguises the real experience, substitutes itself for it, ultimately achieving a generalized hoax. Exploration of the different forms of the novel reveals what is contingent in the form we are used to, unmasks it, releases us from it, allows us to rediscover beyond this fixed narrative everything it camouflages or passes over in silence: that fundamental narrative in which our whole life is steeped.

Further, it is obvious that since form is a principle of choice (and style in this regard appears as one of the aspects of form, being the way in which the details of the language are actually linked together, the thing that determines the choice of one word or turn of phrase rather than another), new forms will reveal new things in reality, new connections, and naturally, the more the internal coherence of these new forms is stressed in relation to others, the more rigorous they will be.

Inversely, different forms of narrative correspond to different realities. Now, it is clear that the world in which we live is being transformed with great rapidity. Traditional narrative techniques are incapable of integrating all the new relations thus created. There results a perpetual uneasiness; it is impossible for our consciousness to organize all the information which assails it, because it lacks adequate tools.

The search for new novelistic forms with a greater power of

integration thus plays a triple role in relation to our consciousness of reality: unmasking, exploration, and adaptation. The novelist who refuses to accept this task, never discarding old habits, never demanding any particular effort of his reader, never obliging him to confront himself, to question attitudes long since taken for granted, will certainly enjoy a readier success, but he becomes the accomplice of that profound uneasiness, that darkness, in which we are groping for our way. He stiffens the reflexes of our consciousness even more, making any awakening more difficult; he contributes to its suffocation, so that even if his intentions are generous, his work is in the last analysis a poison.

Formal invention in the novel, far from being opposed to realism as shortsighted critics often assume, is the *sine qua non* of a greater realism.

III

But the novel's relationship to the reality which surrounds us is not confined to the fact that what it describes is presented as an illusory fragment of that reality, a very isolated, pliable fragment which it is then possible to study at close range. The difference between the events of a novel and those of life does not lie only in the fact that we can verify the latter while the former can be reached only through the text which creates them. For the events of a novel are also, to use the common expression, more 'interesting' than real ones. The emergence of these fictions corresponds to a need, fulfils a function. Imaginary characters fill the gaps in reality and enlighten us about it.

Not only the creation but also the reading of a novel is a kind of waking dream. It is thus susceptible to psychoanalysis in the broad sense. Further, if I want to explain a given theory, whether psychological, sociological, ethical or whatever, it is often convenient to take a fictitious example. The characters of a novel will play this part to perfection; and I will recognize these characters in my friends and acquaintances, I will elucidate the conduct of the latter by relying on the adventures of the former, and so on.

This application of the novel to reality is extremely complex, and the novel's 'realism', the fact that it is presented as an illusory fragment of daily life, is only one particular aspect of it, the one which allows us to isolate it as a literary genre.

I call the 'symbolism' of a novel the sum of the relationships of what it describes to the reality we experience.

These relationships are not the same in all novels, and it seems to me that the critic's essential undertaking is to unravel them, to illuminate them so that we can extract from each particular work its entire lesson.

But since, in the creation of a novel and in that recreation which is attentive reading, we are exposed to a complex system of relationships of extremely varied significance. If the novelist sincerely tries to share his experience, if his realism is carried far enough, if the form he employs is sufficiently integrative, he will necessarily be led to account for these diverse types of relationships within his work itself. The external symbolism of a novel tends to be reflected in an internal symbolism, certain portions playing in relation to the whole the same part that the whole plays in relation to reality.

IV

This general relationship of the 'reality', described by the novel to the reality which surrounds us is, obviously, the relationship which determines what is commonly called the novel's theme or subject, which appears as a response to a certain state of consciousness. But this theme, this subject, as we have seen, cannot be separated from the way in which it is presented, from the form in which it is expressed. A new state of consciousness, a new awareness of what a novel is, of its relationships to reality, of its status, corresponds to new subjects, to new forms on every level – language, style, technique, composition, structure. Inversely, the search for new forms, revealing new subjects, reveals new relationships.

After a certain degree of reflection, realism, formalism, and symbolism in the novel appear to constitute an indissoluble unity.

The novel tends naturally towards its own elucidation, and so it should; but we know that there are certain states of consciousness characterized by an incapacity to reflect upon themselves, states which subsist only by the illusion they maintain, and to these states of consciousness correspond those works in which that indissoluble unity cannot appear, those attitudes of novelists who refuse to question themselves about the nature of their work and the validity of the forms they employ: those forms which could not be reflected upon without immediately revealing their inadequacy, their untruthfulness, those forms which give us an image of reality in flagrant contradiction to the reality which gave them birth and which they are concerned to pass over in silence. These are impostures which it is the duty of criticism to expose; for such works, for all their charms and merits, preserve and deepen the darkness, imprison consciousness in its contradictions, in its blindness, which risks leading it into the most fatal disorders.

The consequence of all this is that any genuine transformation of the novel's form, any fruitful research in this realm, can be situated only within a transformation of the concept of the novel itself, which evolves very slowly but inevitably (all the great novels of the twentieth century attest to the fact) toward a new kind of poetry at once epic and didactic, within a transformation of the very notion of literature, which begins to appear no longer as a simple pastime or luxury, but in its essential role within the workings of society, and as a systematic experiment.

translated by Gerald Fabian

SAUL BELLOW

Some Notes on Recent American Fiction

(1963)

Gertrude Stein is supposed to have explained to Hemingway that 'remarks are not literature'. Here I am offering some remarks, and I make no claim for them whatever. A writer's views on other writers may have a certain interest, but it should be clear that he reads what they write almost always with a special attitude. If he should be a novelist, his own books are also a comment on his contemporaries and reveal that he supports certain tendencies and rejects others. In his own books he upholds what he deems necessary, and usually by the method of omission he criticizes what he understands as the errors and excesses of others.

I intend to examine the view taken by recent American novelists and short-story writers of the individual and his society, and I should like to begin with the title of the new book by Wylie Sypher: *Loss of the Self in Modern Literature and Art*. I do not propose to discuss it; I simply want to cite the title, for in itself it tells us much about the common acceptance of what the Spanish critic Ortega y Gasset described some years ago as 'the dehumanization of the arts'. One chapter is devoted to the Beats, but, for the most part, Sypher finds, as we might have expected, that the theme of annihilation of Self, and the description of an 'inauthentic' life which can never make sense, is predominantly European and particularly French. The names he most often mentions are those of André Gide, Sartre, Beckett, Sarraute, and Robbe-Grillet: writers whose novels and plays are derived from definite theories which make a historical reckoning of the human condition and are peculiarly responsive to new

53

physical, psychological, and philosophical theories. American writers, when they are moved by a similar spirit to reject and despise the Self, are seldom encumbered by such intellectual baggage, and this fact pleases their European contemporaries, who find in them a natural, that is, a brutal or violent acceptance of the new universal truth by minds free from intellectual preconceptions.

In the early twenties D. H. Lawrence was delighted to discover a blunt, primitive virtue in the first stories of Ernest Hemingway, and twenty years later André Gide praised Dashiell Hammett as a good barbarian.

European writers take strength from German phenomenology and from the conception of entropy in modern physics in order to attack a romantic idea of the Self, triumphant in the nineteenth century but intolerable in the twentieth. The feeling against this idea is well-nigh universal. The First World War with its millions of corpses gave an aspect of the horrible to romantic over-valuation of the Self. The leaders of the Russian Revolution were icy in their hatred of bourgeois individualism. In the communist countries millions were sacrificed in the building of socialism, and almost certainly the Lenins and the Stalins, the leaders who made these decisions, serving the majority and the future, believed they were rejecting a soft, nerveless humanism which attempted in the face of natural and historical evidence to oppose progress.

A second great assault on the separate Self sprang from Germany in 1939. Just what the reduction of millions of human beings into heaps of bone and mounds of rag and hair or clouds of smoke betokened, there is no one who can plainly tell us, but it is at least plain that something was being done to put in question the meaning of survival, the meaning of pity, the meaning of justice and of the importance of being oneself, the individual's consciousness of his own existence.

It would be odd, indeed, if these historical events had made no impression on American writers, even if they are not on the whole given to taking the historical or theoretical view. They characteristically depend on their own observations and appear at times obstinately empirical.

But the latest work of writers like James Jones, James Baldwin, Philip Roth, John O'Hara, J. F. Powers, Joseph Bennett, Wright Morris and others shows the individual under a great strain. Labouring to maintain himself, or perhaps an idea of himself (not always a clear idea), he feels the pressure of a vast public life, which may dwarf him as an individual while permitting him to be a giant in hatred or fantasy. In these circumstances he grieves, he complains, rages, or laughs. All the while he is aware of his lack of power, his inadequacy as a moralist, the nauseous pressure of the mass media and their weight of money and organization, of cold war and racial brutalities.

Adapting Gresham's theorem to the literary situation one might say that public life drives private life into hiding. People begin to hoard their spiritual valuables. Public turbulence is largely coercive, not positive. It puts us into a passive position. There is not much we can do about the crises of international politics, the revolutions in Asia and Africa, the rise and transformation of masses. Technical and political decisions, invisible powers, secrets which can be shared only by a small elite, render the private will helpless and lead the individual into curious forms of behaviour in the private sphere.

Public life, vivid and formless turbulence, news, slogans, mysterious crises, and unreal configurations dissolve coherence in all but the most resistant minds, and even to such minds it is not always a confident certainty that resistance can ever have a positive outcome. To take narcotics has become in some circles a mark of rebellious independence, and to scorch one's personal earth is sometimes felt to be the only honourable course. Rebels have no bourgeois certainties to return to when rebellions are done. The fixed points seem to be disappearing. Even the Self is losing its firm outline.

One recent American novel deals openly and consciously with these problems: *The Thin Red Line* by James Jones, a book which, describing the gross and murderous conditions of jungle combat, keeps a miraculously sensitive balance and does not weary us with a mere catalogue of horrors. What Mr Jones sees very precisely is the fluctuation in the value of the life of the individual soldier. Childhood in some cases ends for the fighting man as he accepts the lesson of realism. The attitude of Storm, one of the older soldiers, towards Fife, a younger man, is described as follows: 'He [Fife] was a good enough kid. He just hadn't been away from home long enough. And Storm, who had started off bumming during the Depression when he was only fourteen, couldn't find kids like that very interesting.' Storm, the mess sergeant, tolerates the inexperienced Fife, but First Sergeant Welsh has no such tolerance. He cannot abide softness and the lack of realism, and he cruelly and punitively teaches the hard lesson to his undeveloped subordinates. Real knowledge as he sees it is brutal knowledge and it must be painfully and brutally learned. The heart of the lesson, as Welsh understands it, is that it matters little – it matters, therefore, not at all – whether any single man survives or falls. Welsh offers no indulgence to anyone and asks none for himself. His message to mankind is that you must cast the cold eye on life, on death.

Mr Jones shrewdly understands that the philosophy of Welsh is not ultimately hard. Towards himself the sergeant is not fanatically severe, and his toughness betrays a large degree of self-pity. What Jones describes here is the casting off of a childish or feminine or false virtue, despised because it cannot meet the test of survival. In apprehending what is real, Jones's combat soliders learn a bitter and levelling truth and in their realism revenge themselves on the slothful and easy civilian conception of the Self. The new idea cruelly assails the old, exposing its conventionality and emptiness. Young Fife, after he has gone the rugged course, kills like the rest, becomes quarrelsome, drinks and brawls, and casts off his hesitant, careful, and complaining childishness.

A very different sort of novel, in a peaceful sphere far removed from the explosions and disembowellings of Guadalcanal, is J. F. Powers's *Morte d'Urban*, which does not so much study as brood over the lives of priests belonging to the Order of St

Clement. Father Urban, a well-known preacher and a man of some talent, is transferred for reasons not clearly understood from Chicago, where he has worked effectively, to a new Foundation of the Order in Duesterhaus, Minnesota. To Urban, a sociable and civilized priest, this transfer can only be seen as a mysterious banishment, and he is described by Mr Powers looking from the train windows at the empty country beyond Minneapolis.

> ... flat and treeless, Illinois without people. It didn't attract, it didn't repel. He saw more streams than he'd see in Illinois, but they weren't working. November was winter here. Too many white frame farmhouses, not new and not old, not at all what Father Urban would care to come to for Thanksgiving or Christmas. Rusty implements. Brown dirt. Grey skies. Ice. No snow. A great deal of talk about this on the train. Father Urban dropped entirely out of it after an hour or so. The Voyageur arrived in Duesterhaus a few minutes before eleven that morning, and Father Urban was the only passenger to get off.

In more ways than one, Father Urban is viewed as the only passenger. At the new Foundation he is, without complaint, in a solitary situation. In charge of the Duesterhaus Foundation is Father Wilfred '... who, on account of his broad nose and padded cheeks, had been called Bunny in the Novitiate. Bunny Bestudik.' Father Wilfred's concerns are all of a practical nature. His interests are the interests of any Midwestern American who has to run a place efficiently; he watches the fuel bills, thinks about the pick-up truck and its rubber, the cost of paint, and is anxious to have good public relations. This religious Order is described as a community of consumers. It is the American and average character of activities whose ultimate aim is religious that Mr Powers wants to describe. His tone is dry and factual and he tells of the discussions of the Fathers who have to heat, paint, and renovate their buildings, sand the floors, tear up old linoleum, lay new tiles in the bathrooms, and this light and dry comedy cannot be maintained through such a long account of the effort to fill up a great emptiness with activity which is insufficiently purposeful. The religion of Father Urban is expressed in steadiness and patience, in endurance, not in fiery strength. His resistance to the prolonged barrenness and vacant busyness of this thoroughly American Order is made in a spirit of mild and decent martyrdom. Indeed, the only violent and passionate person in the book is a certain Billy Cosgrove. Billy is rich and generous. He gives lavishly to the Order but he expects also to have his way. He and Father Urban eat shish kebab and drink champagne, play golf and go fishing. With Billy one talks of cars and sailing boats. Urban gets along rather well with spoiled and boisterous Billy until Billy tries to drown a deer in the water of Bloodsucker Lake. Billy has been fishing and is in an ugly mood because his luck has been bad. Seeing a swimming deer, he decides to seize it by the antlers and hold its head under water. As hungry for trophies as the soldiers in *The Thin Red Line*, Billy wants those antlers. Father Urban, who cannot bear his cruelty, starts up the motor of the boat, and Billy falls into the water. For this outrage Billy will never forgive him.

What Father Urban had been thinking just before the appearance of the deer was that in the Church there was perhaps too great an emphasis on dying for the faith and winning the martyr's crown.

> How about living for the faith? Take Lanfranc and William the Conqueror – of whom it was written (in the Catholic Encyclopædia and Father Urban's notes on a book he might write some day): 'He was mild to good men of God and stark beyond all bounds to those who withsaid his will.'

Billy Cosgrove turns out to occupy the position of the Conqueror. He is stark beyond all bounds, and Urban is never again to see his face. Nor does Urban seem destined to write his book. He goes to the Novitiate of the Order as Father Provincial, there to deal with practical matters to the best of his ability. But he appears to be succumbing to a brain injury he received while playing golf. He had been struck on the head by a golf ball in Minnesota and is now subject to fits of dizziness. A martyr's crown seems to be waiting Urban as the book ends.

Powers does not look at the issue of the single Self and the multitude as nakedly as Jones does, and it is a pity that he chose not to do so, for he might have been able to offer us a more subtle development of the subject. He would have been examining what Mr Sypher calls 'Loss of the Self' from the point of view of a Christian, that is, from the point of view of one who believes in the existence of something more profound than the romantic or secular idea of Selfhood, namely, a soul. But there is curiously little talk of souls in this book about a priest. Spiritually, its quality is very thin. That perhaps is as Mr Powers meant it to be. Even at play Father Urban is serving the Church, and, if he is hit on the head by a golf ball, we can perhaps draw our own conclusions from that about the present age viewed as a chapter in the spiritual history of mankind. Here great things will only be dimly apprehended even by the most willing servant of God. Still this seems to me unsatisfactory, and I am not sure that I can bring myself to admire such meekness. A man might well be meek in his own interests, but furious at such abuses of the soul and eager to show what is positive and powerful in his faith. The lack of such power makes faith itself shadowy, more like obscure tenacity than spiritual conviction. In this sense Mr Powers's book is disappointing.

The individual in American fiction often comes through to us, especially among writers of 'sensibility', as a colonist who has been sent to a remote place, some Alaska of the soul. What he has to bring under cultivation, however, is a barren emptiness within himself. This is, of course, what writers of sensibility have for a long time been doing and what they continue to do. The latest to demonstrate his virtuosity with exceptional success is John Updike, who begins the title story of his new collection, *Pigeon Feathers*, 'When they moved to Firetown, things were upset, displaced, rearranged.' The rearrangement of things in new and hostile solitude is a common theme with writers of sensibility. David, the only child of a family which has moved to the country, is assailed by terror when he reads in H. G. Wells's *The Outline of History* that Jesus was nothing more than a rather communistic Galilean, '. . . an obscure political agitator, a kind of hobo in a minor colony of the Roman Empire'. The effect of this is to open the question of death and immortality. David is dissatisfied with answers given by the Reverend Dobson and by his parents. He cannot understand the pleasure his mother takes in her solitary walks along the edge of the woods. '. . . to him the brown stretches of slowly rising and falling land expressed only a huge exhaustion.'

' "What do you want Heaven to be?" ' asks David's mother. 'He was becoming angry, sensing her surprise at him. She had assumed that Heaven had faded from his head long ago. She had imagined that he had already entered in the secrecy of silence, the conspiracy that he now knew to be all around him.'

Young David in the end resolves the problem for himself aesthetically. Admiring the beauty of pigeon feathers he feels consoled by the sense of a providence. '. . . the God who had lavished such craft upon these worthless birds would not destroy His whole Creation by refusing to let David live forever.' The story ends with a mild irony at the expense of the boy. Nevertheless, there is nothing to see here but the writer's reliance on beautiful work, on an aesthetic discipline and order. And sensibility, in such forms, incurs the dislike of many because it is perceptive inwardly, and otherwise blind. We suspect it of a stony heart because it functions so smoothly in its isolation. The writer of sensibility assumes that only private exploration and inner development are possible, and accepts the opposition of public and private as fixed and indissoluble.

We are dealing with modern attitudes towards the ancient idea of the individual and the many, the single Self in the midst of the mass or species. In modern times the idea of the unique Self has become associated with the name of Rousseau. Nietzsche identified the Self with the God Apollo, the god of light, harmony, music, reason and proportion, and the many, the tribe, the species, the instincts and passions, with Dionysus. Between these two principles, the individual and the generic, men and civilizations supposedly work out their destinies. It is to Nietzsche, too, that we owe the concept of the 'last man'. His 'last man' is an obituary on the unitary and sufficient Self produced by a proud bourgeois and industrial civilization. Dostoevsky's Underground Man is an analogous figure. Atheism, rationalism, utilitarianism, and revolution are signs of a deadly sickness in the human soul, in his scheme of things. The lost Selves whose souls are destroyed he sees as legion. The living soul clearly discerns them. It owes this illumination to Christ the Redeemer. More optimistically, an American poet like Walt Whitman imagined that the single Self and the democratic mass might complement each other. But on this side of the Atlantic, also, Thoreau described men as leading lives of quiet desperation, accepting a deadly common life: the individual retires from the community to define or re-define his real needs in isolation beside Walden Pond.

Still later a French poet tells us '*Je est un autre.*' Rimbaud and Jarry launch their bombs and grenades against the tight little bourgeois kingdom of the Self, that sensitive sovereign. Darwin and the early anthropologists unwittingly damage his sovereignty badly. Then come the psychologists, who explain that his Ego is a paltry shelter against the unendurable storms that rage in outer reality. After them come the logicians and physical scientists who tell us that 'I' is a grammatical expression. Poets like Valéry describe this Self as a poor figment, a thing of change, and tell us that consciousness is interested only in what is eternal. Novelists like Joyce turn away from the individualism of the romantics and the humanists to contemplate instead qualities found in dreams and belonging to the entire species – Earwicker is everybody. Writers like Sartre, Ionesco, and Beckett or like our own William Burroughs and Allan Ginsberg are only a few of the active campaigners on this shrinking front against the Self. One would like to ask these contemporaries, 'After nakedness, what?' 'After absurdity, what?'

But, on the whole, American novels are filled with complaints over the misfortunes of the sovereign Self. Writers have inherited a tone of bitterness from the great poems and novels of this century, many of which lament the passing of a more stable and beautiful age demolished by the barbarous intrusion of an industrial and metropolitan society of masses or proles who will, after many upheavals, be tamed by bureaucracies and oligarchies in brave new worlds, human anthills.

These works of the first half of our century nourish the imagination of contemporary writers and supply a tonal background of disillusion or elegy.

There are modern novelists who take all of this for granted as fully proven and implicit in the human condition and who complain as steadily as they write, viewing modern life with a bitterness to which they themselves have not established clear title, and it is this unearned bitterness that I speak of. What is truly curious about it is that often the writer automatically scorns contemporary life. He bottles its stinks artistically. But, seemingly, he does not need to study it. It is enough for him that it does not allow his sensibilities to thrive, that it starves his instincts for nobility or for spiritual qualities.

But what the young American writer most often appears to feel is his *own* misfortune. The injustice is done to *his* talent if life is brutish and ignorant, if the world seems overcome by Spam and beer, or covered with detergent lathers and poisonous monoxides. This apparently is the only injustice he feels. Neither for himself nor for his fellows does he attack power and injustice directly and hotly. He simply defends his sensibility.

Perhaps the reason for this is the prosperity and relative security of the middle class from which most writers come. In educating its writers it makes available to them the radical doctrines of all the ages, but these in their superabundance only cancel one another out. The middle-class community trains its writers also in passivity and resignation and in the double enjoyment of selfishness and goodwill. They are taught that they can have it both ways. In fact they are taught to expect to enjoy everything that life can offer. They can live dangerously while managing somehow to remain safe. They can be both bureaucrats and bohemians, they can be executives but use pot, they can raise families but enjoy bohemian sexuality, they can observe the laws while in their hearts and in their social attitudes they may be as subversive as they please. They are both conservative and radical. They are everything that is conceivable. They are not taught to care genuinely for any man or any cause.

A recent novel like Philip Roth's *Letting Go* is a consummate example of this. Roth's hero, Gabriel, educated to succeed in this world and to lead a good life come hell or high water, is slightly uncomfortable in his selfishness. But nevertheless he wants his, as the saying goes, and he gets his. But he feels obscurely the humiliation of being a private bourgeois Self, the son of an unhappy but prosperous dentist, and he senses that a 'personal life' with its problems of personal adjustment and personal responsibility and personal happiness, its ostensibly normal calculations of profit and loss, safety and danger, lust and prudence is a source of shame. But Gabriel's middle-class parents sent him into life to make the grade and that is precisely, with tough singlemindedness, what he does. His shame therefore becomes a province of his sensibility, and it is something he can be rather proud of as he does what he was going to do anyway.

Roth's hero clings to the hope of self-knowledge and personal improvement, and he concludes that, with all his faults, he loves himself still. His inner life, if it may be called that, is a rather feeble thing of a few watts. Conceivably it may guide him to a more satisfactory adjustment, but it makes me think of the usher's flashlight in the dark theatre guiding the single ticket-holder to his reserved seat. We are supposed to feel that Gabriel is unusually sensitive, but what we find is that he is a tough young man who cannot be taken in and who will survive the accidents of life that madden or kill genuinely sensitive young men.

* * *

I would like now to list the categories suggested by my reading of current novels: the documentation of James Jones, the partially Christian approach of Powers, the sensibility of Updike, and the grievance of Philip Roth. I do not retract my earlier statement that in American novels – for I have decided rather arbitrarily to limit myself to examining these – the tone of complaint prevails. The public realm, as it encroaches on the private, steadily reduces the powers of the individual; but it cannot take away his power to despair, and sometimes he seems to be making the most of that. However, there are several other avenues commonly taken: stoicism, nihilistic anger, and comedy. Stoicism and comedy are sometimes mixed, as in the case of the late German dramatist Bertolt Brecht, but our own contemporary American stoicism comes from Hemingway, and its best American representative at present is John O'Hara.

O'Hara is properly impatient with people who suffer too intensely from themselves. The characters in his latest collection of stories, *The Cape Cod Lighter*, for whom he shows a decided preference, appear to be bluff, natural people, who know how to endure hurt and act with an elementary and realistic sense of honour. When Ernest Pangborn in the story 'The Professors' learns that he has misjudged his colleague Jack Veech and understands at last that Veech's behaviour has been decent and manly, he is moved to say something to him but does not know what to say.

> A compliment would be rejected, and a word of pity would be unthinkable. Indeed the compliment was being paid to Pangborn; Veech honoured him with his confidence and accorded him honour more subtly, more truly, by asking no further assurances of his silence.

The emotion we feel here is made possible by long reticence, by the deep burial of self-proclamation or self-assertion. We recall the pure decencies of schooldays, and the old chivalrous or military origins of these. These, surely, are virtues of silence and passivity. We endure. We are rewarded by a vision of one another's complexities, but there is no possibility of a flourish, or of rhetoric, or anything that would make an undue personal claim.

This is no longer the sovereign Self of the Romantics, but the decent Self of Kipling whose great satisfaction it is to recognize the existence of a great number of others. These numerous others reduce personal significance, and both realism and dignity require us to accept this reduction. Such stoicism of separateness is the opposite of sensibility with its large claims for the development of internal riches.

But the O'Haras are curiously like the Updikes in at least one respect. They are scrupulous craftsmen and extraordinarily strict about their writing. Nothing unrealistic, unnatural, or excessive (as they define those qualities) is suffered to appear. O'Hara insists upon a hard literalness in his language which reminds one of the simple crystalline code of his characters. There is a roughness in O'Hara which may make the writer of sensibility feel like a dude. O'Hara's self-identification is obviously with the workman, with the average, with plain people. Or perhaps he feels himself to be a part of the majority, which is to say, of the crowd. Certainly he does not merely react against what he judges an incorrect definition of the individual; he hates it violently. And conceivably he hates it in himself. His view of sensibility or of an intricate and conceivably self-indulgent privacy is, like Hemingway's (in *The Sun Also Rises*, for instance), entirely negative. He sees the romantic Self with the eyes of the crowd. And the crowd is a leveller. The average it seeks is anything but Whitman's divine average.

The absolute individualism of the Enlightenment has fallen. Contemporary writers like Brecht, or Beckett, or the Beats, and recently and most atrociously William Burroughs in his *Naked Lunch*, have repudiated it in a spirit of violence. Some have been violently comic at its expense, others ruthlessly nihilistic and vengeful. Among them there are some who gather unto themselves more and more and more power only to release it destructively on this already discredited and fallen individualism. In this they seem at times to imitate the great modern consolidations of power, to follow the example of parties and states and their scientific or military instruments. They act, in short, like those who hold the real power in society, the masters of the Leviathan. But this is only an imitation of the real power. Through this imitation they hope perhaps to show that they are not inferior to those who lead the modern world. Joint Chiefs or Pentagons have power to do as they will to huge populations. But there are writers who will not reckon themselves among these subordinate masses and who aim to demonstrate an independent power equal to the greatest. They therefore strike one sometimes as being extraordinarily eager to release their strength and violence against an enemy, and that enemy is the false conception of Self created by Christianity and by Christianity's successors in the Enlightenment. Modern literature is not satisfied simply to dismiss a romantic, outmoded conception of the Self. In a spirit of deepest vengefulness it curses it. It hates it. It rends it, annihilates it. It would rather have the maddest chaos it can invoke than a conception of life it has found false. But after this destruction, what?

I have spoken of complaint, stoicism, sensibility, and nihilistic rage, and I would like to touch now on recent American writers who have turned to comedy. It is obvious that modern comedy has to do with the disintegrating outline of the worthy and humane Self, the bourgeois hero of an earlier age. That sober, prudent person, the bourgeois, although he did much for the development of modern civilization, built factories and railroads, dug canals, created sewage systems, and went colonizing, was indicted for his shallowness and his ignoble and hypocritical ways. The Christian writer (see Dostoevsky's portrait of Luzhin in *Crime and Punishment*) and the revolutionary (see Mangan in Shaw's *Heartbreak House*) repudiated him and all his works. The First World War dealt a blow to his prestige from which it never recovered. Dada and surrealism raised a storm of laughter against him. In the movies René Clair and Charlie Chaplin found him out. He became the respectable little person, the gentlemanly tramp. Poets of the deepest subversive tendencies came on like bank clerks in ironic masquerade.

The trick is still good, as J. P. Donleavy has lately shown in his novel *The Ginger Man*. His hero, Sebastian Dangerfield, a free-wheeling rascal and chaser, presents himself with wickedly comic effect as an ultra-respectable citizen with an excellent credit rating, one who doesn't know what it is to hock other people's property for the price of a drink, the gentlemanly sack-artist.

The private and inner life which was the subject of serious books until very recently now begins to have an antique and funny look. The earnestness of a Proust towards himself would seem old-fashioned today. Indeed, Italo Svevo, a contemporary of Proust, in *The Confessions of Zeno*, made introspection, hypochondria, and self-knowledge the subjects of his comedy. *My* welfare, *my* development, *my* advancement, *my* earnestness, *my* adjustment, *my* marriage, *my* family – all that will make the modern reader laugh heartily. Writers may not wholly agree with Bertrand Russell that 'I' is no more than a grammatical expression, but they do consider certain claims of the 'I' to be definitely funny. Already in the nineteenth century Stendhal became bored with the persistent 'I-I-I' and denounced it in characteristic terms.

Perhaps the change that has occurred can be clearly illustrated by a comparison of Thomas Mann's *Death in Venice* with Nabokov's *Lolita*. In both stories an older man is overcome by sexual desire for a younger person. With Mann, however, this sad occurrence involves Apollo and Dionysus. Gustave von Aschenbach, an overly civilized man, an individual estranged from his instincts which unexpectedly claim their revenge, has gone too far, has entered the realm of sickness and perversity and is carried away by the plague. This is a typically Nietzschean theme. But in *Lolita* the internal life of Humbert Humbert has become a joke. Far from being as Aschenbach, a great figure of European literature, he is a fourth- or fifth-rate man of the world and is unable to be entirely serious about his passion. As for Lolita's mother, the poor thing only makes him laugh when she falls in love with him – a banal woman. To a very considerable extent Humbert's judgement of her is based on the low level of her culture. Her banality makes her a proper victim. If her words about love and desire had not come out of a bin in which the great American public finds suitable expressions to describe its psychological and personal needs, she might have been taken more seriously. The earnestness of Mann about love and death might be centuries old. The same subject is sadly and maliciously comical in *Lolita*. Clare Quilty cannot be made to take even his own death seriously and while he is being murdered by Humbert, ridicules his own situation and Humbert's as well, losing at last a life that was not worth having anyway. The contemporary Aschenbach does not deny his desires, but then he is without the dignity of the old fellow and is always on the verge of absurdity. Wright Morris in his new novel *What a Way to Go* explicitly makes comedy of the *Death in Venice* theme. His American professors in Venice, discussing *Death in Venice* all the while, seem to feel that there is small hope for them. They decline to view themselves with full seriousness. They believe their day is over. They are unfit, and dismiss themselves with a joke.

We must carefully remind ourselves that, if so many people today exist to enjoy or deplore an individual life, it is because prodigious public organizations, scientific, industrial, and political, support huge populations of new individuals. These organizations both elicit and curtail private development. I myself am not convinced that there is less 'Selfhood' in the modern world. I am not sure anyone knows how to put the matter properly. I am simply recording the attitudes of modern writers, including contemporary Americans, who are convinced that the jig of the Self is up.

What is the modern Self in T. S. Eliot's *Waste Land*? It is the many, crossing the bridge in the great modern city, who do not know that death has already undone them; it is the 'clerk carbuncular' taking sexual liberties of brief duration with the 'lovely lady' who, after she has stooped to folly, puts a record on the gramophone. What is the Self for French novelists of the first post-war era like Louis Ferdinand Céline, or for writers like Curzio Malaparte or Albert Camus in the second post-war era? Man, in a book like *The Stranger*, is a creature neither fully primitive nor fully civilized, a Self devoid of depths. We have come a long way from Montaigne and his belief in a self-perfecting, self-knowing character.

Recent American comic novels like *Lolita*, or *The Ginger Man*, or Burt Blechman's *How Much?*, or Bruce Friedman's first novel *Stern* examine the private life. It is as if they were testing the saying of Socrates, that the unexamined life was not worth living. Apparently they find the examined life funny too. Some cannot find the life they are going to examine. The power of public life has become so vast and threatening that private life cannot maintain a pretence of its importance. Our condition of destructibility is ever-present in everyone's mind. Our submission seems required by public ugliness in our cities, by the public nonsense of television which threatens to turn our brains to farina within our heads, by even such trifling things as Muzak broadcasts in the elevators of public buildings. The Self is asked to prepare itself for sacrifice, and this is the situation reflected in contemporary American fiction.

As for the future, it cannot possibly shock us since we have already done everything possible to scandalize ourselves. We have so completely debunked the old idea of the Self that we can hardly continue in the same way. Perhaps some power within us will tell us what we are, now that old misconceptions have been laid low. Undeniably the human being is not what he commonly thought a century ago. The question nevertheless remains. He is something. What is he?

And this question, it seems to me, modern writers have answered poorly. They have told us, indignantly or nihilistically or comically, how great our error is, but for the rest they have offered us thin fare. The fact is that modern writers sin when they suppose that they *know*, as they conceive that physics *knows* or that history *knows*. The subject of the novelist is not knowable in any such way. The mystery increases, it does not grow less as types of literature wear out. It is, however, Symbolism or Realism or Sensibility wearing out, and not the mystery of mankind.

JOHN BARTH

The Literature of Exhaustion

(1967)

> The fact is that every writer *creates* his own precursors. His work
> modifies our conception of the past, as it will modify the future.
>
> JORGE LUIS BORGES, *Labyrinths*

> You who   listen   give me life   in a
> manner   of speaking.   I won't hold you respon-
> sible.   My first words weren't my first words. I wish
> I'd begun differently.
>
> JOHN BARTH, *Lost in the Fun House*

I want to discuss three things more or less together: first, some
old questions raised by the new intermedia arts; second, some
aspects of the Argentine writer Jorge Luis Borges, whom I
greatly admire; third, some professional concerns of my own,
related to these other matters and having to do with what I'm
calling 'the literature of exhausted possibility' – or, more chicly,
'the literature of exhaustion'.

By 'exhaustion' I don't mean anything so tired as the subject
of physical, moral, or intellectual decadence, only the used-
upness of certain forms or exhaustion of certain possibilities –
by no means necessarily a cause for despair. That a great many
Western artists for a great many years have quarrelled with
received definitions of artistic media, genres, and forms goes
without saying: pop art, dramatic and musical 'happenings', the
whole range of 'intermedia' or 'mixed-means' art, bear recentest
witness to the tradition of rebelling against Tradition. A catalogue I received some time ago in the mail, for example,
advertises such items as Robert Filliou's *Ample Food for Stupid*

Thought, a box full of postcards on which are inscribed 'apparently meaningless questions', to be mailed to whomever the purchaser judges them suited for; Ray Johnson's *Paper Snake*, a collection of whimsical writings, 'often pointed', once mailed to various friends (what the catalogue describes as The New York Correspondence School of Literature); and Daniel Spoerri's *Anecdoted Typography of Chance*, 'on the surface' a description of all the objects that happen to be on the author's parlour table – 'in fact, however ... a cosmology of Spoerri's existence'.

'On the surface', at least, the document listing these items is a catalogue of The Something Else Press, a swinging outfit. 'In fact, however', it may be one of their offerings, for all I know: The New York Direct-Mail Advertising School of Literature. In any case, their wares are lively to read about, and make for interesting conversation in fiction-writing classes, for example, where we discuss Somebody-or-other's unbound, unpaginated, randomly assembled novel-in-a-box and the desirability of printing *Finnegans Wake* on a very long roller-towel. It's easier and sociabler to talk technique than it is to make art, and the area of 'happenings' and their kin is mainly a way of discussing aesthetics, really; illustrating 'dramatically' more or less valid and interesting points about the nature of art and the definition of its terms and genres.

One conspicuous thing, for example, about the 'intermedia' arts is their tendency (noted even by *Life* magazine) to eliminate not only the traditional audience – 'those who apprehend the artists' art' (in 'happenings' the audience is often the 'cast', as in 'environments', and some of the new music isn't intended to be performed at all) – but also the most traditional notion of the artist: the Aristotelian conscious agent who achieves with technique and cunning the artistic effect; in other words, one endowed with uncommon talent, who has moreover developed and disciplined that endowment into virtuosity. It's an aristocratic notion on the face of it, which the democratic West seems eager to have done with; not only the 'omniscient' author of older fiction, but the very idea of the controlling artist, has been condemned as politically reactionary, even fascist.

Now, personally, being of the temper that chooses to 'rebel along traditional lines', I'm inclined to prefer the kind of art that not many people can *do*: the kind that requires expertise and artistry as well as bright aesthetic ideas and/or inspiration. I enjoy the pop art in the famous Albright-Knox collection, a few blocks from my house in Buffalo, like a lively conversation for the most part, but was on the whole more impressed by the jugglers and acrobats at Baltimore's old Hippodrome, where I used to go every time they changed shows: genuine *virtuosi* doing things that anyone can dream up and discuss but almost no one can do.

I suppose the distinction is between things worth remarking – preferably over beer, if one's of my generation – and things worth doing. 'Somebody ought to make a novel with scenes that pop up, like the old children's books,' one says, with the implication that one isn't going to bother doing it oneself.

However, art and its forms and techniques live in history and certainly do change. I sympathize with a remark attributed to Saul Bellow, that to be technically up to date is the least important attribute of a writer, though I would have to add that this least important attribute may be nevertheless essential. In any case, to be technically *out* of date is likely to be a genuine defect: Beethoven's Sixth Symphony or the Chartres Cathedral if executed today would be merely embarrassing. A good many current novelists write turn-of-the-century-type novels, only in more or less mid-twentieth-century language and about contemporary people and topics; this makes them considerably less interesting (to me) than excellent writers who are also technically contemporary: Joyce and Kafka, for instance, in their time, and in ours, Samuel Beckett and Jorge Luis Borges. The intermedia arts, I'd say, tend to be intermediary too, between the traditional realms of aesthetics on the one hand and artistic creation on the other; I think the wise artist and civilian will regard them with quite the kind and degree of seriousness with

73

which he regards good shoptalk: he'll listen carefully, if non-committally, and keep an eye on his intermedia colleagues, if only the corner of his eye. They may very possibly suggest something usable in the making or understanding of genuine works of contemporary art.

The man I want to discuss a little here, Jorge Luis Borges, illustrates well the difference between a technically old-fashioned artist, a technically up-to-date civilian, and a technically up-to-date artist. In the first category I'd locate all those novelists who for better or worse write not as if the twentieth century didn't exist, but as if the great writers of the last sixty years or so hadn't existed (*nota bene* that our century's more than two-thirds done; it's dismaying to see so many of our writers following Dostoevsky or Tolstoy or Flaubert or Balzac, when the real technical question seems to me to be how to succeed not even Joyce and Kafka, but those who've *succeeded* Joyce and Kafka and are now in the evenings of their own careers). In the second category are such folk as an artist-neighbour of mine in Buffalo who fashions dead Winnie-the-Poohs in sometimes monumental scale out of oilcloth stuffed with sand and impaled on stakes or hung by the neck. In the third belong the few people whose artistic thinking is as hip as any French new-novelist's, but who manage nonetheless to speak eloquently and memorably to our still-human hearts and conditions, as the great artists have always done. Of these, two of the finest living specimens that I know of are Beckett and Borges, just about the only contemporaries of my reading acquaintance mentionable with the 'old masters' of twentieth-century fiction. In the unexciting history of literary awards, the 1961 International Publishers' Prize, shared by Beckett and Borges, is a happy exception indeed.

One of the modern things about these two is that in an age of ultimacies and 'final solutions' – at least *felt* ultimacies, in everything from weaponry to theology, the celebrated dehuman-ization of society, and the history of the novel – their work in separate ways reflects and deals with ultimacy, both technically and thematically, as, for example, *Finnegans Wake* does in its different manner. One notices, by the way, for whatever its symptomatic worth, that Joyce was virtually blind at the end, Borges is literally so, and Beckett has become virtually mute, musewise, having progressed from marvellously constructed English sentences through terser and terser French ones to the unsyntactical, unpunctuated prose of *Comment C'est* and 'ultimately' to wordless mimes. One might extrapolate a theoretical course for Beckett: language, after all, consists of silence as well as sound, and the mime is still communication – 'that nineteenth-century idea', a Yale student once snarled at me – but by the language of action. But the language of action consists of rest as well as movement, and so in the context of Beckett's progress, immobile, silent figures still aren't altogether ultimate. How about an empty, silent stage, then, or blank pages (an ultimacy already attained in the nineteenth century by that *avant-gardiste* of East Aurora, New York, Elbert Hubbard, in his *Essay on Silence*) – a 'happening' where nothing happens, like Cage's *4' 33"* performed in an empty hall? But dramatic communication consists of the absence as well as the presence of the actors; 'we have our exits and our entrances'; and so even that would be imperfectly ultimate in Beckett's case. Nothing at all, then, I suppose: but Nothingness is necessarily and inextricably the background against which Being et cetera; for Beckett, at this point in his career, to cease to create altogether would be fairly meaningful: his crowning work, his 'last word'. What a convenient corner to paint yourself into! 'And now I shall finish,' the valet Arsene says in *Watt*, 'and you will hear my voice no more.' Only the silence *Molloy* speaks of, 'of which the universe is made'.

After which, I add on behalf of the rest of us, it might be conceivable to rediscover validly the artifices of language and literature – such far-out notions as grammar, punctuation ... even characterization! Even *plot*! – if one goes about it the right way, aware of what one's predecessors have been up to.

Now J. L. Borges is perfectly aware of all these things. Back in the great decades of literary experimentalism he was associated with *Prisma*, a 'muralist' magazine that published its pages on walls and billboards; his later *Labyrinths* and *Ficciones* not only anticipate the farthest-out ideas of The Something Else Press crowd – not a difficult thing to do – but being marvellous works of art as well, illustrate in a simple way the difference between the *fact* of aesthetic ultimacies and their artistic *use*. What it comes to is that an artist doesn't merely exemplify an ultimacy; he employs it.

Consider Borges's story 'Pierre Menard, Author of the Quixote': the hero, an utterly sophisticated turn-of-the-century French Symbolist, by an astounding effort of imagination, produces – not *copies* or *imitates*, mind, but *composes* – several chapters of Cervantes's novel.

> It is a revelation [Borges's narrator tells us] to compare Menard's *Don Quixote* with Cervantes's. The latter, for example, wrote (part one, chapter nine):
>
> ... truth, whose mother is history, rival of time, depository of deeds, witness of the past, exemplar and adviser to the present, the future's counsellor.
>
> Written in the seventeenth century, written by the 'lay genius' Cervantes, this enumeration is a mere rhetorical praise of history. Menard, on the other hand, writes:
>
> ... truth, whose mother is history, rival of time, depository of deeds, witness of the past, exemplar and adviser to the present, the future's counsellor.
>
> History, the *mother* of truth: the idea is astounding. Menard, a contemporary of William James, does not define history as an enquiry into reality but as its origin ...

Et cetera. Now, this is an interesting idea, of considerable intellectual validity. I mentioned earlier that if Beethoven's Sixth were composed today, it would be an embarrassment; but clearly it wouldn't be, necessarily, if done with ironic intent by a composer quite aware of where we've been and where we are. It would have then potentially, for better or worse, the kind of significance of Warhol's Campbell's Soup ads, the difference being that in the former case a work of art is being reproduced instead of a work of non-art, and the ironic comment would therefore be more directly on the genre and history of the art than on the state of the culture. In fact, of course, to make the valid intellectual point one needn't even re-compose the Sixth Symphony any more than Menard really needed to recreate the *Quixote*. It would've been sufficient for Menard to have *attributed* the novel to himself in order to have a new work of art, from the intellectual point of view. Indeed, in several stories Borges plays with this very idea, and I can readily imagine Beckett's next novel, for example, as *Tom Jones*, just as Nabokov's last was that multivolume annotated translation of Pushkin. I myself have always aspired to write Burton's version of *The 1001 Nights*, complete with appendices and the like, in twelve volumes, and for intellectual purposes I needn't even write it. What evenings we might spend (over beer) discussing Saarinen's Parthenon, D. H. Lawrence's *Wuthering Heights*, or the Johnson Administration by Robert Rauschenberg!

The idea, I say, is intellectually serious, as are Borges's other characteristic ideas, most of a metaphysical rather than an aesthetic nature. But the important thing to observe is that Borges doesn't attribute the *Quixote* to himself, much less recompose it like Pierre Menard; instead, he writes a remarkable and original work of literature, the implicit theme of which is the difficulty, perhaps the unnecessity, of writing original works of literature. His artistic victory, if you like, is that he confronts an intellectual dead end and employs it against itself to accomplish new human work. If this corresponds to what mystics do – 'every moment leaping into the infinite', Kierkegaard says, 'and every moment falling surely back into the finite' – it's only one more aspect of that old analogy. In homelier terms, it's a matter of every moment throwing out the bath water without for a moment losing the baby.

Another way of describing Borges's accomplishment is in a

pair of his own favourite terms, *algebra* and *fire*. In his most often anthologized story, 'Tlön, Uqbar, Orbis Tertius', he imagines an entirely hypothetical world, the invention of a secret society of scholars who elaborate its every aspect in a surreptitious encyclopaedia. This *First Encyclopaedia of Tlön* (what fictionist would not wish to have dreamed up the *Britannica?*) describes a coherent alternative to this world complete in every aspect from its algebra to its fire, Borges tells us, and of such imaginative power that, once conceived, it begins to obtrude itself into and eventually to supplant our prior reality. My point is that neither the algebra nor the fire, metaphorically speaking, could achieve this result without the other. Borges's algebra is what I'm considering here – algebra is easier to talk about than fire – but any intellectual giant could equal it. The imaginary authors of the *First Encyclopaedia of Tlön* itself are not artists, though their work is in a manner of speaking fictional and would find a ready publisher in New York nowadays. The author of the story 'Tlön, Uqbar, Orbis Tertius', who merely *alludes* to the fascinating *Encyclopaedia*, is an artist; what makes him one of the first rank, like Kafka, is the combination of that intellectually profound vision with great human insight, poetic power, and consummate mastery of his means, a definition which would have gone without saying, I suppose, in any century but ours.

Not long ago, incidentally, in a footnote to a scholarly edition of Sir Thomas Browne (*The Urn Burial*, I believe it was), I came upon a perfect Borges datum, reminiscent of Tlön's self-realization: the actual case of a book called *The Three Impostors*, alluded to in Browne's *Religio Medici* among other places. *The Three Impostors* is a non-existent blasphemous treatise against Moses, Christ, and Mohammed, which in the seventeenth century was widely held to exist, or to have once existed. Commentators attributed it variously to Boccaccio, Pietro Aretino, Giordano Bruno, and Tommaso Campanella, and though no one, Browne included, had ever seen a copy of it, it was frequently cited, refuted, railed against, and generally discussed as if everyone had read it – until, sure enough, in the *eighteenth* century a spurious work appeared with a forged date of 1598 and the title *De Tribus Impostoribus*. It's a wonder that Borges doesn't mention this work, as he seems to have read absolutely everything, including all the books that don't exist, and Browne is a particular favourite of his. In fact, the narrator of 'Tlön, Uqbar, Orbis Tertius' declares at the end:

> ... English and French and mere Spanish will disappear from the globe. The world will be Tlön. I pay no attention to all this and go on revising, in the still days at the Adrogué hotel, an uncertain Quevedian translation (which I do not intend to publish) of Browne's *Urn Burial*.

(Moreover, on rereading 'Tlön', etc., I find now a remark I'd swear wasn't in it last year: that the eccentric American millionaire who endows the *Encyclopaedia* does so on condition that 'the work will make no pact with the impostor Jesus Christ'.)

This 'contamination of reality by dream', as Borges calls it, is one of his pet themes, and commenting upon such contaminations is one of his favourite fictional devices. Like many of the best such devices, it turns the artist's mode or form into a metaphor for his concerns, as does the diary-ending of *Portrait of the Artist as a Young Man* or the cyclical construction of *Finnegans Wake*. In Borges's case, the story 'Tlön', etc., for example, is a real piece of imagined reality in our world, analogous to those Tlönian artifacts called *hronir*, which imagine themselves into existence. In short, it's a paradigm of or metaphor for itself; not just the *form* of the story but the *fact* of the story is symbolic; 'the medium is the message'.

Moreover, like all of Borges's work, it illustrates in other of its aspects my subject: how an artist may paradoxically turn the felt ultimacies of our time into material and means for his work – *paradoxically* because by doing so he transcends what had appeared to be his refutation, in the same way that the mystic who transcends finitude is said to be enabled to live, spiritually and physically, in the finite world. Suppose you're a writer by vocation – a 'print-oriented bastard', as the McLuhanites call us

– and you feel, for example, that the novel, if not narrative literature generally, if not the printed word altogether, has by this hour of the world just about shot its bolt, as Leslie Fiedler and others maintain. (I'm inclined to agree, with reservations and hedges. Literary forms certainly have histories and historical contingencies, and it may well be that the novel's time as a major art form is up, as the 'times' of classical tragedy, grand opera, or the sonnet sequence came to be. No necessary cause for alarm in this at all, except perhaps to certain novelists, and one way to handle such a feeling might be to write a novel about it. Whether historically the novel expires or persists seems immaterial to me; if enough writers and critics *feel* apocalyptical about it, their feeling becomes a considerable cultural fact, like the feeling that Western civilization, or the world, is going to end rather soon. If you took a bunch of people out into the desert and the world didn't end, you'd come home shame-faced, I imagine; but the persistence of an art form doesn't invalidate work created in the comparable apocalyptic ambience. That's one of the fringe benefits of being an artist instead of a prophet. There are others.) If you happened to be Vladimir Nabokov you might address that felt ultimacy by writing *Pale Fire*: a fine novel by a learned pedant, in the form of a pedantic commentary on a poem invented for the purpose. If you were Borges you might write *Labyrinths*: fictions by a learned librarian in the form of footnotes, as he describes them, to imaginary or hypothetical books. And I'll add, since I believe Borges's idea is rather more interesting, that if you were the author of this paper, you'd have written something like *The Sot-Weed Factor* or *Giles Goat-Boy*: novels which imitate the form of the Novel, by an author who imitates the role of Author.

If this sort of thing sounds unpleasantly decadent, nevertheless it's about where the genre began, with *Quixote* imitating *Amadis of Gaul*, Cervantes pretending to be the Cid Hamete Benengeli (and Alonso Quijano pretending to be Don Quixote), or Fielding parodying Richardson. 'History repeats itself as farce' – meaning, of course, in the form or mode of farce, not that history is farcical. The imitation (like the Dadaist echoes in the work of the 'intermedia' types) is something new and *may be* quite serious and passionate despite its farcical aspect. This is the important difference between a proper novel and a deliberate imitation of a novel, or a novel imitative of other sorts of documents. The first attempts (has been historically inclined to attempt) to imitate actions more or less directly, and its conventional devices – cause and effect, linear anecdote, characterization, authorial selection, arrangement, and interpretation – can be and have long since been objected to as obsolete notions, or metaphors for obsolete notions: Robbe-Grillet's essays *For a New Novel* come to mind. There are replies to these objections, not to the point here, but one can see that in any case they're obviated by imitations-of-novels, which attempt to represent not life directly but a representation of life. In fact such works are no more removed from 'life' than Richardson's or Goethe's epistolary novels are: both imitate 'real' documents, and the subject of both, ultimately, is life, not the documents. A novel is as much a piece of the real world as a letter, and the letters in *The Sorrows of Young Werther* are, after all, fictitious.

One might imaginably compound this imitation, and though Borges doesn't he's fascinated with the idea: one of his frequenter literary allusions is to the 602nd night of *The 1001 Nights*, when, owing to a copyist's error, Scheherezade begins to tell the King the story of the 1001 nights, from the beginning. Happily, the King interrupts; if he didn't there'd be no 603rd night ever, and while this would solve Scheherezade's problem – which is every storyteller's problem: to publish or perish – it would put the 'outside' author in a bind. (I suspect that Borges dreamed this whole thing up: the business he mentions isn't in any edition of *The 1001 Nights* I've been able to consult. Not *yet*, anyhow: after reading 'Tlön, Uqbar', etc., one is inclined to recheck every semester or so.)

Now Borges (whom someone once vexedly accused *me* of inventing) is interested in the 602nd night because it's an instance of the story-within-the-story turned back upon itself, and his interest in such instances is threefold: first, as he himself declares, they disturb us metaphysically: when the characters in a work of fiction become readers or authors of the fiction they're in, we're reminded of the fictitious aspect of our own existence, one of Borges's cardinal themes, as it was of Shakespeare, Calderón, Unamuno, and other folk. Second, the 602nd night is a literary illustration of the *regressus in infinitum*, as are almost all Borges's principal images and motifs. Third, Scheherezade's accidental gambit, like Borges's other versions of the *regressus in infinitum*, is an image of the exhaustion, or attempted exhaustion, of possibilities – in this case literary possibilities – and so we return to our main subject.

What makes Borges's stance, if you like, more interesting to me than, say, Nabokov's or Beckett's is the premise with which he approaches literature; in the words of one of his editors: 'For [Borges] no one has claim to originality in literature; all writers are more or less faithful amanuenses of the spirit, translators and annotators of pre-existing archetypes.' Thus his inclination to write brief comments on imaginary books: for one to attempt to add overtly to the sum of 'original' literature by even so much as a conventional short story, not to mention a novel, would be too presumptuous, too naïve; literature has been done long since. A librarian's point of view! And it would itself be too presumptuous, if it weren't part of a lively, passionately relevant metaphysical vision and slyly employed against itself precisely, to make new and original literature. Borges defines the Baroque as 'that style which deliberately exhausts (or tries to exhaust) its possibilities and borders upon its own caricature'. While his own work is *not* Baroque, except intellectually (the Baroque was never so terse, laconic, economical), it suggests the view that intellectual and literary history has been Baroque, and has pretty well exhausted the possibilities of novelty. His *ficciones* are not only footnotes to imaginary texts, but postscripts to the real corpus of literature.

This premise gives resonance and relation to all his principal images. The facing mirrors that recur in his stories are a dual *regressus*. The doubles that his characters, like Nabokov's, run afoul of suggest dizzying multiples and remind one of Browne's remark that 'every man is not only himself . . . men are lived over again'. (It would please Borges, and illustrate Browne's point, to call Browne a precursor of Borges. 'Every writer,' Borges says in his essay on Kafka, 'creates his own precursors.') Borges's favourite third-century heretical sect is the Histriones – I think and hope he invented them – who believe that repetition is impossible in history and therefore live viciously in order to purge the future of the vices they commit: in other words, to exhaust the possibilities of the world in order to bring its end nearer.

The writer he most often mentions, after Cervantes, is Shakespeare; in one piece he imagines the playwright on his deathbed asking God to permit him to be one and himself, having been everyone and no one; God replies from the whirlwind that He is no one either; He has dreamed the world like Shakespeare, and including Shakespeare. Homer's story in Book IV of the *Odyssey*, of Menelaus on the beach at Pharos, tackling Proteus, appeals profoundly to Borges: Proteus is he who 'exhausts the guises of reality' while Menelaus – who, one recalls, disguised his own identity in order to ambush him – holds fast. Zeno's paradox of Achilles and the Tortoise embodies a *regressus in infinitum* which Borges carries through philosophical history, pointing out that Aristotle uses it to refute Plato's theory of forms, Hume to refute the possibility of cause and effect, Lewis Carroll to refute syllogistic deduction, William James to refute the notion of temporal passage, and Bradley to refute the general possibility of logical relations; Borges himself uses it, citing Schopenhauer, as evidence that the world is our dream, our idea, in which 'tenuous and eternal crevices of unreason' can be found to remind us that our creation is false, or at least fictive.

The infinite library of one of the most popular stories is an image particularly pertinent to the literature of exhaustion; the 'Library of Babel' houses every possible combination of alphabetical characters and spaces, and thus every possible book and statement, including your and my refutations and vindications, the history of the actual future, the history of every possible future, and, though he doesn't mention it, the encyclopaedias not only of Tlön but of every imaginable other world – since, as in Lucretius's universe, the number of elements, and so of combinations, is finite (though very large), and the number of instances of each element and combination of elements is infinite, like the library itself.

That brings us to his favourite image of all, the labyrinth, and to my point. *Labyrinths* is the name of his most substantial translated volume, and the only full-length study of Borges in English, by Ana Maria Barrenechea, is called *Borges the Labyrinth-Maker*. A labyrinth, after all, is a place in which, ideally, all the possibilities of choice (of direction, in this case) are embodied, and – barring special dispensation like Theseus's – must be exhausted before one reaches the heart. Where, mind, the Minotaur waits with two final possibilities: defeat and death, or victory and freedom. Now, in fact, the legendary Theseus is non-Baroque; thanks to Ariadne's thread he can take a shortcut through the labyrinth at Knossos. But Menelaus on the beach at Pharos, for example, is genuinely Baroque in the Borgesian spirit, and illustrates a positive artistic morality in the literature of exhaustion. He is not there, after all, for kicks (any more than Borges and Beckett are in the fiction racket for their health): Menelaus is *lost*, in the larger labyrinth of the world, and has got to hold fast while the Old Man of the Sea exhausts reality's frightening guises so that he may extort direction from him when Proteus returns to his 'true' self. It's a heroic enterprise, with salvation as its object – one recalls that the aim of the Histriones is to get history done with so that Jesus may come again the sooner, and that Shakespeare's heroic metamorphoses culminate not merely in a theophany but in an apotheosis.

Now, not just any old body is equipped for this labour, and Theseus in the Cretan labyrinth becomes in the end the aptest image of Borges after all. Distressing as the fact is to us liberal Democrats, the commonality, alas, will *always* lose their way and their souls; it's the chosen remnant, the virtuoso, the Thesean *hero*, who, confronted with Baroque reality, Baroque history, the Baroque state of his art, need *not* rehearse its possibilities to exhaustion, any more than Borges needs actually to *write* the *Encyclopaedia of Tlön* or the books in the Library of Babel. He need only be aware of their existence or possibility, acknowledge them, and with the aid of *very special* gifts – as extraordinary as saint- or hero-hood and not likely to be found in The New York Correspondence School of Literature – go straight through the maze to the accomplishment of his work.

DAVID LODGE

The Novelist at the Crossroads

(1969)

Marvin asks Sam if he has given up his novel, and Sam says, 'Temporarily.' He cannot find a form, he explains. He does not want to write a realistic novel, because reality is no longer realistic.

NORMAN MAILER: *The Man Who Studied Yoga*

Robert Scholes's recent book *The Fabulators* (OUP, 1967) has given a new impetus to the old guessing game of 'Whither the Novel?' At least, it has prompted me to try to organize my own tentative thoughts on the subject. To do this, however, and to understand *The Fabulators*, it is necessary to go back, first, to an earlier book of Mr Scholes, *The Nature of Narrative* (1966), written in collaboration with Robert Kellogg. There, the authors proposed that there are two main, antithetical modes of narrative: the *empirical*, whose primary allegiance is to the real, and the *fictional*, whose primary allegiance is to the ideal. Empirical narrative subdivides into history, which is true to fact, and what the authors call mimesis (i.e. realistic imitation), which is true to experience. Fictional narrative subdivides into romance, which cultivates beauty, and aims to delight, and allegory, which cultivates goodness and aims to instruct. This genre theory is combined with a large-scale historical scheme, according to which the primitive oral epic was a synthesis of empirical and fictional modes that under various cultural pressures (chiefly the transition from oral to written forms of communication) broke up into its component parts; and this fragmentation occurred twice — once in late classical literature, and again in the

European vernacular literatures, where the different modes were developed independently, or in partial combinations. In the late Middle Ages and the Renaissance there is a perceptible movement in narrative literature towards a new synthesis of empirical and fictional modes which finally produces, in the eighteenth century, the novel. In the experiments of modern narrative writers, however, and in the advent of new media such as motion pictures, Scholes and Kellogg saw evidence that the synthesis is about to dissolve once more.

Now, while this ambitious scheme is obviously vulnerable to scholarly sniping on points of detail, it is, I think, a suggestive and useful one when we try to take an overview of the nature and development of the novel. It gives some substance, for instance, to our vague intuition that the novel stands to modern, post-Renaissance civilization as the epic did to ancient civilization. Perhaps more important, by suggesting that the novel is a new synthesis of pre-existing narrative traditions, rather than a continuation of one of them or an entirely unprecedented phenomenon, it accounts for the great variety and inclusiveness of the novel form: its capacity for being pushed, by different authors, in the directions of history (including autobiography), allegory or romance while still remaining somehow 'the novel'. It will be noticed that I do not invoke, here, the fourth of Scholes's and Kellogg's categories – what they call 'mimesis', and what I should prefer to call 'realism'. To talk of the novel 'being pushed in the direction of realism while still remaining somehow a novel' does not make immediate sense because it is difficult to conceive of there being a conflict of interests between the novel and realism – whether one uses that elastic term primarily in a formal sense (as I do), to denote a particular mode of presentation which, roughly speaking, treats fictional events as if they were a kind of history, or in a more qualitative sense, to denote a literary aesthetic of truth-telling. For most of the novel's life-span, one of these notions of realism has tended to imply the other. If realism of presentation was not actually invented by the eighteenth-century novelists and their nine-teenth-century successors, it was certainly developed and exploited by them on a scale unprecedented in earlier literature; and when all the necessary exceptions and qualifications have been made, it is generally true that the major novelists of this period justified the form, and their own particular contributions to it, by appealing to some kind of 'realist' aesthetic.

Thus, if Scholes and Kellogg are right to see the novel as a new synthesis of pre-existing narrative modes, the dominant mode, the synthesizing element, is realism. It is realism which holds history, romance and allegory together in precarious synthesis, making a bridge between the world of discrete facts (history) and the patterned, economized world of art and imagination (allegory and romance). The novel, supremely among literary forms, has satisfied our hunger for the meaningful ordering of experience *without* denying our empirical observation of its randomness and particularity. It is therefore based on a kind of compromise, but one which has permitted many varieties of emphasis, on one side or the other, from Richardson and Fielding onwards, and which has survived numerous attempts to break it up. The Gothic novel was one such attempt: a revolt against realism, sponsored for the most part by second-class minds, it was by the major novelists of the nineteenth century either ridiculed out of countenance (e.g. Jane Austen) or tamed, domesticated, and assimilated into a more realistic account of experience (e.g. the Brontës). To be sure, the compromise (or synthesis) was always more stable in Europe than in America. But even in Hawthorne and Melville, writers strongly attracted to history, allegory and romance, realism exerts a strong if intermittent influence; while in *Huckleberry Finn*, the book from which Hemingway traced all significant modern American literature, we have a classic novelistic achievement: mythic and thematic interests controlled and expressed through the realistic rendering of particular experience.

If the above argument is granted, it follows that the disintegration of the novel-synthesis should be associated with a radical undermining of realism as a literary mode; and that is precisely what is claimed in *The Nature of Narrative*. Literary realism, we may say, depicts the individual experience of a common phenomenal world, and Scholes and Kellogg point out that both parts of this undertaking are under pressure in modern culture. As, influenced by developments in human knowledge, particularly in the field of psychology, the writer pursues the reality of individual experience deeper and deeper into the subconscious or unconscious, the common perceptual world recedes and the concept of the unique person dissolves: the writer finds himself in a region of myths, dreams, symbols and archetypes that demand 'fictional' rather than 'empirical' modes for their expression. 'The mimetic impulse towards the characterization of the inner life dissolves inevitably into mythic and expressionistic patterns upon reaching the citadel of the psyche.' On the other hand, if the writer persists in seeking to do justice to the common phenomenal world he finds himself, today, in competition with new media, such as tape and motion pictures, which can claim to do this more effectively.

This latter point is taken up and developed by Mr Scholes in *The Fabulators*, which is a more topical and polemical sequel to *The Nature of Narrative*:

> the cinema gives the *coup de grâce* to a dying realism in written fiction. Realism purports – has always purported – to subordinate the words themselves to their referents, to the things words point to. Realism exalts life and diminishes art, exalts things and diminishes words. But when it comes to representing *things*, one picture is worth a thousand words, and one motion picture is worth a million. In face of competition from cinema, fiction must abandon its attempt to 'represent reality' and rely more on the power of words to stimulate the imagination.

Mr Scholes's book consists largely of appreciative studies in a number of contemporary narrative writers who have, in his view, already recognized the obsolescence of realism and hence of the traditional novel, and are exploring, with modern sophistication, the purely 'fictional' modes of allegory and romance. To describe this kind of narrative he has revived the archaic word 'fabulation'. It is, as will be evident, a development he welcomes. 'The novel may be dying,' he says, 'but we need not fear for the future.'

Lawrence Durrell, Iris Murdoch, John Hawkes, Terry Southern, Kurt Vonnegut and John Barth are the writers principally discussed. Durrell's *Alexandria Quartet* is seen as a sophisticated exploitation of the labyrinthine intrigues and reversals of (appropriately) Alexandrian romance. Murdoch's *The Unicorn* is interpreted as an elaborate and multifaceted allegory, worked out in terms of Gothic fiction, about the conflict of secular and religious attitudes. Hawkes, and the 'Black Humorists' Southern and Vonnegut, are seen as practising a surrealistic form of picaresque. Barth's *Giles Goat-boy*, with its rich and exuberant mixture of mythic, romantic and allegorical modes, is the perfect exemplification of Scholes's theory, and his prize exhibit.

'The only legitimate way to approach "intention" in a literary work,' Mr Scholes observes, 'is through a highly discriminated sense of genre.' In this respect his explications are useful and perceptive, but as evaluations they are somewhat undiscriminating. Reading *The Unicorn* for the first time under Mr Scholes's guidance, I felt I understood what Miss Murdoch was up to more clearly than in previous readings of her novels; but whether the 'ideas' in that book, or its involved and melodramatic plot, or the process of abstracting the former from the latter, yield any great pleasure or instruction seemed to me still open to question. It is a question that Mr Scholes scarcely faces: for him the intention to reject realism in favour of fabulation is itself a guarantee of value.

In considering this point of view it behoves the English reader to proceed carefully, and with a certain self-awareness. There is a good deal of evidence that the English literary mind is peculiarly committed to realism, and resistant to non-realistic literary modes to an extent that might be described as prejudice. It is something of a commonplace of recent literary history, for instance, that the 'modern' experimental novel, represented diversely by Joyce, Virginia Woolf and D. H. Lawrence, which threatened to break up the stable synthesis of the realistic novel, was repudiated by two subsequent generations of English novelists. And, reviewing the history of the English novel in the twentieth century it is difficult to avoid associating the restoration of traditional literary realism with a perceptible decline in artistic achievement. There is a certain uncomfortable truth in Mr Rubin Rabinovitz's comments at the end of his recent book, *The Reaction Against Experiment in the English Novel 1950–1960* (Columbia UP, 1968):

> The critical mood in England has produced a climate in which traditional novels can flourish and anything out of the ordinary is given the denigratory label 'experiment' and neglected . . . The greatest fear of the English contemporary novelist is to commit a *faux pas*; every step is taken within prescribed limits, and the result is intelligent, technically competent, but ultimately mediocre . . . The successful novelist in England becomes, too quickly, a part of the literary establishment . . . All too often he uses his position as a critic to endorse the type of fiction he himself is writing and he attacks those whose approach is different.

Though Mr Rabinovitz has little to offer that is either new or interesting, by way of critical comment on the English novel of the fifties, he has burrowed deep into the journalistic archives of the period and produced some interesting documentation. It is instructive, for instance, to learn (or be reminded) that *Lord of the Flies* (1954) was reviewed by Walter Allen in the *New Statesman* in these terms:

> *Lord of the Flies* is like the fragment of a nightmare, for all that it is lightly told. It commands a reluctant assent: yes, doubtless it could be like that, with the regression from choir school to Mau Mau only a step. The difficulty begins when one smells allegory. 'There's not a child so small and weak but has his little cross to take.' These children's crosses, it seemed to me, were altogether too

unnaturally heavy for it to be possible to draw conclusions from Mr Golding's novel, and if that is so, it is,
however skilfully told, only a rather unpleasant and too-
easily affecting story.

The unexamined assumptions behind this critique, that allegory
is necessarily a literary vice, because it makes the action of the
book 'unnatural', undermining the essential criterion of 'it could
be like that', without the satisfaction of which all 'skill' is vain
– these essentially realist assumptions are entirely typical of the
post-war English literary temper. It now seems fairly obvious
that this was an inappropriate response to *Lord of the Flies* (at
least Mr Allen has acknowledged as much by his praise of the
book in *Tradition and Dream* [1964]), but the instance is a
cautionary one. Most of Golding's subsequent novels have
provoked similar objections, at least initially.

Turning to the writers Scholes holds up for admiration we
find two English novelists (Murdoch and Durrell) who have
generally enjoyed a higher reputation abroad than at home, and
whose later work has been received with less and less favour in
England; and four American writers who have made compara-
tively little impact on English readers. Vonnegut is not widely
read in England, and although Southern is well known for the
scandalous *Candy*, this scarcely amounts to a literary reputation.
Hawkes's novels failed disastrously in England until the determined efforts of a few admirers, notably Christopher Ricks,
recently obtained for them a respectful but grudging attention.
Barth's *Giles Goat-boy*, rapturously received in America, was
put down by most English reviewers.

The picture we get by putting Rabinovitz's and Scholes's
books together – of an incorrigibly insular England defending
an obsolete realism against the life-giving invasions of fabulation
– is, however, an oversimplification. For one thing, the consen-
sus of English literary opinion as described by Mr Rabinovitz
has been greatly shaken up since 1960; for another, fabulation
is not the only alternative to traditional realism that is being
explored by contemporary narrative writers.

I shall take the latter point first. Mr Scholes may be right to see the novel as closer to disintegration today than it has ever been in its always hectic and unstable history, but his diagnosis of its condition in *The Fabulators* is one-sided. Since, in his view, the synthesis of empirical and fictional modes is no longer worth the trouble of maintaining, he recommends that narrative should exploit the fictional modes, for which he has a personal predilection, more or less exclusively. Logic suggests, however, that it would be equally possible to move in the opposite direction – towards empirical narrative, and away from fiction. This in fact is what we find happening.

The term 'non-fiction novel' was first coined, I believe, by Truman Capote to describe his book *In Cold Blood*, an account of a brutal multiple murder committed in Kansas in 1959. Every detail of this book is 'true', discovered by painstaking research – Capote spent many hours with the murderers in prison, for instance, getting to know their characters and backgrounds. Yet *In Cold Blood* also reads like a novel. It is written with a novelist's eye for the aesthetic possibilites of his *donnée*, for the evocative and symbolic properties of circumstantial detail, for shapeliness and ironic contrast in structure. The moral protests the book provoked in some quarters – the charge, for instance, that there was something callous and inhuman about so 'literary' a treatment of experience so painfully actual and immediate – is one indication of the way the book straddles the conventional boundary between fiction and reportage.

That Norman Mailer's *The Armies of the Night* (1968) straddles this boundary is very clearly advertised by its subtitle: 'History as a Novel – The Novel as History'. The first part ('History as a Novel') of this account of the anti-Vietnam War march on the Pentagon in 1967 is a detailed account of the author's own experience of the event, from his initial, reluctant agreement to participate, through the riotous eve-of-march gathering at the Ambassador Theatre in Washington, where Mailer drunkenly insisted on chairing the proceedings, scandalizing or embarrassing most of those present, to the early stages of the March, Mailer's self-sought arrest, imprisonment, trial and release. This section is, in Mailer's words, 'nothing but a personal history which while written as a novel was to the best of the author's memory scrupulous to facts'. It is distinguished from a straight autobiographical narrative primarily by the fact that Mailer writes about himself in the third person, thus achieving an ironic distance on his own complex personality which is one of the chief delights of the book:

> 'Let's sing them a song, boys,' Mailer called out [on the bus taking arrested demonstrators to jail]. He could not help it – the mountebank in him felt as if he were playing Winston Churchill. Ten minutes ago he had been mired in long slow thoughts of four wives – now he had a stage again and felt not unheroic. 'Can it be?' he wondered to himself, 'that I have mis-spent twenty years as a novelist, and all along have been languishing as an actor?'

This self-irony enabled by the third-person narrative method also licenses Mailer to describe his fellow-participants, such as Dwight MacDonald and Robert Lowell, with a mischievous candour that might have seemed impertinent in a conventional autobiography, and to indulge in a good deal of prophetic cultural generalization about America which, like 'ideas' in a novel, we judge by their plausibility, rhetorical force and relevance to context rather than by the stricter criteria of logic and verifiability – for example:

> the American small town ... had grown out of itself again and again, its cells travelled, worked for government, found security through wars in foreign lands, and the nightmares which passed on the winds in the old small towns now travelled on the nozzle of the tip of the flame thrower, no dreams now of barbarian lusts, slaughtered villages, battles of blood, no, nor any need for them – technology had driven insanity out of the wind and out of the attic, and out of all the lost primitive places: one had to find it now wherever fever, force, and machines

could come together, in Vegas, at the race track, in pro football, race riots for the Negro, suburban orgies – none of it was enough – one had to find it in Vietnam; that was where the small town had gone to get its kicks.

It makes a significant difference to such passages if one transposes the free indirect speech into the declarative present tense of the conventional essay.

It is less easy to describe the narrative principles of the second part of *The Armies of the Night*, partly because Mailer himself seems confused about them. When, at the beginning of this section, 'The Novel as History', he speaks of 'the novelist ... passing his baton to the Historian', he seems to mean that the narrative method of Part I, in which events were seen from one limited point of view, in the manner of a Jamesian novel, will be exchanged for the method of the historian, who assembles and collates data from various sources and presents a coherent account of a complex sequence of events.

> The mass media which surrounded the March on the Pentagon created a forest of inaccuracy which would blind the efforts of a historian; our novel has provided us with the possibility, no, even the instrument to view our facts and conceivably study them in that light a labour of lens-grinding has produced.

I take this to mean that, both for the writer and for us the readers, the research into the self that is carried out in Part I has exposed and purged the inevitable bias of any human report. Thus the 'novel' has given the 'history' a unique kind of reliability. About half-way through Part II, however, Mailer abandons this claim. When he gets to the point in his narrative where the massed troops and demonstrators confront each other across 'six inches of no-man's-land' he announces that Part II 'is now disclosed as some sort of condensation of a collective novel – which is to admit that an explanation of the mystery of the events at the Pentagon cannot be developed by the methods of history – only by the instincts of the novelist'. Mailer thus claims the freedom to enhance his narrative with vivid invention – for instance, the briefing he imagines the troops getting:

> 'Well, men,' says the major, 'our mission is to guard the Pentagon from rioters and out-of-march scale pre-arranged-upon levels of defacement, meaning clear? Well the point to keep in mind, troopers, is those are going to be American citizens out there expressing their constitutional right to protest – that don't mean we're going to let them fart in our face – but the Constitution is a complex document with circular that is circulating sets of conditions – put it this way, I got my buddies being chewed up by VC right this minute maybe I don't care to express personal sentiments now, negative, keep two things in mind – those demos out there could be carrying bombs or bangelore torpedoes for all we know, and you're going out with no rounds in your carbines so thank God for the ·45. And first remember one thing more – they start trouble with us, they'll wish they hadn't left New York unless you get killed in the stampede of us to get to them. Yessir, you keep a tight asshole and the fellow behind you can keep his nose clean.'

This, certainly, uses to advantage a novelist's gift for caricature by violating the rules of modern historical method (though the convention is a very familiar one in classical historiography).

The Armies of the Night implies no disillusionment on the author's part with the novel as a literary form: on the contrary, it reaffirms the primacy of that form as a mode of exploring and interpreting experience. The non-fiction novel, however, is, like fabulation, often associated with such disillusionment. A case in point is the young English writer B. S. Johnson, whose break with the conventional novel was very explicitly made in *Albert Angelo* (1964). This, for about three-quarters of its length, is the story of a young architect who is unable to practise his profession, and is obliged to earn his living as a supply teacher in a number of tough London schools. He is a fairly familiar kind of English post-war hero, or anti-hero: young, frustrated, classless, mildly delinquent, disappointed in love. Though Johnson uses a number of experimental expressive techniques (simultaneous presentation of dialogue and thought in double columns, holes cut in the pages so that the reader can see what is coming), the narrative reads like realistic fiction. Then, at the beginning of the fourth section, comes the shock:

> – fuck all this lying look what im really trying to write about is writing not all this stuff about architecture trying to say something about writing about my writing im my hero though what a useless appellation, my first character then im trying to say something about me through him albert an architect when whats the point in covering up covering up covering over pretending pretending i can say anything through him that is anything i would be interested in saying . . .

In brief, Johnson goes on to expose and destroy the fictiveness of the narrative he has elaborately created, telling us the 'true' facts behind the story – for instance, the real name of the girl and the fact that while in the novel the girl jilted Albert, in actuality Johnson jilted her. Of course, one has to take the author's word that he *is* telling the truth in this section; but even if one doubts this, the story of Albert has been drastically stripped of what Henry James called 'authority'. It is an extreme strategy for achieving an effect of sincerity and authenticity, though coming so late in the work it is more of a gesture than an achievement. Having blown up his fictional bridges behind him, the author stands at the end of the book defiant and vulnerable on the bare ground of fact. And there in his subsequent books, *Trawl* (1967) and *The Unfortunates* (1969) he has remained, taking the fundamentalist Platonic position that 'telling stories is telling lies', but at the same time experimenting with form to bring writing into closer proximity with living.

The Unfortunates, for instance, consists of twenty-seven unbound sections, in a box. The first and last sections are marked as such, but the rest are in random order, and the reader is invited to shuffle them further if he so wishes. According to the blurb, this unconventional format is designed to 'represent the random workings of the mind without the forced consecutiveness of a book', but this is not in fact the case. The random flow of sensation and association in the narrator's mind is imitated by the movement of the words, clauses and sentences *within each section* – a stream-of-consciousness technique in the manner of Joyce. The randomness only affects the narrative presentation of this consciousness in time. It makes explicit the almost infinite choice a writer has in representing a particular sequence of events by refusing to commit itself to any one choice. Such is the nature of the human mind, however, that, working with the key of the marked first section, we mentally arrange the events of the book in their chronological order as we read; and the puzzle or game element thus introduced into the reading experience has the effect (ironically, in view of the author's declared intentions, but also advantageously in my opinion) of putting the painful, personal, 'real' experience of the book at an aesthetic distance, making it read more like fiction than autobiography.

For Johnson, one may gather readily from his books, the effort required to throw off the burden of the great tradition of the realistic novel has been considerable. For Frank Conroy, a young American writer whose first book *Stop-time* (1967) attracted considerable attention, it was evidently no effort at all. Where the young writer of an earlier generation would have worked his experience of growing up into a *Bildungsroman*, he simply wrote his autobiography (a form traditionally thought to be the privilege of maturity, if not fame) – but an autobiography with, in the words of Norman Mailer's significant tribute, 'the intimate and unprotected candour of a novel'. Here is a specimen – the author's memories of his father:

> I try to think of him as sane, and yet it must be admitted
> he did some odd things. Forced to attend a rest-home
> dance for its therapeutic value, he combed his hair with
> urine and otherwise played it out like the Southern
> gentleman he was. He had a tendency to take off his

trousers and throw them out the window. (I harbour some secret admiration for this.) At a moment's notice he could blow a thousand dollars at Abercrombie and Fitch and disappear into the Northwest to become an out-doorsman. He spent an anxious few weeks convinced that I was fated to become a homosexual. I was six months old. And I remember visiting him at one of the rest-homes when I was eight. We walked across a sloping lawn and he told me a story, which even then I recognized as a lie, about a man who sat down on the open blade of a penknife embedded in a park bench. (Why, for God's sake would he tell a story like that to his eight-year-old son?)

'The history of the realistic novel,' Harry Levin has observed in his book on Joyce, 'shows that fiction tends towards auto-biography. The increasing demands for social and psychological detail that are made upon the novelist can only be satisfied out of his own experience. The forces which make him an outsider focus his observation upon himself.' Johnson and Conroy (and one might mention Henry Miller here as a precursor of this form of the non-fiction novel) take this principle to its logical con-clusion. If the fictional reworking of personal experience inevi-tably falsifies it, and if the writer no longer feels the need or obligation to protect his own and others' privacy, the autobio-graphical *novel* is, in this perspective, redundant.

Scholes and Kellogg seem to endorse this point of view in *The Nature of Narrative*:

> If any distinction can be said to exist between the autobiography and the autobiographical novel it resides not in their respective fidelity to facts but rather in their respective originality in perceiving and telling the facts. It is in the knowing and the telling, and not in the facts, that the art is to be found (p. 156).

The last sentence is obviously true, but it obscures the point that the autobiographical novelist is free to alter, rearrange and add to 'the facts'; and that this freedom is exercised not merely to protect his privacy, but in the interest of literary values such as representative significance and formal coherence. In practice the reader is rarely in a position to judge with any confidence the 'fidelity to facts' of either the autobiography or the autobiographical novel, but he makes a different 'contract' with each kind of book, and brings different expectations to the reading experience. Works like *The Unfortunates* and *Stop-time* complicate and delay this process by combining the properties of both forms; but sooner or later one decides, I think, to read the former as a novel and the latter as an autobiography.

One can detect in B. S. Johnson's work the influence of Samuel Beckett and of some younger French practitioners of the *nouveau roman*. In French experiments with the non-fiction novel, however, the fiction that is purged from the novel is not so much a matter of invented characters and actions as a philosophical 'fiction', or fallacy, which the traditional novel encourages – namely, that the universe is susceptible of human interpretation. The purest statement of this point of view is to be found in the theoretical writings of Alain Robbe-Grillet. Essentially his argument is that traditional realism has distorted reality by imposing human meanings upon it. That is, in describing the world of things, we are not willing to admit that they are *just* things, with their own existence, indifferent to ours. We make things reassuring by attributing human meanings or 'significations' to them. In this way we create a false sense of solidarity between man and things.

> In the realm of literature this solidarity is expressed mainly through the systematic search for analogies or for analogical relationships . . . Metaphor is never an innocent figure of speech . . . the choice of an analogical vocabulary, however simple, always goes beyond giving an account of purely physical data . . . setting up a constant rapport between the universe and the human being who inhabits it . . . It is the whole literary language that has to change . . . the visual or descriptive adjective

THE NOVELIST AT THE CROSSROADS

- the word that contents itself with measuring, locating, limiting, defining — indicates a difficult but most likely direction for the novel of the future.

Now, the language of analogy to which Robbe-Grillet objects is exploited much more elaborately in non-realistic narrative (such as allegory) than in the novel, which can claim to have honoured the world of discrete 'things' more than any other previous form of literature, by virtue of what Henry James called its 'solidity of specification'. But Robbe-Grillet is right to see that the use of descriptive particularity in realistic fiction assumes a meaningful connection between the individual and the common phenomenal world; and from his point of view the way in which traditional realism *conceals* this connection while simultaneously exploiting it — smuggling metaphorical significance into apparently inno-cent factual descriptions of furniture, dress, weather, etc. — makes it all the more subversive.

Of Robbe-Grillet's attempt to disinfect his own narratives of analogical implication, Scholes says in *The Fabulators*:

> This cannot solve the problem, because all language is a human product and thus must humanize everything it touches. The writer must either acknowledge this and accept it as one of the terms of his work or turn to a wordless art like cinema — as M. Robbe-Grillet has so brilliantly done on occasion.

With the first part of this statement I entirely agree; but it is precisely for this reason that I cannot accept Mr Scholes's contention (quoted earlier) that literary realism 'subordinates words . . . to things'. Being a verbal medium it cannot do so — it is constantly making 'things' over into 'words'. It may indeed create the *illusion* of subordinating words to things, and this may involve a certain restraint in exploiting the literary resources of language. But the extreme exercise of such restraint in Robbe-Grillet or (much more poignantly and meaningfully) in Beckett is not the norm of realistic fiction, which has, historically, given many great writers quite as much freedom as they needed to develop the expressive possibilities of their medium. It is difficult to think of Jane Austen or George Eliot or Flaubert or Henry James as being less creative users of words because of their commitment to realism.

I am not convinced, either, that the camera is, in human hands, any more neutral than language, or that it renders literary realism redundant. It is true that Robbe-Grillet himself invokes the film to define the 'new realism' he wants to impart to the novel; and other novelists have invoked the film medium in a similar spirit. The narrator of J. D. Salinger's *Zooey* describes the story as a 'sort of prose home-movie'. The main character of Doris Lessing's *The Golden Notebook* – that anguished account of a writer's effort to fix, identify and express reality – finds herself constantly alluding to the cinema to indicate the completely truthful, mimetic quality she is seeking in her writing; and her final, most satisfactory insight into her own experience comes in the form of a hallucination in which she seems to see her life as a film which she has directed herself. There are, however, rhetorical strategies – the visual medium is invoked to reinforce a verbal communication. For this purpose the film is made to stand for a highly mimetic art. Indeed, it is; but it is a commonplace that there is a language of the film which is as much a 'human product' as verbal language. It has its own rules, conventions and possibilities of choice, which have to be learned by both artist and audience, and which make possible an infinite variety of effects, none of them entirely neutral and objective. The contemporary cinema, in fact, exhibits as wide a spectrum of styles as the contemporary novel, all the way from 'non-fiction' underground movies of the Empire State Building or people's bottoms to 'fabulations' like Stanley Kubrick's *2001*, Godard's *Weekend* or *Yellow Submarine*.

Much the same situation obtains in the contemporary theatre, where the 'well-made play' of scrupulously realistic illusion (the dramatic equivalent of the realistic novel and, in many ways, a by-product of the cultural dominance of the novel form) has been to a large extent displaced by experiments corresponding roughly to fabulation and the non-fiction novel in narrative. On the one hand we have drama that exploits the artificiality of theatrical presentation, inventing and often fantasizing freely (e.g. Brecht, Ionesco, N. F. Simpson), and on the other the 'theatre of fact' (Hochhuth, Weiss) or efforts like those of the American Living Theatre Company, who seek to break down the formal conventions that separate audience from performers and to physically involve both in an uncontrolled and unpredictable 'happening'.

We seem, indeed, to be living through a period of unprecedented cultural pluralism which allows, in all the arts, an astonishing variety of styles to flourish simultaneously. Though they are in many cases radically opposed on aesthetic and epistemological grounds, no one style has managed to become dominant. In this situation, the critic has to be very fast on his feet. He is not, of course, obliged to like all the styles equally, but he must avoid the cardinal error of judging one style by criteria appropriate to another. He needs what Mr Scholes calls 'a highly discriminated sense of genre'. For the practising artist, however, the existence of a bewildering plurality of styles presents problems not so easily solved; and we should not be surprised that many contemporary writers manifest symptoms of extreme insecurity, nervous self-consciousness and even at times a kind of schizophrenia.

The situation of the novelist today may be compared to a man standing at a crossroads. The road on which he stands (I am thinking primarily of the English novelist) is the realistic novel, the compromise between fictional and empirical modes. In the fifties there was a strong feeling that this was the main road, the central tradition, of the English novel, coming down through the Victorians and Edwardians, temporarily diverted by modernist experimentalism, but subsequently restored (by Orwell, Isherwood, Greene, Waugh, Powell, Angus Wilson, C. P. Snow, Amis, Sillitoe, Wain, etc., etc.) to its true course. That wave of enthusiasm for the realistic novel in the fifties has, however, considerably abated. For one thing, the novelty of the social experience the fiction of that decade fed on — the break-up of a bourgeois-dominated class society – has faded. More important, the literary theorizing behind the 'Movement' was fatally thin. For example, C. P. Snow:

> Looking back, we can see what an odd affair the 'experimental' novel was. To begin with, the 'experiment' stayed remarkably constant for thirty years. Miss Dorothy Richardson was a great pioneer, so were Virginia Woolf and Joyce: but between *Pointed Roofs* in 1915 and its successors, largely American, in 1945, there was no significant development. In fact there could not be; because this method, the essence of which was to represent brute experience through the moments of sensation, effectively cut out precisely those aspects of the novel where a living tradition can be handed on. Reflection had to be sacrificed; so did moral awareness; so did the investigatory intelligence. That was altogether too big a price to pay and hence the 'experimental novel' . . . died from starvation, because its intake of human stuff was so low.

Or Kingsley Amis:

> The idea about experiment being the life-blood of the English novel is one that dies hard. 'Experiment', in this context, boils down pretty regularly to 'obtruded oddity', whether in construction – multiple viewpoints and such – or in style; it is not felt that adventurousness in subject matter or attitude or tone really counts. Shift from one scene to the next in mid-sentence, cut down on verbs or definite articles, and you are putting yourself right up in the forefront, at any rate in the eyes of those who were reared on Joyce and Virginia Woolf and take a jaundiced view of more recent developments.

Simply as literary history, Snow's comment does not survive the most cursory examination (no development between *A Portrait of the Artist* and *Finnegans Wake?* Between *Pointed Roofs* and *The Sound and the Fury?*). Amis's has a certain satiric force and cogency, and is aimed at a more vulnerable target, but that kind of 'cultivated Philistinism', refreshing in its time, could not be maintained indefinitely, even by Amis, let alone anyone else.

Realistic novels continue to be written – it is easy to forget that most novels published in England still fall within this category – but the pressure of scepticism on the aesthetic and epistemological premises of literary realism is now so intense that many novelists, instead of marching confidently straight ahead, are at least considering the two routes that branch off in opposite directions from the crossroads. One of these routes leads to the non-fiction novel, and the other to what Mr Scholes calls 'fabulation'.

To fill out the latter category we may add to the examples discussed in *The Fabulators*: Günter Grass, William Burroughs, Thomas Pynchon, Leonard Cohen (*Beautiful Losers*), Susan Sontag (*Death Kit*), some of the novels of Anthony Burgess, and individual works by novelists who have remained generally faithful to realism, such as Bellow's *Henderson the Rain King*, Updike's *The Centaur*, Malamud's *The Natural*, Angus Wilson's *The Old Men at the Zoo*, and Andrew Sinclair's *Gog*. Such narratives suspend realistic illusion in some significant degree in the interests of a freedom in plotting characteristic of romance or in the interest of an explicitly allegorical manipulation of meaning, or both. They also tend to draw inspiration from certain popular forms of literature, or subliterature, in which the arousal and gratification of very basic fictional appetites (such as wonder, wish fulfilment, suspense) are only loosely controlled by the disciplines of realism: especially science fiction, pornography and the thriller.

Of these three, science fiction has the most respectable pedigree, going back to Utopian speculation, apocalyptic prophecy, and satirical fantasy like *Gulliver's Travels*, *Candide*, *Alice in Wonderland*, and *Erewhon*. It was this tradition that kept fabulation alive through the period of the realistic novel's dominance, and it continues to offer the most obvious vehicle for the novelist who wants to experiment with a more 'fictional' kind of narrative. Pornography and the thriller, being more debased forms, are approached more gingerly, but the fascination they hold for the contemporary literary imagination cannot be missed in such phenomena as the cult of James Bond (which was a high brow cult before it was a mass cult). Kingsley Amis seems a representative figure here. His absorption with Fleming (see *The James Bond Dossier*), like his enthusiasm for science fiction (see *New Maps of Hell*), is difficult to reconcile with the stance he adopted in the fifties, both as novelist and critic, as a defender of a traditional kind of literary realism, except as a lust for fabulation, repressed by his literary 'censor', seeking outlet in certain licensed areas where traditional literary values are not expected to obtain. His publication of a James Bond novel, *Colonel Sun* (1968), under the pen-name Robert Markham, is surely a case of the realistic novelist taking a holiday from realism, finding a way to enjoy the forbidden fruit of romance without fully committing himself to the enterprise. (It is, I hope, unnecessary to labour the point that the James Bond novels are essentially romances, and that their superficial realism of presentation – the descriptive set-pieces, the brand-name dropping, the ostentatious display of technical knowledge of various kinds – does not convert the romantic stereotypes into anything individually realized, but merely gives them a gloss of contemporary sophistication and facilitates the reader's willing suspension of disbelief.) In fact *Colonel Sun* is considerably more realistic than most of the Fleming novels (Amis's Bond, for instance, survives by virtue of his wits and good luck rather than the gadgetry which, like the magical weapons of medieval romance, preserves Fleming's hero) and also duller. This is not surprising since the whole enterprise, undertaken, apparently, in a spirit of pious imitation, required Amis to keep in check his natural talent for parody and deflating comic realism. Anthony Burgess's *Tremor of Intent* (1966) is a much more entertaining highbrow contribution to the genre partly because of its parodic exaggerations of Bondian themes and motifs. This is a work of extraordinary virtuosity, in which Burgess sets himself to cap every effect exploited by Fleming and succeeds triumphantly: the sex is sexier, the violence more visceral, the high-living more

THE NOVELIST AT THE CROSSROADS

extravagant, the intrigues and reversals of the plot more stun-
ning, and the style, naturally, infinitely more vivid and evocative.
Yet in its overall effect the book wobbles uncertainly between
parodying Bond by extravagant exaggeration and reaching after
something genuinely felt and realized. Thus at one point in the
story a precocious teenage boy has to shoot a man to save the
hero and is violently sick immediately after: 'He went and stood,
like a naughty boy, in the corner. His shoulders heaved as he
tried to throw up the modern world.' This striking image sounds
a note too serious for the narrative to bear, and only serves to
remind us that it is not the modern world which this character
is throwing up but a grotesque comic-strip version of it.

There is, I think, a similar ambiguity of motive, an insecurity
of stance, an impression that regressive or perverse fantasies are
being indulged under cover of pretensions to satirical caricature
or displays of stylistic virtuosity, in so-called 'parodies' or
'spoofs' of pornography, such as *Candy* (1958), or Stephen
Schneck's *The Nightclerk* (1965), or Gore Vidal's *Myra Breckinridge* (1968). Of these three novels, Vidal's is easily the most
complex and accomplished, parodying and commenting acutely
upon not only pornography but also the non-fiction novel of the
French variety:

> Nothing is *like* anything else. Things are themselves
> entirely and do not need interpretation, only a minimal
> respect for their precise integrity. The mark on the wall
> is two feet three inches wide and four feet eight and a
> fraction inches high. Already I have failed to be com-
> pletely accurate. I must write 'fraction' because I can't
> read the little numbers on the ruler without my glasses
> which I never wear.

– and the kind of argument advanced by Mr Scholes, that the
cinema has superseded the mimetic possibilities of literature:

> Tyler's close scrutiny of the films of the Forties makes
> him our age's central thinker, if only because *in the
> decade between 1935 and 1945 no irrelevant film was*

made in the United States. During those years, the entire range of human (which is to say, American) legend was put on film, and any profound study of these extra-ordinary works is bound to make clear the human condition. For instance, to take an example at random, Johnny Weismuller, the zahftic Tarzan, still provides the last word on the subject of soft man's relationship to hard environment . . . that glistening overweight body set against a limestone cliff at noon says the whole thing. Auden once wrote an entire poem praising limestone, unaware that any one of a thousand frames from *Tarzan and the Amazons* had not only anticipated him but made irrelevant his efforts.

Myra Breckinridge is a brilliant, but somehow sterile and despairing work: as if Vidal, deeply contemptuous of the contemporary *avant garde* and the cultural climate, 'post-Gutenberg, pre-Apocalypse', that fosters it, has abandoned hope of positively resisting either, and cynically set himself to match their wildest excesses.

There are indeed good reasons for anticipating with some-thing less than enthusiasm the disappearance of the novel and its replacement by the non-fiction novel or fabulation. Especially to anyone whose imagination has been nourished by the great realistic novelists of the past, both these side roads will seem to lead all too easily into desert or bog – self-defeating banality or self-indulgent excess. Yet, as I have already suggested, there are formidable discouragements to continuing serenely along the road of fictional realism. The novelist who has any kind of self-awareness must at least hesitate at the crossroads; and the solution many novelists have chosen in their dilemma is to *build their hesitation into the novel itself*. To the novel, the non-fiction novel, and the fabulation, we must add a fourth category: the novel which exploits more than one of these modes without fully committing itself to any, the novel-about-itself, the trick-novel, the game-novel, the puzzle-novel, the novel that leads the reader (who wishes, naïvely, only to be told what to believe) through a fairground of illusions and deceptions, distorting mirrors and trap-doors that open disconcertingly under his feet, leaving him ultimately not with any simple or reassuring message or meaning but with a paradox about the relation of art to life.

This kind of novel, which I shall call the 'problematic novel', clearly has affinities with both the non-fiction novel and fabulation, but it remains distinct precisely because it brings both into play. Mr Scholes's fabulators, for instance, play tricks on their readers, expose their fictive machinery, dally with aesthetic paradoxes, in order to shed the restricting conventions of realism, to give themselves freedom to invent and manipulate. In the kind of novel I am thinking of, however, the reality principle is never allowed to lapse entirely – indeed, it is often invoked, in the spirit of the non-fiction novel, to expose the artificiality of conventional realistic illusion. Whereas the fabulator is impatient with 'reality', and the non-fiction novelist is impatient with fiction, the kind of novelist I am talking about retains a loyalty to both, but lacks the orthodox novelist's confidence in the possibility of reconciling them. He makes the difficulty of his task, in a sense, his subject.

The father and mother of this kind of novel is *Tristram Shandy* – to say which is to concede that we are not dealing with a totally new phenomenon. But it is significant that, while it is difficult to think of anything (apart from feeble imitations) comparable to *Tristram Shandy* in the eighteenth and nineteenth centuries, when the realistic novel developed into maturity, it is not hard to think of parallels in modern literature. Take, for example, J. D. Salinger's Glass stories. When one puts them mentally beside *Tristram Shandy* the essential similarity of each writer's undertaking is striking: the loving, minutely circumstantial evocation and celebration of a richly eccentric family, observed mainly in domestic life, with extraordinary attention to detail of speech, mannerism and gesture, recorded by a narrator who is himself a member of the family (though with certain very pointed, teasing resemblances to the actual, historic author), who is partly dependent on the other members for his information, who addresses the reader directly in a whimsical, garrulous, digressive flow of complex reminiscence and reconstruction, commenting freely on the difficulty of his undertaking, and incorporating into the narrative an account of his personal circumstances at the time of composition. Salinger's stories, it seems to me, have been received with increasing disfavour because they have been taken too much at their face value as disingenuous gospels of a new religion, to the neglect of their literary experimentation. This feature, though less obvious than in *Tristram Shandy*, is clear enough when one reads the stories through in the order of their composition. Then, one cannot fail to notice how, as the record of the Glass family comes more and more to follow the shapelessness and randomness of actuality, as the tone of the narrator (Buddy Glass) becomes more and more personal, idiosyncratic, non-literary – as, in short, the narrator begins to appeal to our interest more and more at the level of anecdote about 'real' people, so a subtly growing amount of highly unusual, objectively improbable and in fact irrational information is conveyed. Thus, in *Raise High the Roofbeam, Carpenters*, Franny Glass is said to remember her brother Seymour (the family *guru*) reading to her when she was ten months old, and Seymour records in his diary the experience of stigmata from touching certain things. In *Seymour; an Introduction* Buddy tells us how he eased the pain of pleurisy by placing 'a perfectly innocent-looking Blake lyric in my shirt pocket', and claims that from early childhood till he was thirty he seldom read fewer than 200,000 words a day, and often 400,000. In other words, as the manner of the saga inclines more and more to that of non-fictional narrative, the matter becomes more and more 'fictive'. There is a similar tension between the bizarre obsessions and eccentricities of the Shandy family and the minutely faithful, realistically particular rendering of them by Tristram. In both cases the normal conventions of narrative fiction are exposed and undermined by the narrator himself, and the stability of the reader's stance towards the experience of the book is always threatened.

It is in fact the transference of the writer's own sense (which may be humorous or deadly serious) of the problematic nature of his undertaking – making the reader *participate* in the aesthetic and philosophical problems the writing of fiction presents, by embodying them directly in the narrative – that characterizes the 'problematic novel'. I would want to make this a large enough category to include such works as Gide's *The Counterfeiters*, Flann O'Brien's *At Swim Two-birds*, Nabokov's *Pale Fire*, Sartre's *La Nausée*, the labyrinthine fables of Jorge Luis Borges, Waugh's *The Ordeal of Gilbert Pinfold*, Amis's *I Like It Here*, Muriel Spark's *The Comforters*, and Doris Lessing's *The Golden Notebook*. No doubt the reader can think of other examples, if not of the fully developed problematic novel, at least of novels that incorporate to some degree its characteristic note of self-consciousness. As Elizabeth Hardwick has written recently:

> Many good novels show a degree of panic about the form. Where to start and where to end, how much must be believed and how much a joke, a puzzle; how to combine the episodic and the carefully designed and consequential ... the mood of the writer is to admit manipulation and design, to exploit the very act of authorship in the midst of the imagined scene.
> [A passage discussing Julian Mitchell's *The Undiscovered Country* (1968) has been cut here. (Ed.)]

This brings me to my conclusion, which is a modest affirmation of faith in the future of realistic fiction. In part this is a rationalization of a personal preference. I like realistic novels, and I tend to write realistic fiction myself. The elaborate code of literary decorum that governs the composition of realistic fiction – consistency with history, solidity of specification, and so on – which to many of the writers discussed above seems inhibiting, or evasive, or redundant – is to my mind a valuable discipline and source of strength – or at least can be. Like metrical or stanzaic form in verse, which prevents the poet from saying what he wants to say in the way that comes most readily to his mind, involving him in a laborious struggle with sounds and meanings that, if he is resourceful enough, yields results superior to spontaneous expression, so the conventions of realistic fiction prevent the narrative writer from telling the first story that comes into his head – which is likely to be either autobiography or fantasy – and compel him to a kind of concentration on the possibilities of his *donnée* that may lead him to new and quite unpredictable discoveries of what he has to tell. In the novel personal experience must be explored and transmuted until it acquires an authenticity and persuasiveness independent of its actual origins; while the fictive imagination through which this exploration and transmutation is achieved is itself subject to an empirical standard of accuracy and plausibility. The problem of reconciling these two opposite imperatives is essentially rhetorical and (contrary to Mr Scholes) requires great linguistic resourcefulness and skill for its successful solution. (I am not of course denying that fabulation or autobiography or the non-fiction novel have their own internal disciplines and challenges, but merely trying to define those of the realistic novel.)

If the case for realism has any ideological content it is that of liberalism. The aesthetics of compromise go naturally with the ideology of compromise, and it is no coincidence that both are under pressure at the present time. The non-fiction novel and fabulation are *radical* forms which take their impetus from an extreme reaction to the world we live in – *The Armies of the Night* and *Giles Goat-boy* are equally products of the apocalyptic imagination. The assumption behind such experiments is that our 'reality' is so extra-ordinary, horrific or absurd that the methods of conventional realistic imitation are no longer adequate. There is no point in carefully creating fiction that gives an illusion of life when life itself seems illusory. (This argument, interestingly, was used by the Marquis de Sade, writing at the time of the French Revolution, to explain the Gothic novel and, by implication, his own pornographic contributions to the genre.) Art can no longer compete with life on equal terms, showing the universal in the particular. The alternatives are either to cleave to the particular – to 'tell it like it is' – or to abandon history altogether and construct pure fictions which reflect in an emotional or metaphorical way the discords of contemporary experience.

The realist – and liberal – answer to this case must be that while many aspects of contemporary experience encourage an extreme, apocalyptic response, most of us continue to live most of our lives on the assumption that the reality which realism imitates actually exists. History may be, in a philosophical sense, a fiction, but it does not feel like that when we miss a train or somebody starts a war. We are conscious of ourselves as unique, historic individuals, living together in societies by virtue of certain common assumptions and methods of communication; we are conscious that our sense of identity, of happiness and unhappiness, is defined by small things as well as large; we seek to adjust our lives, individually and communally, to some order or system of values which, however, we know is always at the mercy of chance and contingency. It is this sense of reality which realism imitates; and it seems likely that the latter will survive as long as the former.

Writing in 1939, at the beginning of the Second World War, George Orwell voiced many of the doubts about the future of the novel reviewed in this essay. The novel, he said in 'Inside the Whale', was inextricably tied up with liberal individualism and could not survive the era of totalitarian dictatorships he saw ahead. In his appreciation of Henry Miller's *Tropic of Cancer* he seems to endorse the confessional non-fiction novel as the only viable alternative ('Get inside the whale . . . Give yourself over to the world process, stop fighting against it or pretending you control it, simply accept it, endure it, record it. That seems to be the formula that any sensitive novelist is likely to adopt.') Orwell's prophecy was, however, incorrect. Shortly after the War there was a significant revival of the realistic novel in England, inspired partly by Orwell's own fiction of the thirties; and although none of this fiction is of the very first rank, it is not an inconsiderable body of work. Many of the most talented post-war American novelists – John Updike, Saul Bellow, Bernard Malamud and Philip Roth, for example – have worked, for the most part, within the conventions of realistic fiction. Obsequies over the novel may be as premature today as they were in 1939.

FRANK KERMODE

The House of Fiction

Interviews with Seven Novelists

(1963)

These conversations are abridged from longer talks; they were
entirely free and unprepared. In cutting them I have naturally
preferred to leave out whatever seemed most remote from the
centre represented by the title. If this seems a somewhat abstract
topic, I can only say that it proved reasonably easy to keep the
mind of the contributors fixed upon it. Clearly it is a relationship
that they all think about in a more or less abstract way, as well
as handling it daily in terms of technique.

I planned to ask each of the novelists about this abstract issue,
and then to get them on to the subject of their own books.
Sometimes this method didn't work, and the two questions got
involved with each other, beneficially I think. Though there
were no striking divergencies of opinion, there were considerable
and interesting differences of emphasis. But if I had to decide
what this selection of good living English novelists had most
obviously in common I should say it was a kind of modesty.
Not only do they emphasize their own limitations; for the most
part they're happy to ignore all the larger claims that can be
made for their craft. Obviously none of them subscribes to
apocalyptic views such as Lawrence's: 'Being a novelist, I
consider myself superior to the saint, the scientist, the philosopher and the poet. The novel is the one bright book of life.'
There is probably no living English novelist who even wants to
believe that. Again, though none of them would accept the old

criterion of naturalism unrevised, none on the other hand throws it out with the arrogance of Gide: 'Please understand, I should like to put everything into my novel.' The old realism will not do, nor the old formalism, for none of these writers sees himself as making a universe. Each looks out, as if from one of the windows of James's house of fiction – 'a number of possible windows not to be reckoned,' as he said – and senses not merely that reality has the limited shape of his window, but also that he has a deep obligation to things as they are – or a not too extraordinary view of them.

For this modesty has a philosophical aspect, too. You might expect that English writers would partake of the national character, at any rate to the extent of dodging discussion of the metaphysics of their form. In fact they were all willing to talk about such matters. But they did so in a peculiarly modest way. Just as they avoid the idea of the novel as an image of all reality, so they don't seem to think of their imaginative powers as a component of or even as a complement to reality. Indeed their concern with this problem seems on the whole strongly ethical rather than epistemological, as we see for instance in Mrs Spark's discriminations between truth and absolute truth, between one kind of lie and another which you render harmless by calling it a story. Not for the English novelists the sophisticated epistemology of the new French writers (of whom few of our subjects were willing, by the way, to speak). Not for them the banner of the antinovel. A French author – M. Butor for instance – might have said that a novel contributes substantially to reality and that a new writer's task might always be seen to be the correction of obsolete versions of reality imposed by earlier novels (hence any good novel is an antinovel). But for the most part our authors see the whole problem of the relation between fiction and reality in terms of their own struggle to be faithful to themselves as perceivers and to fact, as perceived by the eye of informed commonsense. Some of them have performed extraordinary feats of construction – I think here especially of Mr Greene – yet it will be observed that the names of Conrad and Ford Madox Ford are not so much as mentioned.

There already exist learned articles with such titles as 'The Epistemology of the Good Soldier', and there is no reason why someone should not write similarly about *The End of the Affair*; but for Mr Greene this is an inconceivable activity, and though what he says about himself has strong roots in Turgeniev and James, he thinks of the problem as largely his own, and in the first place technical rather than as a matter for philosophic enquiry.

I

It seemed to me that a recent article by Miss Iris Murdoch expressed most of the issues we wanted discussed in a clear, usable way. Most of the contributors did in fact find her terminology convenient, so we began with what she said about it. The antithesis of 'crystalline' and 'journalistic', plot and myth, will in fact echo through the conversations.

I first asked Miss Murdoch to enlarge on one of her points, this distinction between 'crystalline' and 'journalistic' modes:

MURDOCH: It's one of these epigrammatic distinctions which are probably themselves rather inexact. This distinction was suggested to me in a way by worrying about my own work and about what was wrong with it. There is a tendency, I think, on the one hand, and especially now, to produce a closely-coiled, carefully-constructed object wherein the story rather than the people is the important thing, and wherein the story perhaps suggests a particular, fairly clear moral. On the other hand, there is and always has been in fiction a desire to describe the world around one in a fairly loose and cheerful way. And it seemed to me at present in the novel that there was a flying apart of these two different aims. Some ideal state of affairs would combine the merits of both.

KERMODE: You spoke of the consolation of form in your article as being a deceptive presentation of reality. Is this a certain kind of form? It doesn't apply to the sort which combines crystalline and journalistic, but only to the crystalline sort?

MURDOCH: This is a delicate question. It's absurd to say that form in art is in any sense a menace, because form is the absolute essence of art. But there can be a tendency too readily to pull a form or a structure out of something one's thinking about and to rest upon that. The satisfaction of the form is such that it can stop one from going more deeply into the contradictions or paradoxes or more painful aspects of the subject matter.

KERMODE: You didn't want myth to the degree that it interferes with the representation of character in a rather old-fashioned sense?

MURDOCH: Yes, this is perhaps my main thought in that article you referred to. I think that it would be coming back to character in the old-fashioned sense which would save one from being too readily consoled.

KERMODE: You also say that writers write what they can and not what they should. May I ask you whether in work that you perhaps have in hand there's any attempt to carry out this programme?

MURDOCH: I always attempt to carry it out but I find it very difficult to do so.

KERMODE: Because of the strength of the myth?

MURDOCH: This sounds pretentious, as if one were thinking of one's work in a rather grandiose way, but yes, I suppose it is. Another way of putting it would be just that one isn't good enough at creating character. One starts off – at least I start off – hoping every time that this is going to happen and that a lot of people who are not me are going to come into existence in some wonderful way. Yet often it turns out in the end that something about the structure of the work itself, the myth as it were of the work, has drawn all these people into a sort of spiral, or into a kind of form which ultimately is the form of one's own mind.

KERMODE: Yes. And in so far as they are absorbed into that, they lose identity.

MURDOCH: I think this tends to happen.

KERMODE: So that the myth is a sort of safety net under the tightrope?

MURDOCH: Well, yes, if you put it so, it's a form of safety. I don't take a low view of it. I think it can be important and beautiful; but I think it comes more easily to writers now than the other thing.

KERMODE: Yes. And although myth is in itself, as you say, a high matter, if it is ultimately something that distorts reality, then it is the enemy, however dignified, of the kind of novel that you feel ought to be written.

MURDOCH: Well, not altogether the enemy. It should be present also. It's perhaps the thing which at the moment one should guard against giving in to.

KERMODE: One of the more sensible definitions of myth in this connection would be one which allowed it to look after itself, wouldn't it?

MURDOCH: Yes.

KERMODE: May I now bring the discussion a little closer to your own books? Would you feel free to say that in your books since *Under the Net* there has been any movement towards the kind of fiction that you say ought to be written?

MURDOCH: It's very hard to say. Leaving aside the question of whether they're better or worse or anything – well, I don't know that you can leave this question aside quite, but trying to leave it aside – I think they oscillate rather between attempts to portray a lot of people and giving in to a powerful plot or story. I think the last one, *A Severed Head*, probably represents a giving in to the myth; and the previous one, *The Bell*, has more people in it; and the one I've just written now I think again has more people in it. But it's always rather a problem. Given that one hasn't achieved the kind of synthesis which I think is desirable and which would make one's stuff of some use, there is a tendency to oscillate between achieving a kind of intensity through having a very powerful story and sacrificing character, and having the characters and losing the intensity.

KERMODE: It might seem, perhaps, using myth in too crude a sense, that there was more of it, or that it was more openly to be met with in *The Bell* and *The Severed Head* than in *Under the Net*, for example.

MURDOCH: *Under the Net* has in fact got its own myth, but I think it probably just hasn't emerged very clearly in the story.

KERMODE: It's a philosopher's novel?

MURDOCH: In a very simple sense. It plays with a philosophical idea. The problem which is mentioned in the title is the problem of how far conceptualizing and theorizing, which from one point of view are absolutely essential, in fact, divide you from the thing that is the object of theoretical attention. And Hugo is a sort of non-philosophical metaphysician who is supposed to be paralysed in a way by this problem.

KERMODE: And you set this novel quite deliberately in places which are given a good deal of actuality, in London and Paris, for example, as I remember it rendered in some detail.

MURDOCH: That was just self-indulgence. It hadn't any particular significance.

KERMODE: The technical excursions which we all like so much in your novels, how a car turns over, or how you get a bell out of a lake and so on, are they also self-indulgence under this very strict definition?

MURDOCH: Yes. That is just a kind of fascination with completely theoretical amateur mechanics.

KERMODE: Well, someone will come along and call them a myth all the same.

MURDOCH: Of course, the bell itself has significance, and is quite explicitly used as a symbol by the characters. But I think the majority of my 'technical excursions' are pure play.

II

Miss Murdoch, then, finds it clear that the trouble nowadays lies in an over-willingness to depend upon 'myth', and that this premature dependence is falsely consoling; that it takes the bitter flavour out of reality, reduces the identity of characters, and, morally speaking, is a self-indulgence on the part of the writer. Graham Greene uses the term 'myth' differently, and accordingly sees the whole problem in another light. In fact he almost echoes Turgeniev, who said, 'I would, I think, rather have too little architecture than too much – when there's a danger of its interfering with my measure of the truth.'

KERMODE: Mr Greene, in the book in which you describe the genesis of your last novel, *The Burnt Out Case*, you make this remark: 'Am I beginning to plot, to succumb to that abiding temptation to tell a good story?' I'd like to ask you, if I may, in what sense the abiding temptation to tell a good story is to be regarded as inimical, as it presumably is, to the production of a good novel?

GREENE: I'm not sure that one can generalize on that; I feel it's inimical to *my* producing a good novel. My own wish always is to produce a central figure who represents some idea of reasonable simplicity – a mythical figure if you like. And the simplicity often gets damaged by plot making. For instance, if I can just illustrate a point from a book I don't like much called *The Heart of the Matter*, there one wanted to draw a fairly simple portrait of a man who was corrupted by his sense of pity. But in the course of that book, perhaps because one was rusty, not having written for some years during the war, one began to overload the plot, and I felt the effect of the character was whittled away.

KERMODE: This is a curious comment on the terms plot and myth, because we have had Iris Murdoch telling us that she regarded myth as the great temptation to self-indulgence, when what one ought to be concerned with was the texture of reality. And you are really saying something which is not quite the opposite, but quite close to the opposite, aren't you?

GREENE: Yes, very nearly the opposite.

KERMODE: And it's interesting in that connection that Miss Murdoch's stories do, as she would put it herself, descend into myth-making from time to time, whereas you are a plot-builder, are you not?

GREENE: And I would like to ascend into myth, but find my boots so often muddy with plot. My own feeling is that the nearest I came to hitting the mythical element was in *The Power and the Glory*, where I feel the plot was sufficiently simple for the main purpose of this story to remain clear throughout.

KERMODE: May I mention a novel of yours, which I especially admire, and which I dare say would incur your own criticism that it's too heavily plotted in a slightly different way? That's *The End of the Affair*. What do you feel about that?

GREENE: I like a lot of the book, but I made an appalling mistake, I think, in the last third of the book, which has always spoilt – though I don't read my books – any retrospective enjoyment I might have.

KERMODE: It would be very interesting to know what you thought that mistake was.

GREENE: The introduction of something which had not got a natural explanation. I had intended a much longer last part of the book after the woman had died, where there was to be a succession of coincidences, until the lover became maddened by the coincidences which would not cease. I found it very difficult to continue the book with the loss of the principal figure, and I foreshortened badly by introducing something which was not easily accountable for in natural terms.

KERMODE: This encourages me to believe that I am right in my own view of the book, which is that it is in a way a novel about plot-making, isn't it – not only about a novelist making a plot, but about God making a plot?

GREENE: Yes.

KERMODE: And if you had put in these additional coincidences, you would have strengthened that element?

GREENE: Yes.

KERMODE: Of course, I think in *The End of the Affair* God the novelist is quite a strong figure in the myth, as it were.

GREENE: Yes.

KERMODE: In *A Burnt Out Case*, for example, you didn't feel that your plot had that kind of function as a kind of mirror image of providence?

GREENE: No.

KERMODE: So this is a different case, in that the element of plot in it tends to be destructive rather than to augment the myth?

GREENE: Yes, in a curious way it was more simple plotting, wasn't it, than, say, *The Heart of the Matter* – less details, less events, less action. And yet what little action there was seemed to take too strong a part. Perhaps it would have seemed less plotted if there had been more plot.

KERMODE: I had intended to ask you whether you feel that there is a point beyond which you can't dispense with plot. I mean there obviously is such a point, but where does this point lie? On what you said at the beginning of our conversation, it would seem that the less plot a novel had, the better it was likely to be, broadly speaking.

GREENE: Yes, in a way I agree – but that's my feeling often when I'm trying to write a novel which conflicts with passionate liking for melodrama. And a reaction, when I was a young man, I suppose a reaction from the books of Virginia Woolf, where narrative was very subordinated to mood. And I still have a liking for action in the novel.

KERMODE: But on the whole you think that the representation of reality, of the real truth about the world, in a novel is primarily the burden of what we have agreed to call myth?

GREENE: Yes.

KERMODE: And that plot on the whole is in opposition, at any rate, has to be controlled.

GREENE: Yes, it must be controlled. Because after all in *Tom Jones* there is a tremendous amount of plot, but it's subordinated the whole time to the main character, isn't it?

KERMODE: I suppose it's a good case of a novel in which you have a strong myth of a rather ethical cast, and also an extremely complex plot, well timed, and thoroughly worked out and so on.

GREENE: Yes.

KERMODE: Without any sense that the things collide; in fact when they do seem to collide, as in the case of Sophia's muff on the bed, for example, they have a very strong ethical flavour.

GREENE: Yes.

KERMODE: And this is the direction in which you would like to . . .

GREENE: I would like to be able to write.

KERMODE: So in fact there is no real argument against having very complex plots?

GREENE: No, as long as it does not damage the mythical centre.

III

Mr Greene is very actively torn between his ethical myth, a matter largely of character, of 'showing my people', as Turgeniev said; but unlike Turgeniev, who was short on 'story', he regards plot as his self-indulgence, much as myth is Miss Murdoch's. When I asked Angus Wilson about the relation between myth and the significant rendering of 'real life', he said this:

WILSON: That is an essential problem for me. It seems to me that all the novelists that I value have projected a real world which is nevertheless entirely their own vision. How far this will coincide with a myth which they may also discover in life I'm not quite so sure. One shouldn't be too careful about bringing this myth out, because I think it will come through, so long as you are absolutely true to your own vision of life. Of course you must shore yourself up with little bits of facts about real life. The myth element has grown stronger with me as I've written. It was there very strongly in *Hemlock* but I didn't try to bring it out, although the title after all does so. It was there in *Anglo-Saxon Attitudes*, and now I have really tried to deal with the myth in a very much more allegorical way in my last novel.

KERMODE: So on the whole, apart from the last novel, you would say that the deliberate distortion of reality is not one of your aims?

WILSON: No. I'm immensely interested, as you know from my novels, in the shaping of the total novel, but not to reduce life to some sort of formal pattern. I think what I want to do is quite other. It is to amass various reactions to life, strong reactions, to amass various distortions and caricatures, scenes, pictures, and to bombard my readers with these things, having previously, I hope, put them into as strict a formal pattern in the sense of a designed novel as I possibly can. That is why I think people are mistaken when they ask what my novel is telling them. I don't believe, as Snow does, for example, in the didactic novel.

KERMODE: I sometimes have felt, although I wouldn't argue very strongly for this in your novels, that there is a degree of reality, of actuality in the representation of certain kinds of society which diminishes as one moves down the social scale.

WILSON: I think that might be true. The only plea for myself I would put in there is that even though this may be the case, it seems to me that I have a wider range than most novelists writing now. I do want to say something about the total society, and I can't refuse to do that simply because I'm not quite sure whether in working-class homes today you still find those ladies with borzois on the ends of leads. I could go and find this out, probably, but that is not the way I would set about it. I would take a chance on it.

KERMODE: I don't think anybody would think that mattered, provided that the persons involved didn't seem to lose a certain degree of moral reality, if I can use that phrase. But on this question of middle-class, or, as I suspect many people would want to call them, upper middle-class characters in your books, there is a general idea, which one can understand, I think, that all Wilson's characters turn out nasty.

WILSON: I would have said that not all but a good number of the characters in my books are highly self-conscious. I'm interested in very self-conscious, self-aware people, and on the whole, like Miss Compton-Burnett's characters, they make their own judgement about themselves, almost before I can do so. But it's true that I do make some. Meg Eliot [in *The Middle Age of Mrs Eliot*] was for me a very heroic character and, if you like, she was a bit drawn from myself, much more so than any other character I've written about. She was the one who could face collapse most easily, but on the other hand she had this same kind of capacity for almost being stultified, as her brother even more so, by self-observation. I regard this as a disease, but a necessary disease, of civilized people. I agree that my characters may not often be entirely virtuous, or even entirely likeable, but they don't try to make themselves into God very much, or if they do, they are very much aware of it.

KERMODE: Yes, well this is a very George Eliot-like way to write books. (Laughter) I don't know if this strengthens the link between you and Mrs Eliot at all.

WILSON: Well, I really don't know why one shouldn't try to write like George Eliot but I –

KERMODE: Not at all – except that when she wants characters to be nasty, even in a complicated way like Rosamund Vincey, she is nasty in a way recognizable by a great many people.

WILSON: Yes, yes.

KERMODE: Your notion of reality is more alien, perhaps, to that of many people than George Eliot's was.

WILSON: I suppose it is. I think that I'm a kinder person really than George Eliot: that is to say that my nasty characters get through better, but perhaps my good characters don't get through so well. I reduce people to a greyer level than she does probably.

KERMODE: You would say that the difference is really a kind of difference in reality rather than difference in your approach, that you have the same kind of approach to fiction, but what you are talking about is a different thing now.

WILSON: Well, I don't know that I would have the right to say that. I would say that there is a great deal of what you call the George Eliot approach. But above all that, and mixed with it, and perhaps swirling it round and distorting it and so on, is a great lump of a kind of Dickensianism, and this is the thing which distinguishes me from that sort of George Eliot writing: that I have got this – how can I say it? – this grand guignol side. I am sure that I have in my character strong sadistic impulses which do come out in my books, and I try to choke that down when I see it in the books, but nevertheless that again is difficult because the modern world is a world in which sadistic impulses have run very rife. Therefore how am I to know whether they are mine, or those of the world in which I live?

IV

At the start of Mr Wilson's remarks we have the already familiar notion, that myths should be left to look after themselves; of course, the difficulty of this in our time is obvious. And he ends by suggesting that his own myth or fantasy may overthrow the whole antithesis on which I was basing the questions by representing not only a 'sadistic impulse' in himself, but a pattern in contemporary reality: this amounts to a theory which it would be difficult to defend in so far as it would make universally valid, for instance, a schizophrenic's account of the world; but of course Mr Wilson is also strongly and self-consciously concerned with the technical and moral problems of justly representing the facts.

It is a good notion, therefore, to turn now to a novelist whose myth might, at first blush, seem to flourish in rarefied isolation from the facts of contemporary existence, indeed its habits of speech and living. Miss Compton-Burnett, however, questions this: of all our contributors she is the most empirically minded; of course there has to be form, of course form doesn't distort reality. Neither does her dialogue.

COMPTON-BURNETT: A novel must have a form and has to be adapted in that way. I don't think that there is any way out of that.

KERMODE: I gather then that you would say that the mere act of devising a plot involves a degree of distortion of reality.

COMPTON-BURNETT: No, not distortion, but I think that it makes a frame to put reality in. I think the reality and the plot have to be adapted a little to each other, not distorted, I think. I don't see why it should.

KERMODE: Well, may I just take another aspect of your work which obviously comes to people's minds when they are thinking about this question, namely the nature of your dialogue, and the relative uniformity of dialect, shall we say. Among people of all classes, parents, children and so on.

COMPTON-BURNETT: It never seems to me that they talk alike, that the servants talk like the children, or that the children or the servants talk like the other people. Some people think they do, and some people think they don't. And I of course think they don't.

KERMODE: Well, I would say as a reader of your novels that they clearly are not talking exactly alike, but that they are all talking the same language.

COMPTON-BURNETT: We all do that, don't we?

KERMODE: Er – yes. Let me return to the word dialect then. They are all talking the same upper-class dialect.

COMPTON-BURNETT: I shouldn't have thought they did. You see, the servants echoed the other people. But I think – I think their talk has, or should have, quite a different – quite a different tone, you know. But of course if people miss it, it may be my fault. Some people miss it, and some people don't. Miss it is perhaps my own word, you see.

KERMODE: Yes, in other words you would explain the similarity – as it falsely appears to me to be . . .

COMPTON-BURNETT: Yes, you put it rather unkindly from your point of view.

KERMODE: Well, let's be unkind to me. The similarity is really a symptom of a sociological situation.

COMPTON-BURNETT: Yes, I think it is, and I should have thought that the children talk quite differently. But children, you know, do really talk rather formally if you listen to them. Colloquialism comes later. It is what people pick up.

KERMODE: May I ask one thing again, with an attempt to save my position, and establish a certain degree of conventionality about the dialect that your people speak. I notice in a good many of your novels a tendency to use what in a play would be called an 'aside', and not to observe the dramatic convention that the aside is never overheard; asides are always overheard in your dialogues.

COMPTON-BURNETT: Yes, I think they are. I put them in to have them overheard. I don't see how you can help it if you write a book that's – in my case – something rather between a novel and a play.

KERMODE: In one of your recent books, one of the characters says: 'None of it is fit to be uttered aloud.' Do you remember that remark? Do you think that that is true of most of your conversation?

COMPTON-BURNETT: Well – not most of it – some of it, I dare say. But I think if you write in dialogue, things must be uttered aloud, otherwise there is no book.

KERMODE: Now, just as you limit the text of your novel to dialogue largely, so you limit the scene of it, as everyone knows, to a particular kind of house, to a particular kind of family, at a time which most people would regard as being about sixty years ago, I suppose.

COMPTON-BURNETT: Yes. Well, I think that when that kind of time comes to an end, you know the time, you understand the time and know the life. But I think there is a lot of that life still left, you know – perhaps more in the country than in London – and I think that people will gradually join it, you know. I think that there is an ambition in a great many people to join that sort of life, and I think human relationships – although they may be more easy to depict and portray in a more or less narrow scene – I think in narrow scenes, in broad scenes, in any scenes, they must be the same.

KERMODE: You regard this kind of family history as archetypal?

COMPTON-BURNETT: No, I don't think I do. I think it must get modified as the years go by. But I think history will repeat itself – and it is beginning to repeat itself a little, and has never really stopped going on in the same way.

KERMODE: You're speaking now of the social conditions, and I'm speaking more of the relationship between parents and children.

COMPTON-BURNETT: I'm speaking of both.

KERMODE: But if one takes that pattern, it's interesting, for example, that the kind of society that you describe would possibly be rather similar to the kind of family life upon which Freud based his observations, so that there is this sense . . .

COMPTON-BURNETT: I think family life will always have its own essence you know. *If* people have family life. They tell me – of course, I don't know if it is true – that some parents leave their children entirely to the state, and there isn't so much family life; but of course I shouldn't meet those people, you see. I think really family life goes on.

KERMODE: Oh, yes. Some of the incidents that occur in the families in your novels aren't of the sort that occur in ordinary families perhaps.

COMPTON-BURNETT: They might occur – I think they did occur more than people know.

KERMODE: So that you would want to say, would you, that for example in the book *A Heritage and its History*, the seduction of the old man's wife by his son, and the consequent embroilment in another generation, that is the kind of thing that you would regard as a not too improbable aspect of family . . .?

COMPTON-BURNETT: I think it might happen.

KERMODE: What we see is the normal tension that exists in families, in a very pure state.

COMPTON-BURNETT: Yes – er – yes, in a way. Perhaps it is rather keyed up, and a plot has to be imposed if you like because a book must have a form, you see.

KERMODE: Of course, and the similarity between your plots and certain ancient plots which has sometimes been pointed out is because families are always alike.

COMPTON-BURNETT: I think so. But it is true that I was classically educated, and it is possible that I was influenced without knowing it. It isn't conscious. It is true that I read Greek plays when I was young.

KERMODE: So, on the whole, you wouldn't want to say, as some novelists do, that there is an element of myth construction in your plots?

COMPTON-BURNETT: No, I don't think I should.

V

If life isn't like her novels, Miss Compton-Burnett suggests, it was and it will be again and she cannot be bothered to discuss the conventions which distinguish her manner, since to imagine them away is to imagine away the books. Similarly, she will have no nonsense about myth. Yet her characters themselves have been known to pause and consider how absurd it is for them to have got into such primitive situations; and the truth as one sees it in her books seems to be that Miss Compton-Burnett is endlessly aware of the remarkable artifice of her plots and the implications, moral and aesthetic, of her procedures.

For another view of the myth-fact relation we turn to C. P. Snow, who alone of all the contributors does in a sense write the antinovel, in that he is continuously in reaction from the formalist myth-makers of the twenties and thirties. He starts by trying out Miss Murdoch's terms 'journalistic' and 'crystalline' on Tolstoy.

SNOW: Now Tolstoy, for instance, if he comes into either of these categories, certainly must come into the journalistic. That makes me suspicious of the entire dichotomy.

KERMODE: Yes. Miss Murdoch doesn't indeed want novels to be either of these things. She is just as opposed to the crystalline, as I understand her, as she is to the other kind.

SNOW: Yes. Then absence of formal restriction is a thing I find slightly bewildering. You can't invent mystery, it seems to me.

KERMODE: Now, Sir Charles, if this distinction were workable, I suppose we should want to place your novels a little nearer, allowing for the pejorative sound of the word, to the journalistic rather than the crystalline. Would this be fair?

SNOW: Oh, certainly.

KERMODE: Does this mean that you have some kind of mistrust of formal patterning and the suggestions of myth and so on in novels?

SNOW: I'll have to distinguish between those two. I have no objection to formal patterning, and indeed I think it can give great strength to a novel, and a great many novels which would come under the journalistic side of this division would have deep formal patterning. Myth I'm much more suspicious of — unless it comes quite naturally and innately. I don't believe you can put in the myths any more than you can put in the symbols.

KERMODE: On the whole you would certainly at any rate reject the idea of a discontinuity between the real world — in the terms which we are using in this discussion — and the reality of the novel. They must be continuous?

SNOW: Yes, yes, quite certainly. Here of course we are begging terms in using the word 'real' like that, but I think we both know what we mean.

KERMODE: May we pass on to the idea of novels considered as social history — novels as related very closely and continuously to fact. Would you say that your novels have some kind of meaning in these terms?

SNOW: I should think they have some meaning. That is, I believe that persons live in their time, and they are tagged down by their time, and if you try to loosen their feet from that particular earth, then you get them wrong. But a novel is never really social history in the exact sense. Even the novels which seem deeply documentary, like Balzac's, really are much farther away from real social history than many of us think, and I believe that's also true of mine.

KERMODE: To what degree would you say that your being a scientist has conditioned the view of reality that you propose in your books?

SNOW: Quite a bit. How much, it is harder for me to say than it would be for you. But certainly part of my training would make me suspicious of a lot of the categories which certain writers think in, and also would give me, I think, a rather simpler view of the kind of truth which I should like to aim at.

I believe there are certain things you can say about people in their society which are – slightly begging the terms but not too much – which are objectively true. That is, people are like that in those places at that time. Their temperaments are like that, and their reaction on their environment, and their environment's reaction on them, can be with some kind of accuracy stated. Now I believe a realistic novelist ought to do that, often does do it. And that seems to me not grossly dissimilar from the scientific process, or a part of the scientific process. At least, the spirit behind it is not grossly different.

KERMODE: So that the degree to which you impose, have to impose, formal patterns on reality when you make fiction of any sort, does not seem to you to distort that reality, any more than a scientific experiment would do?

SNOW: To an extent more, but not grossly more. I mean the sort of formal patterns of narrative which are very important in a novel, to an extent, of course, are slightly neater than anything you get in a slice of documentary life, but I don't think it need affect the particular persons, or even the particular scenes, which are really the bread and butter and the heart of the novel.

KERMODE: So that one can't draw any analogy between what you do as a novelist and the degree of distortion that I believe is involved in some kinds of physical experiment. It is the different kind of change that the mind induces in the facts.

SNOW: Yes, I think that is actually a very deep question, because the degree of abstraction, of course, at which physical experiments have to be thought of and constructed is so very far away from the immediate world of reality that the same conditions don't apply. But I think a certain amount of the same spirit can and probably does apply. I would have thought what Tolstoy was trying to do in *War and Peace*, and to an extent what George Eliot tried to do in *Middlemarch*, is very deeply near the spirit of certain scientific processes.

Tolstoy wanted to tell a lot of truths, and none of them imagined truths, and none of them things which he was drawing from myth, or drawing from a particular shaping of his own interior experience. He wanted to say that this and this happened, this person behaved so; how they were moved by the mysterious forces of history was deeply occupying him. But this was all going to be expressed, or this was at least the intention, in terms of particular persons in particular situations. And this seemed to me to have the degree of objectivity which you don't get in, say, physical science, I think, so much as, say, in the more observational sciences, like some parts of biology.

KERMODE: I gather from what you say that you don't feel with, say, the new novelists in France that the novel itself has imposed a kind of conventionalized reality upon us, and that this has become evidently obsolete and a new way of looking is required.

SNOW: Well, you know as well as I do, this was being said with the utmost vigour about 1917, by our Bloomsbury forebears. It was exactly the same doctrine which was propounded by Dorothy Richardson, by Virginia Woolf and what not, and it made the novel totally meaningless in a very short time. And some of my colleagues and I have to spend quite a lot of time – unnecessary time – getting rid of that particular legacy and finding a different way of doing things. And I think that in fact it's a curious example of French provincialism that they should think that this is new.

VI

Sir Charles, of course, robustly opposes the notion that there is anything special about the problem of reality in novels, and even the notion that the novel to any serious extent translates fact into its own conventional notations. His own books, most people would say, have their myth or mystique; but he believes that this is to be inferred from an honest account of people behaving, rather than 'put in' by the author. This 'neo-realist' view evidently exercises a powerful appeal at the moment. A much younger writer, with a strong interest in Arnold Bennett, is John Wain; and he certainly does not believe that myth has a free hand with reality; indeed, reality is for him something you stand firmly outside of, that you select from.

WAIN: I don't believe that there is one fixed reality. I think that there is the huge flux of raw experience, experiences of every kind – personal experience, political experience, philosophical, physical, emotional experience. It is all there as a raw welter. All you can do is to select the bit you feel you can handle at the moment, and devise some means of handling it, and make a complete start. So many writers, even quite good ones, write the same book over and over again. And the great danger is that if they keep on doing it year after year, they will begin to feel that the kind of reality they are presenting is something genuinely fixed. I don't really believe it is fixed.

KERMODE: Now, you write other kinds of books besides novels. But just because you think the novel imposes a certain fixed view, fixed within very wide limits of reality, and that this doesn't always please you, you want to do other things?

WAIN: There are certain kinds of experience, and certain kinds of perception, which are very well suited to be handled with certain kinds of form. For instance, Virginia Woolf's criticism of Arnold Bennett resolved itself into the point that the realistic novel will take care of certain kinds of experience, and other kinds simply can't be caught in that particular scoop, and she wanted to propose another kind of scoop, which I don't think is a valid point at all. The only thing is a complete freedom of attitude, where you are ready to pick up any form once you've taken the trouble to train yourself in any form, whether it be the realistic novel, the romantic or surrealist novel, the play, the ballet, the circus – I don't care what it is as long as you are ready to pick up the form that will take the piece of reality that you have in mind.

KERMODE: Now, may we talk for a moment or two about your novels? A lot of the other people have suggested that there's something they tend to call myth, which is a kind of pattern that their own mind imposes, and which occasionally falsifies the truth, as they sometimes see afterwards. Do you feel that in your novels you've ever indulged yourself in myth in this way, and have you found it a problem?

WAIN: Not all my novels come equally close to being more or less readable and successful, and in one particular case, which is a very bad book, I did impose a certain interpretation upon the events I was going to write about before I wrote about it, and my perception of the way characters actually work and exist, and the way things really work out, was tied from the beginning to an intellectual concept.

KERMODE: What about the odd exception, or apparent exception, as in William Golding, for example, where a series of events clearly suggests a myth, and a myth suggests a series of events which don't in their extent go very much beyond the scope of that myth – at least that would seem to be the way he works?

WAIN: William Golding, a writer I admire enormously, is not a novelist as far as I can see. He is an allegorist. He has certain perceptions about the human condition which he, I should imagine at a guess, goes ahead and creates an allegory to represent.

KERMODE: But you were saying how loose the novel and how undefined a thing it is; is there no reason why this kind shouldn't be included presumably as well as the kind you've been describing?

WAIN: You go a long way before you reach a frontier in the novel, but you do finally reach one; and at the point where you ultimately come up against a frontier, Mr Golding's work is still beyond it, I think.

KERMODE: And what about the frontier on the other side – the frontier where Arnold Bennett is on the novel side of it? What would you place on the far side of it?

WAIN: The newspaper.

KERMODE: Ah, but something that's as near to being a novel, as William Golding's books are?

WAIN: No, because the realistic novel as understood by French writers who invented it, and by writers like Bennett who took it over, is in fact right on the very edge of the newspaper report. It's simply the newspaper report which did not actually take place and which is done at enormous length and with complete fullness of detail.

KERMODE: Finally, holding the views that you've expressed as I understand them, it is not one of your problems to worry about whether you are distorting reality by the mere act of imposing a form upon it?

WAIN: Distorting it, no. Scooping it out with a specially shaped scoop, yes. I feel like a mouse biting into some gigantic cheese. There is the cheese – mile upon mile of it – at least as big in relation to me as Mount Everest is physically, and I am doing all right if I can take a piece of this cheese and shape it into anything; because the whole object of writing is to tell the truth and if you can tell any portion of the truth, and continue to make it truthful, although you are putting it into literary form, then goodness me, that is enough.

VII

The mouse and the cheese is a homely allegory of fiction-writing on the borders of fact, as far as possible from the crystalline or mythic pole. Our last contributor, though, upsets these categories by saying, very reasonably, that myth *is* plot, myth is what you make up about reality. What seems to concern Muriel Spark more than the myth-fact antithesis is a much purer and much more ancient issue, which lies behind all these conversations, and is, simply, are novelists liars? If not, what kind of truth are they telling?

SPARK: To me the plot is the basic myth. I don't know much about myths, you see. If I think of a plot, I take it for granted that that's a myth. I don't bother about myths apart from that, but I hope that a plot's got something universal in it.

KERMODE: May I bring into the conversation a particular book of yours, *The Comforters*, because here we have something which is very handy to the whole discussion, including what other people have said. This is a book in which you've got your myth, but you've deliberately made it in a sense a game about novels, haven't you? There you are – the novelist herself is mixed up in the story, keeps on breaking in. Is this because you've got a kind of interest in the form of fiction, which some people rather morally think extrudes reality from the whole thing? It becomes a game instead of a transcript?

SPARK: No, I don't think so. It really depends on the fact that this book *The Comforters* was my first novel. I was asked to write a novel, and I didn't think much of novels – I thought it was an inferior way of writing. So I wrote a novel to work out the technique first, to sort of make it all right with myself to write a novel at all – a novel about writing a novel, about writing a novel sort of thing, you see. I think that the set-up of my writing is probably just a justification of the time I wasted doing something else. And it is an attempt to redeem the time, you see.

KERMODE: You use the word 'wasted' advisedly, do you?

SPARK: It wouldn't be wasted if I had my way. It won't be wasted – it won't be known to be wasted until I'm dead.

KERMODE: The novels that you've written since *The Comforters* have not had quite this wantonness, as I called it, about the form which you are employing, though they've had some.

SPARK: Yes. Well, because I observed a kind of wantonness, as you call it, I decided the best thing to do was to stick to a plot, and stick to a formal outline and say what I wanted to say in that limit. And then I decided that I was writing minor novels deliberately, and not major novels. An awful lot of people are telling me to write big long novels – Mrs Tolstoy, you know – and I decided it is no good filling a little glass with a pint of beer.

KERMODE: You tend to pick not a Tolstoyan society, but a rather limited society of very old people, for example. Is this because the other things are on too big a scale for what you want to do?

SPARK: Well, partly because of my own temperament, and my own constitution. When I become interested in a subject, say old age, then the world is peopled for me – just peopled with them. And it is a narrow little small world, but it's full of old people, full of whatever I'm studying. They're the centre of the world, and everyone else is on the periphery. It is an obsession until I've finished writing about them. And that's how I see things. I wrote a book about bachelors and it seemed to me that everyone was a bachelor. It is true, just strangely enough, those people come my way while I am writing – I don't take a long time, so it is not difficult.

KERMODE: And you don't feel that it is necessary to explain the difference between this temporary world and the permanent one in terms of saying that you are a writer of fantasy, that you might as well make the world full of insects, or of very large or very small men?

SPARK: I don't claim that my novels are truth – I claim that they are fiction, out of which a kind of truth emerges. And I keep in my mind specifically that what I am writing is fiction because I am interested in truth – absolute truth – and I don't pretend that what I'm writing is more than an imaginative extension of the truth – something inventive. I don't say that such and such a person lived and such and such a person crossed the road, simply because I write it – in a court of law it wouldn't carry any weight, and it's not true, what I write is not true – it is a pack of lies. There is metaphorical truth and moral truth, and what they call anagogical, you know, the different sorts of truth; and there is absolute truth, in which I believe things which are difficult to believe, but I believe them because they are absolute. And this is one aspect of truth, perhaps. But in fact if we are going to live in the world as reasonable beings, we must call it lies. But simply because one puts it out as a work of fiction, then one is not a liar. I do think that this ought to be recognized by people. People get very annoyed if you say, look here, Goldilocks and the three bears is a pack of lies.

KERMODE: One of the many senses in which the word myth has been used in these discussions is to cover this unconscious element in any story and any plot – and a lot of people seem to think that the quicker you get down to this level the better the book is going to be, and some others, like Iris Murdoch, think that the minute that you lapse into it, you've started writing badly, self indulgently.

SPARK: Perhaps she is right. I think the best thing is to be conscious of everything that one writes, and let the unconscious take care of itself, if it exists, which we don't know. If we knew it, it wouldn't be the unconscious. I think you should be as conscious as possible of what you are doing, and never give in to the temptation – it comes upon most writers – of 'Oh, I did that wonderfully – now I must go on doing that unconsciously'. It is terribly wrong. The unconscious is completely limitless. The best thing is to know what you are doing, I think.

KERMODE: It's an old charge that poets are liars, and we include novelists among poets; and the old defence is that he nothing affirmeth and therefore never lieth. Is this very much what you have been saying in this conversation?

SPARK: Yes, I think so. I think that the novelist is out just to say what happened. I express it in the past tense, but in the actual process, as far as I am concerned, it happens in the present tense. Things just happen and one records what has happened a few seconds later. I don't mean, of course, that one is that recording instrument that Blake thought of himself, just a kind of medium between the angels and the creatures, but I do know events occur in my mind, and I record them.

Whether it fits in with this theory, that theory, this myth, that myth, has nothing to do with me.

For Mrs Spark the novel is true because it happens in the author's mind as he writes; in this sense it is a completely accurate transcript of events, and as an account of character not to be faulted. It may be a corollary of this that the outside world becomes, momentarily for such a novelist, a world populated by a limited class of persons behaving in unusual ways; but the novelist is not affirming this, and in any case distinguishes between absolute truth (revealed religion) and other less important kinds of truth, of which the novel might produce one.

This is a question which will look different according as you believe or do not believe in absolute truth. Yet to the agnostic Wilson and the Catholic Spark the 'myth' is something best left to take care of itself; whereas to Miss Murdoch it is a temptation to abandon uncompleted the great task of exploring personality; and I have an idea that Miss Murdoch would include Mrs Spark's 'absolute truths' among the myths because they too 'break bitter furies of complexity'. On the other hand, to Mr Greene it is precisely those furies of complexity that damage the important thing, the central static myth.

The house of fiction has many windows, but at any given period they may all be designed as variations on a few basic shapes. What you see from them varies more considerably within these limits: irreducibly complex personalities, a sadistic landscape, a gaunt country house full of secrets that cannot survive the preternatural explicitness of the inhabitants, a mountain of cheese. And for the most part the people at present standing at these windows are content to say 'My window is shaped thus and thus,' rather than 'all windows should be myth-shaped or fact-shaped' – there may be above all a God-shaped window giving perfect all-round visibility, but theirs is in no case held to resemble it.

JOHN FOWLES

Notes on an Unfinished Novel

(1969)

The novel I am writing at the moment (provisionally entitled *The French Lieutenant's Woman*) is set about a hundred years back. I don't think of it as a historical novel, a genre in which I have very little interest. It started four or five months ago as a visual image. A woman stands at the end of a deserted quay and stares out to sea. That was all. This image rose in my mind one morning when I was still in bed half asleep. It corresponded to no actual incident in my life (or in art) that I can recall, though I· have for many years collected obscure books and forgotten prints, all sorts of flotsam and jetsam from the last two or three centuries, relics of past lives – and I suppose this leaves me with a sort of dense hinterland from which such images percolate down to the coast of consciousness.

These mythopoeic 'stills' (they seem almost always static) float into my mind very often. I ignore them, since that is the best way of finding whether they really are the door into a new world.

So I ignored this image; but it recurred. Imperceptibly it stopped coming to me. I began deliberately to recall it and to try to analyse and hypothesize why it held some sort of imminent power. It was obviously mysterious. It was vaguely romantic. It also seemed, perhaps because of the latter quality, not to belong to today. The woman obstinately refused to stare out of the window of an airport lounge; it had to be this ancient quay – as I happen to live near one, so near that I can see it from the bottom of my garden, it soon became a specific ancient quay. The woman had no face, no particular degree of sexuality. But she was Victorian; and since I always saw her in the same static long shot, with her back turned, she represented a reproach on the Victorian Age. An outcast. I didn't know her crime, but I wished to protect her. That is, I began to fall in love with her. Or with her stance. I didn't know which.

This – not literally – pregnant female image came at a time (the autumn of 1966) when I was already half-way through another novel and had, still have, three or four others planned to follow it. It was an interference, but of such power that it soon came to make the previously planned work seem the intrusive element in my life. This accidentality of inspiration has to be allowed for in writing; both in the work one is on (unplanned development of character, unintended incidents, and so on) and in one's works as a whole. Follow the accident, fear the fixed plan – that is the rule.

Narcissism, or pygmalionism, is the essential vice a writer must have. Characters (and even situations) are like children or lovers, they need constant caressing, concern, listening to, watching, admiring. All these occupations become tiring for the active partner – the writer – and only something akin to love can provide the energy. I've heard people say, 'I want to write a book.' But wanting to write a book, however ardently, is not enough. Even to say, 'I want to be possessed by my own creations,' is not enough; all natural or born writers are possessed, and in the old magical sense, by their own imaginations long before they even begin to think of writing.

This fluke genesis must break all the rules of creative writing; must sound at best childlike, at worst childish. I suppose the orthodox method is to work out what one wants to say and what one has experience of, and then to correlate the two. I have tried that method and started out with an analytically arrived-at theme and a set of characters all neatly standing for something; but the manuscripts have all petered out miserably. *The Magus* (written before *The Collector*, which also originated in a single image) sprang from a very trivial visit to a villa on a Greek island; nothing in the least unusual happened. But in my unconscious I kept arriving at the place again and again; something wanted to happen there, something that had not happened to me at the time. Why it should have been at *that* villa, *that* one visit, among so many thousands of other possible launching-pads, I do not know. Only a month ago someone showed me some recent photographs of the villa, which is now deserted; and it was just a deserted villa. Its mysterious significance to me fifteen years ago remains mysterious.

Once the seed germinates, reason and knowledge, culture and all the rest have to start to grow it. You cannot create a world by hot instinct; but only by cold experience. That is one good reason why so many novelists produce nothing until, or do all their best work after, the age of forty.

I find it very difficult to write if I don't know I shall have several days absolutely clear. All visits, all intrusions, all daily duties become irksome. This is during the first draft. I wrote the first draft of *The Collector* in under a month; sometimes ten thousand words a day. Of course a lot of it was poorly written and had to be endlessly amended and revised. First-draft and revision writing are so different they hardly seem to belong to the same activity. I never do any 'research' until the first draft is finished; all that matters to begin with is the flow, the story, the narrating. Research material then is like swimming in a straitjacket.

During the revision period I try to keep some sort of discipline. I make myself revise whether I feel like it or not; in some ways, the more disinclined and dyspeptic one feels, the better – one is harsher with oneself. All the best cutting is done when one is sick of the writing.

But all this advice from senior writers to establish a discipline always, to get down a thousand words a day whatever one's mood, I find an absurdly puritanical and impractical approach. Writing is like eating or making love; a natural process, not an artificial one. Write, if you must, because you feel like writing; never because you feel you ought to write.

I write memoranda to myself about the book I'm on. On this one: *You are not trying to write something one of the Victorian novelists forgot to write; but perhaps something one of them failed to write.* And: *Remember the etymology of the word. A novel is something new. It must have relevance to the writer's now – so don't ever pretend you live in 1867; or make sure the reader knows it's a pretence.*

In the matter of clothes, social manners, historical background, and the rest, writing about 1867 is merely a question of research. But I soon get into trouble over dialogue, because the genuine dialogue of 1867 (in so far as it can be heard in books of the time) is far too close to our own to sound convincingly old. It very often fails to agree with our psychological picture of the Victorians – it is not stiff enough, not euphemistic enough, and so on; and here at once I have to start cheating and pick out the more formal and archaic (even for 1867) elements of spoken speech. It is this kind of 'cheating', which is intrinsic to the novel, that takes the time.

Even in modern-novel dialogue the most real is not the most comfortable to actual current speech. One has only to read a transcribed tape of actual conversation to realize that it is, in the literary context, not very real. Novel dialogue is a form of shorthand, an *impression* of what people actually say; and besides that it has to perform other functions – to keep the narrative moving (which real conversation rarely does), to reveal character (real conversation often hides it) and so on.

This is the greatest technical problem I have; it is hard enough with modern characters, and doubly so with historical ones.

Memorandum: *If you want to be true to life, start lying about the reality of it.*

And: *One cannot describe reality; only give metaphors that indicate it. All human modes of description (photographic,*

mathematical and the rest, as well as literary) are metaphorical.
Even the most precise scientific description of an object or
movement is a tissue of metaphors.

Alain Robbe-Grillet's polemical essay *Pour un nouveau roman*
(1963) is indispensable reading for the profession, even where it
produces no more than total disagreement. His key question:
Why bother to write in a form whose great masters cannot be
surpassed? The fallacy of one of his conclusions – we must
discover a new form to write in if the novel is to survive – is
obvious. It reduces the purpose of the novel to the discovery of
new forms: whereas its other purposes – to entertain, to satirize,
to describe new sensibilities, to record life, to improve life, and
so on – are clearly just as viable and important. But his obsessive
pleading for new form places a kind of stress on every passage
one writes today. To what extent am I being a coward by
writing inside the old tradition? To what extent am I being
panicked into avant-gardism? Writing about 1867 doesn't lessen
the stress; it increases it, since so much of the subject matter
must of its historical nature be 'traditional'. There are apparent
parallels in other arts: Stravinsky's eighteenth-century rehand-
lings, Picasso's and Francis Bacon's use of Velasquez. But in this
context words are not nearly so tractable as musical notes or
brush-strokes. One can parody a rococo musical ornament, a
baroque face. Very early on I tried, in a test chapter, to put
modern dialogue into Victorian mouths. But the effect was
absurd, since the real historical nature of the characters is
hopelessly distorted; the only people to get away with this
(Julius Caesar speaking with a Brooklyn accent, and so on) are
the professional funny men. One is led inevitably, by such a
technique, into a comic novel.

My two previous novels were both based on more or less
disguised existentialist premises. I want this one to be no
exception; and so I am trying to show an existentialist awareness
before it was chronologically possible. Kierkegaard was, of
course, totally unknown to the British and American Victorians;

but it has always seemed to me that the Victorian Age, especially from 1850 on, was highly existentialist in many of its personal dilemmas. One can almost invert the reality and say that Camus and Sartre have been trying to lead us, in their fashion, to a Victorian seriousness of purpose and moral sensitivity.

Nor is this the only similarity between the 1960s and 1860s. The great nightmare of the respectable Victorian mind was the only too real one created by the geologist Lyell and the biologist Darwin. Until then man had lived like a child in a small room. They gave him – and never was a present less welcome – infinite space and time, and a hideously mechanistic explanation of human reality into the bargain. Just as we 'live with the bomb' the Victorians lived with the theory of evolution. They were hurled into space. They felt themselves infinitely isolated. By the 1860s the great iron structures of their philosophies, religions, and social stratifications were already beginning to look dangerously corroded to the more perspicacious.

Just such a man, an existentialist before his time, walks down the quay and sees that mysterious back, feminine, silent, also existentialist, turned to the horizon.

Magnificent though the Victorian novelists were, they almost all (an exception, of course, is the later Hardy) failed miserably in one aspect; nowhere in 'respectable' Victorian literature (and most of the pornography was based on the brothel – or eighteenth-century accounts) does one see a man and a woman described together in bed. We do not know how they made love, what they said to each other in their most intimate moments, what they felt then.

Writing as I have been today – about two Victorians making love – with no guides except my imagination and vague deductions from the spirit of the age and so on – is really science fiction. A journey is a journey, backwards or forwards.

The most difficult task for a writer is to get the right 'voice' for his material; by voice I mean the overall impression one has of the creator behind what he creates. Now I've always liked the ironic voice that the line of great nineteenth-century novelists, from Austen through to Conrad, all used so naturally. We tend today to remember the failures of that tone – the satirical overkill in Dickens, the facetiousness of Thackeray, the strained sarcasm of Mark Twain, the priggishness in George Eliot – rather than its virtues. The reason is clear enough; irony needs the assumption of superiority in the ironist. Such an assumption must be anathema to a democratic, egalitarian century like our own. We suspect people who pretend to be omniscient; and that is why so many of us twentieth-century novelists feel driven into first-person narration.

I have heard writers claim that this first-person technique is a last bastion of the novel against the cinema, a form where the camera dictates an inevitable third-person point of view of what happens, however much we may identify with one character. But the matter of whether a contemporary novelist uses 'he' or 'I' is largely irrelevant. The great majority of modern third-person narration is 'I' narration very thinly disguised. The real 'I' of the Victorian writers – the writer himself – is as rigorously repressed there (out of fear of seeming pretentious, etc.) as it is, for obvious semantic and grammatical reasons, when the narration is in literal first-person form.

But in this new book, I shall try to resurrect this technique. It seems in any case natural to look back at the England of a hundred years ago with a somewhat ironical eye – and 'I' – although it is my strong belief that history is horizontal in terms of the ratio between understanding and *available* knowledge and (far more important) horizontal in terms of the happiness the individual gets from being alive. In short, there is a danger in being ironic about the apparent follies and miseries of any past age. So I have written myself another memorandum: *You are not the 'I' who breaks into the illusion, but the 'I' who is a part of it.*

In other words, the 'I' who will make first-person commentaries here and there in my story, and who will finally even enter it, will not be my real 'I' in 1967; but much more just another character, though in a different category from the purely fictional ones.

An illustration. Here is the beginning of a minor novel (*Lovel the Widower*, 1861) by Thackeray:

> Who shall be the hero of this tale? Not I who write it. I am but the Chorus of the Play. I make remarks on the conduct of the characters: I narrate their simple story.

Today I think we should assume (not knowing who the writer was) that the 'I' here is the writer's 'I'. For three or four pages more we might still just believe this; but then suddenly Thackeray introduces his eponymous hero as 'my friend Lovel' and we see we've been misled. 'I' is simply another character. But then a few pages on the 'I' cuts in again in the description of a character.

> She never could speak. Her voice was as hoarse as a fishwoman's. Can that immense stout old box-keeper at the —— theatre . . . be the once brilliant Emily Montanville? I am told there are *no* lady box-keepers in the English theatres. This, I submit, is a proof of my consummate care and artifice in rescuing from a prurient curiosity the individual personages from whom the characters of the present story are taken. Montanville is *not* a box-opener. She *may*, under another name, keep a trinket-shop in the Burlington Arcade, for what you know: but this secret no torture shall induce me to divulge. Life has its rises and downfalls, and you have had yours, you hobbling old creature. Montanville, indeed! Go thy ways! Here is a shilling for thee. (Thank you, sir.) Take away that confounded footstool, and never let us see thee more!

We can just still suppose that the 'I' is another character here; but the strong suspicion is that it is Thackeray himself. There is the characteristic teasing of the reader, the shock new angle of the present tense, the compensatory self-mocking in the already revealed 'secret no torture shall induce me to divulge'. But clearly he doesn't mean us to be sure; it is not the whole Thackeray.

Lovel rates poorly by Thackeray's own standards elsewhere; it is nevertheless a brilliant technical exercise in the use of 'voice'. I cannot believe that it is a dead technique. Nothing can get us off the charge of omniscience – and certainly not the *nouveau roman* theory. Even that theory's most brilliant practical demonstrations – say Robbe-Grillet's own *La Jalousie* – fail to answer the accusation. Robbe-Grillet may have removed the writer Robbe-Grillet totally from the text; but he has never denied he wrote it. If the writer really believes in the statement 'I know nothing about my characters except what can be tape-recorded and photographed (and then "mixed" and "cut"),' the logical step is to take up tape-recording and photography – not writing. But if he still writes, and writes well, as Robbe-Grillet does, then he is self-betrayed: he belongs to Cosa Nostra, and is transparently far more deeply implicated than he will admit.

September 2, 1967. Now I am about two-thirds of the way through. Always a bad stage, when one begins to doubt major things like basic motivations, dramatic design, the whole bloody enterprise; in the beginning one tends to get dazzled by each page, by one's fertility, those nice Muses always at one's shoulder . . . but then the inherent faults in the plot and characters begin to emerge. One starts to doubt the wisdom of the way the latter make things go; at the stage in an *affaire*, when one begins to thank God that marriage never raised its ugly head. But here one is condemned to a marriage of sorts – I have the woman on the quay (whose name is Sarah) for better or for worse, so to speak; and all seems worse.

I have to break off for a fortnight to go down to Majorca, where they're filming *The Magus*. I have written the script, but like most scripts it's really a team effort. The two producers have had their say, and the director; and a number of non-human factors, such as the budget, the nature of the locations, and the casting of the main roles, have had theirs. Most of the time I feel like a skeleton at the feast; this isn't what I had imagined, either in the book or in the script.

Yet it is interesting to watch, on a big film production, how buttressed each key man is by the other key men; to see how often one will turn to the other and say, 'Will it work?' I compare this with the loneliness of the long-distance writer; and I come back with a sort of relief, a re-affirmation in my faith in the novel. For all its faults, it is a statement by one person. In my novels I am the producer, director, and all the actors; I photograph it. This may seem a megalomania beside which the more celebrated cases from Hollywood pale to nothingness. There *is* a vanity about it, a wish to play the godgame, which all the random and author-removing devices of avant-garde technique cannot hide. But there must be a virtue, in an age that is out to exterminate both the individual and the enduring, in the individual's attempt to endure by his own efforts alone.

The truth is, the novel is a free form. Unlike the play or the filmscript, it has no limits other than those of the language. It is like a poem; it can be what it wants. This is its downfall and its glory; and explains why both forms have been so often used to establish freedom in other fields, social and political.

A charge all of us who sell film rights have to answer is that we wrote our books with this end in view. What has to be distinguished here is the legitimate and the illegitimate influence of the cinema on the novel. I saw my first film when I was six; I suppose I've seen on average – and discounting television – a film a week ever since; let's say some two and a half thousand films up to now. How can so frequently repeated an experience not have indelibly stamped itself on the *mode* of imagination? At one time I analysed my dreams in detail; again and again I recalled purely cinematic effects . . . panning shots, close shots, tracking, jump cuts, and the rest. In short, this mode of imagining is far too deep in me to eradicate – not only in me, in all my generation.

This doesn't mean we have surrendered to the cinema. I don't share the general pessimism about the so-called decline of the novel and its present status as a minority cult. Except for a brief period in the nineteenth century, when a literate majority and a lack of other means of entertainment coincided, it has always been a minority cult.

One has in fact only to do a filmscript to realize how inalienably in possession of a still vast domain the novel is; how countless the forms of human experience only to be described in and by it. There is too an essential difference in the quality of image evoked by the two media. The cinematic visual image is virtually the same for all who see it; it stamps out personal imagination, the response from individual *visual* memory. A sentence or paragraph in a novel will evoke a different image in each reader. This necessary co-operation between writer and reader, the one to suggest, the other to make concrete, is a privilege of *verbal* form; and the cinema can never usurp it.

Nor is that all. Here (the opening four paragraphs of a novel) is a flagrant bit of writing for the cinema. The man has obviously spent too much time on filmscripts, and can now think only of his movie sale.

> The temperature is in the 90's and the boulevard is absolutely empty.
>
> Lower down, the inky water of a canal reaches in a straight line. Midway between two locks is a barge full of timber. On the bank, two rows of barrels.
>
> Beyond the canal, between houses separated by work-yards, a huge cloudless tropical sky. Under the throbbing sun white façades, slate roofs and granite quays hurt the eyes. An obscure distant murmur rises in the hot air. All seems drugged by the Sunday peace and the sadness of summer days.
>
> Two men appear.

It first appeared on March 25, 1881. The writer's name is Flaubert. All I have done is to transpose his past historic into the present.

* * *

I woke in the small hours, and the book tormented me. All its failings rose up in the darkness. I saw the novel I dropped in order to write *The French Lieutenant's Woman* was much better. This one was not my sort of book; but an aberration, a folly, a delusion. Sentences from vitriolic reviews floated through my mind . . . 'a clumsy pastiche of Hardy', 'pretentious imitation of an inimitable genre', 'pointless exploration of an already over-explored age . . .', and so on and so on.

Now it is day, I am back on it again, and it denies what I felt in the night. But the horror of such realizations is that someone, some reader or reviewer, *will* realize them. The nightmare of the writer is that all his worst private fears and self-criticisms will be made public.

The shadow of Thomas Hardy, the heart of whose 'country' I can see in the distance from my workroom window, I cannot avoid. Since he and Peacock are my two favourite male novelists of the nineteenth century I don't mind the shadow. It seems best to use it; and by a curious coincidence, which I didn't realize when I placed my own story in that year, 1867 was the crucial year in Hardy's own mysterious personal life. It is somehow encouraging that while my fictitious characters weave their own story in their 1867, only thirty miles away in the real 1867 the pale young architect was entering his own fatal life-incident.

My female characters tend to dominate the male. I see man as a kind of artifice, and woman as a kind of reality. The one is cold idea, the other is warm fact. Daedalus faces Venus, and Venus must win. If the technical problems hadn't been so great, I should have liked to make Conchis in *The Magus* a woman. The character of Mrs de Seitas at the end of the book was simply an aspect of his character; as was Lily. Now Sarah exerts this power. She doesn't realize how. Nor do I yet.

I was stuck this morning to find a good answer from Sarah at the climax of a scene. Characters sometimes reject all the possibilities one offers. They say in effect: *I would never say or do a thing like that.* But they don't say what they would say; and one has to proceed negatively, by a very tedious coaxing kind of trial and error. After an hour over this one wretched sentence, I realized that she had in fact been telling me what to do: silence from her was better than any line she might have said.

By the time I left Oxford I found myself much more at home in French than in English literature. There seems to me to be a vital distinction between the French and Anglo-Saxon cultures in this field. Since 1650 French writers have assumed an international audience; and the Anglo-Saxons a national one. This may be no more than a general tendency; the literatures of the two cultures offer hundreds of exceptions, even among the best-known books. Nevertheless I have always found this French assumption that the proper audience of a book is one without frontiers more attractive than the extreme opposite view, which is still widely held in both Britain and America, that the proper job of a writer is to write of and for his own country and countrymen.

I am aware of this when I write, and especially when I revise. English references that will mean nothing to a foreigner I usually cut out, or avoid in the first place. In the present book I have the ubiquity in the West of the Victorian ethos: that helps greatly.

Various things have long made me feel an exile in England. Some years ago I came across a sentence in an obscure French novel: *Ideas are the only motherland.* Ever since I have kept it as the most succinct summary I know of what I believe. Perhaps 'believe' is the wrong verb – if you are without national feeling, if you find many of your fellow countrymen and most of their beliefs and their institutions foolish and antiquated, you can hardly *believe* in anything, but only accept the loneliness that results.

So I live completely away from other English writers and the literary life of London. What I have to think of as my 'public' self is willy-nilly absorbed into or rejected by (mostly the latter, in my case) the national literary 'world'. Even to me it seems, that public self, very remote and often distastefully alien and spurious; just one more thing that I feel my real self in exile from.

My real self is here and now, writing. Whenever I think of this (the writing, not the written) experience, images to do with exploring, singlehanded voyages, lone mountain ascents always spring unwanted to my mind. They sound romantic, but they're not meant to. It's the damned solitude, the fear of failure (by which I do *not* mean bad reviews), the tedium of the novel form, the often nauseating feeling that one is prey to an unhealthy obsession . . .

When I go out and meet other people, become mixed in their lives and social routines, my own solitude, routinelessness, and freedom (which is a subtle imprisonment) from economic 'worries' often make me feel like a visitor from outer space. I like earthmen, but I'm not quite sure what they're at. I mean we regulate things better at home. But there it is – I've been posted here. And there's no transport back.

Something like this lies behind all I write.

This total difference between the written and the writing world is what non-writers never realize about us. They see us as we were; we live with what we are. It is not subjects that matter to writers; but the experience of handling them. In those romantic terms, a difficult pitch scaled, a storm survived, the untrodden moon beneath one's feet. Such pleasures are unholy; and the world in general does right to regard us with malice and suspicion.

I loathe the day a manuscript is sent to the publisher, because on that day the people one has loved die; they become what they are – petrified, fossil organisms for others to study and collect. I get asked what I meant by this and by that. But what I wrote is what I meant. If it wasn't clear in the book, it shouldn't be clear now.

I find Americans, especially the kind people who write and

ask questions, have a strangely pragmatic view of what books are. Perhaps because of the miserable heresy that creative writing can be taught ('creative' is here a euphemism for 'imitative') they seem to believe that a writer always knows exactly what he's doing. Obscure books, for them, are a kind of crossword puzzle. Somewhere, they feel, in some number of a paper they missed, all the answers have been given to all the clues.

They believe, in short, that a book is like a machine; that if you have the knack, you can take it to bits.

Ordinary readers can hardly be blamed for thinking like this. Both academic criticism and weekly reviewing have in the last forty years grown dangerously scientific, or pseudo-scientific, in their general tenor. Analysis and categorization are indispensable scientific tools *in the scientific field*; but the novel, like the poem, is only partly a scientific field. No one wants a return to the kind of bellettrist and onanistic accounts of new books that were fashionable in the early years of the century; but we could do with something better than what we have got.

I am an interested party? I confess it. Ever since I began writing *The French Lieutenant's Woman* I've been reading obituaries of the novel; a particularly gloomy one came from Gore Vidal in the December 1967 issue of *Encounter*. And I have been watching novel-reviewing in England become this last year increasingly impatient and dismissive. Any moment now I expect one of our fashionable newspapers to decide to drop their *New Novels* column for good and give the released space over to television or pop music. Of course I am interested – but, like Mr Vidal, I can hardly be personally resentful. If the novel is dead, the corpse still remains oddly fertile. We are told no one reads novels any more; so the authors of *Julian* and *The Collector* must be grateful to the two million ghosts or more who have bought copies of their respective books. But I don't want to be sarcastic. More is at issue here than self-interest.

One has the choice of two views: either that the novel, along with printed-word culture in general, is moribund, or that there is something sadly shallow and blinded in our age. I know which view I hold; and the people who astound me are the ones who are sure that the first view is true. If you want omniscience, you have it there, and it ought to worry you, you the reader who is neither critic nor writer, that this omniscient contempt for print is found so widely among people who make a living out of literary dissection. Surgery is what we want, not dissection. It is not only the extirpation of the mind that kills the body; the heart will do the trick just as well.

October 27, 1967. I finished the first draft, which was begun on January 25. It is about 140,000 words long, and exactly as I imagined it: perfect, flawless, a lovely novel. But that, alas, is indeed only how I imagine it. When I re-read it I see 140,000 things need to be changed; then it will, perhaps, be less imperfect. But I haven't the energy; the dreaded research now, the interminable sentence-picking. I want to get on with another book. I had a strange image last night . . .

B. S. JOHNSON

Introduction to *Aren't You Rather Young to be Writing Your Memoirs?*

(1973)

It is a fact of crucial significance in the history of the novel this century that James Joyce opened the first cinema in Dublin in 1909. Joyce saw very early on that film must usurp some of the prerogatives which until then had belonged almost exclusively to the novelist. Film could tell a story more directly, in less time and with more concrete detail than a novel; certain aspects of character could be more easily delineated and kept constantly before the audience (for example, physical characteristics like a limp, a scar, particular ugliness or beauty); no novelist's description of a battle squadron at sea in a gale could really hope to compete with that in a well-shot film; and why should anyone who simply wanted to be told a story spend all his spare time for a week or weeks reading a book when he could experience the same thing in a version in some ways superior at his local cinema in only one evening?

It was not the first time that storytelling had passed from one medium to another. Originally it had been the chief concern of poetry, and long narrative poems were bestsellers right up to the works of Walter Scott and Byron. The latter supplanted the former in the favours of the public, and Scott adroitly turned from narrative poems to narrative novels and continued to be a bestseller. You will agree it would be perversely anachronistic to write a long narrative poem today? People still do, of course; but such works are rarely published, and, if they are, the writer is thought of as a literary flat-earther. But poetry did not die when storytelling moved on. It concentrated on the things it was still best able to do: the short, economical lyric, the intense emotional statement, depth rather than scale, the exploitation of rhythms which made their optimum impact at short lengths but which would have become monotonous and unreadable if maintained longer than a few pages. In the same way, the novel may not only survive but evolve to greater achievements by concentrating on those things it can still do best: the precise use of language, exploitation of the technological fact of the book, the explication of thought. Film is an excellent medium for showing things, but it is very poor at taking an audience inside characters' minds, at telling it what people are thinking. Again, Joyce saw this at once, and developed the technique of interior monologue within a few years of the appearance of the cinema. In some ways the history of the novel in the twentieth century has seen large areas of the old territory of the novelist increasingly taken over by other media, until the only thing the novelist can with any certainty call exclusively his own is the inside of his own skull: and that is what he should be exploring, rather than anachronistically fighting a battle he is bound to lose.

Joyce is the Einstein of the novel. His subject-matter in *Ulysses* was available to anyone, the events of one day in one place; but by means of form, style and technique in language he made it into something very much more, a novel, not a story about anything. What happens is nothing like as important as how it is written, as the medium of the words and form through which it is made to happen to the reader. And for style alone *Ulysses* would have been a revolution. Or, rather, styles. For Joyce saw that such a huge range of subject-matter could not be conveyed in one style, and accordingly used many. Just in this one innovation (and there are many others) lie a great advance and freedom offered to subsequent generations of writers.

But how many have seen it, have followed him? Very few. It is not a question of influence, of writing like Joyce. It is a matter of realizing that the novel is an evolving form, not a static one, of accepting that for practical purposes where Joyce left off should ever since have been regarded as the starting point. As Sterne said a long time ago:

> Shall we for ever make new books, as apothecaries make new mixtures, by pouring only out of one vessel into another? Are we for ever to be twisting, and untwisting the same rope? For ever in the same track – for ever at the same pace?

The last thirty years have seen the storytelling function pass on yet again. Now anyone who wants simply to be told a story has the need satisfied by television; serials like *Coronation Street* and so on do very little more than answer the question 'What happens next?' All other writing possibilities are subjugated to narrative. If a writer's chief interest is in telling stories (even remembering that telling stories is a euphemism for telling lies; and I shall come to that) then the best place to do it now is in television, which is technically better equipped and will reach more people than a novel can today. And the most aware film-makers have realized this, and directors such as Godard, Resnais, and Antonioni no longer make the chief point of their films a story; their work concentrates on those things film can do solely and those things it can do best.

Literary forms do become exhausted, clapped out, as well. Look what had happened to five-act blank-verse drama by the beginning of the nineteenth century. Keats, Shelley, Wordsworth and Tennyson all wrote blank-verse, quasi-Elizabethan plays; and all of them, without exception, are resounding failures. They are so not because the men who wrote them were inferior poets, but because the form was finished, worn out, exhausted, and everything that could be done with it had been done too many times already.

That is what seems to have happened to the nineteenth-century narrative novel, too, by the outbreak of the First World War. No matter how good the writers are who now attempt it, it cannot be made to work for our time, and the writing of it is anachronistic, invalid, irrelevant, and perverse.

* * *

Life does not tell stories. Life is chaotic, fluid, random; it leaves myriads of ends untied, untidily. Writers can extract a story from life only by strict, close selection, and this must mean falsification. Telling stories really is telling lies. Philip Pacey took me up on this to express it thus:

> Telling stories is telling lies   is telling
> lies about people   is creating or
> hardening prejudices   is providing an
> alternative to real communication not a stimulus
> to communication and/or communication itself
>   is an escape from the challenge of coming
> to terms with real people

I am not interested in telling lies in my own novels. A useful distinction between literature and other writing for me is that the former teaches one something true about life: and how can you convey truth in a vehicle of fiction? The two terms, *truth* and *fiction*, are opposites, and it must logically be impossible.

The two terms *novel* and *fiction* are not, incidentally, synonymous, as many seem to suppose in the way they use them interchangeably. The publisher of *Trawl* wished to classify it as autobiography, not as a novel. It is a novel, I insisted and could prove; what it is not is fiction. The novel is a form in the same sense that the sonnet is a form; within that form, one may write truth or fiction. I choose to write truth in the form of a novel.

In any case, surely it must be a confession of failure on the part of any novelist to rely on that primitive, vulgar and idle curiosity of the reader to know 'what happens next' (however banal or hackneyed it may be) to hold his interest? Can he not face the fact that it is his choice of words, his style, which ought to keep the reader reading? Have such novelists no pride? The drunk who tells you the story of his troubles in a pub relies on the same curiosity.

And when they consider the other arts, are they not ashamed? Imagine the reception of someone producing a nineteenth-century symphony or a Pre-Raphaelite painting today! The avant-garde of even ten years ago is now accepted in music and painting, is the establishment in these arts in some cases. But today the neo-Dickensian novel not only receives great praise, review space and sales but also acts as a qualification to elevate its authors to chairs at universities. On reflection, perhaps the latter is not so surprising; let the dead live with the dead.

All I have said about the history of the novel so far seems to me logical, and to have been available and obvious to anyone starting seriously to write in the form today. Why then do so many novelists still write as though the revolution that was *Ulysses* had never happened, still rely on the crutch of storytelling? Why, more damningly for my case you might think, do hundreds of thousands of readers still gorge the stuff to surfeit?

I do not know. I can only assume that just as there seem to be so many writers imitating the act of being nineteenth-century novelists, so there must be large numbers imitating the act of being nineteenth-century readers, too. But it does not affect the logic of my case, nor the practice of my own work in the novel form. It may simply be a matter of education, or of communication; when I proposed this book to my publisher and outlined its thesis, he said it would be necessary for me to speak very clearly and very loudly. Perhaps the din of the market-place vendors in pap and propaganda is so high that even doing that will not be enough.

The architects can teach us something: their aesthetic problems are combined with functional ones in a way that dramatizes the crucial nature of their final actions. *Form follows function* said Louis Sullivan, mentor of Frank Lloyd Wright, and just listen to Mies van der Rohe:

> To create form out of the nature of our tasks with the methods of our time – this is our task.

> We must make clear, step by step, what things are possible, necessary, and significant.

> Only an architecture honestly arrived at by the explicit use of available building materials can be justified in moral terms.

Subject-matter is everywhere, general, is brick, concrete, plastic; the ways of putting it together are particular, are crucial. But I recognize that there are not simply problems of form, but problems of writing. Form is not the aim, but the result. If form were the aim then one would have formalism; and I reject formalism.

The novelist cannot legitimately or successfully embody present-day reality in exhausted forms. If he is serious, he will be making a statement which attempts to change society towards a condition he conceives to be better, and he will be making at least implicitly a statement of faith in the evolution of the form in which he is working. Both these aspects of making are radical; this is inescapable unless he chooses escapism. Present-day reality is changing rapidly; it always has done, but for each generation it appears to be speeding up. Novelists must evolve (by inventing, borrowing, stealing or cobbling from other media) forms which will more or less satisfactorily contain an ever-changing reality, their own reality and not Dickens's reality or Hardy's reality or even James Joyce's reality.

Present-day reality is markedly different from, say, nineteenth-century reality. Then it was possible to believe in pattern and eternity, but today what characterizes our reality is the probability that chaos is the most likely explanation; while at the same time recognizing that even to seek an explanation represents a denial of chaos. Samuel Beckett, who of all living is the man I believe most worth reading and listening to, is reported thus:

> What I am saying does not mean that there will hence-forth be no form in art. It only means that there will be new form, and that this form will be of such a type that it admits the chaos, and does not try to say that the chaos is really something else. The forms and the chaos remain separate ... to find a form that accommodates the mess, that is the task of the artist now.

Whether or not it can be demonstrated that all is chaos, certainly all is change: the very process of life itself is growth and decay at an enormous variety of rates. Change is a condition of life. Rather than deplore this, or hunt the chimaerae of stability or reversal, one should perhaps embrace change as all there is. Or might be. For change is never for the better or for the worse; change simply *is*. No sooner is a style or technique established than the reasons for its adoption have vanished or become irrelevant. We have to make allowances and imaginative, lying leaps for Shakespeare, for even Noël Coward, to try to understand how they must have seemed to their contemporaries. I feel myself fortunate sometimes that I can laugh at the joke that just as I was beginning to think I knew something about how to write a novel it is no longer of any use to me in attempting the next one. Even in this introduction I am trying to make patterns, to impose patterns on the chaos, in the doubtful interest of helping you (and myself) to understand what I am saying. When lecturing on the same material I ought to drop my notes, refer to them in any chaotic order. *Order* and *chaos* are opposites, too.

This (and other things I have said) must appear paradoxical. But why should novelists be expected to avoid paradox any more than philosophers?

While I believe (as far as I believe anything) that there may be (how can I know?) chaos underlying it all, another paradox is that I still go on behaving as though pattern could exist, as though day will follow night will follow breakfast. Or whatever the order should be.

I do not really know why I write. Sometimes I think it is simply because I can do nothing better. Certainly there is no single reason, but many. I can, and will, enumerate some of them; but in general I prefer not to think about them.

I think I write because I have something to say that I fail to say satisfactorily in conversation, in person. Then there are things like conceit, stubbornness, a desire to retaliate on those who have hurt me paralleled by a desire to repay those who have helped me, a need to try to create something which may live after me (which I take to be the detritus of the religious feeling), the sheer technical joy of forcing almost intractable words into patterns of meaning and form that are uniquely (for the moment at least) mine, a need to make people laugh with me in case they laugh at me, a desire to codify experience, to come to terms with things that have happened to me, and to try to tell the truth (to discover what is the truth) about them. And I write especially to exorcize, to remove from myself, from my mind, the burden of having to bear some pain, the hurt of some experience: in order that it may be over there, in a book, and not in here in my mind.

The following tries to grope towards it, in another way:

I have a (vision) of something that (happened) to me
    something which (affected) me
    something which meant (something) to me

and I (wrote) (filmed) it
because
I wanted it to be fixed
    so that I could refer to it
    so that I could build on it
    so that I would not have to repeat it

Such a hostage to fortune!

What I have been trying to do in the novel form has been too much refracted through the conservativeness of reviewers and others; the reasons why I have written in the ways that I have done have become lost, have never reached as many people, nor in anything like a definitive form. 'Experimental' to most reviewers is almost always a synonym for 'unsuccessful'. I object to the word *experimental* being applied to my own work. Certainly I make experiments, but the unsuccessful ones are quietly hidden away and what I choose to publish is in my terms successful: that is, it has been the best way I could find of solving particular writing problems. Where I depart from convention, it is because the convention has failed, is inadequate for conveying what I have to say. The relevant questions are surely whether each device works or not, whether it achieves what it set out to achieve, and how less good were the alternatives. So for every device I have used there is a literary rationale and a technical justification; anyone who cannot accept this has simply not understood the problem which had to be solved.

I do not propose to go through the reasons for all the devices, not least because the novels should speak for themselves; and they are clear enough to a reader who will think about them, let alone be open and sympathetic towards them. But I will mention some of them, and deal in detail with *The Unfortunates*, since its form seems perhaps the most extreme.

Travelling People (published 1963) had an explanatory prelude which summed up much of my thinking on the novel at that point, as follows:

> Seated comfortably in a wood and wickerwork chair of eighteenth-century Chinese manufacture, I began seriously to meditate upon the form of my allegedly full-time literary sublimations. Rapidly, I recalled the conclusions reached in previous meditations on the same subject: my rejection of stage-drama as having too many limitations, of verse as being unacceptable at the present time on the scale I wished to attempt, and of radio and television as requiring too many entrepreneurs between the writer and the audience; and my resultant choice of the novel as the form possessing fewest limitations, and closest contact with the greatest audience.
>
> But, now, what kind of novel? After comparatively little consideration, I decided that one style for one novel was a convention that I resented most strongly: it was perhaps comparable to eating a meal in which each course had been cooked in the same manner. The style of each chapter should spring naturally from its subject-matter. Furthermore, I meditated, at ease in far eastern luxury, Dr Johnson's remarks about each member of an

audience always being aware that he is in a theatre could with complete relevance be applied also to the novel reader, who surely knows that he is reading a book and not, for instance, taking part in a punitive raid on the curiously-shaped inhabitants of another planet. From this I concluded that it was not only permissible to expose the mechanism of a novel, but by so doing I should come nearer to reality and truth: adapting to refute, in fact, the ancients:

Artis est monstrare artem

Pursuing this thought, I realized that it would be desirable to have interludes between my chapters in which I could stand back, so to speak, from my novel, and talk about it with the reader, or with those parts of myself which might hold differing opinions, if necessary; and in which technical questions could be considered, and quotations from other writers included, where relevant, without any question of destroying the reader's suspension of disbelief, since such suspension was not to be attempted.

I should be determined not to lead my reader into believing that he was doing anything but reading a novel, having noted with abhorrence the shabby chicanery practised on their readers by many novelists, particularly of the popular class. This applied especially to digression, where the reader is led, wilfully and wantonly, astray; my novel would have clear notice, one way or another, of digressions, so that the reader might have complete freedom of choice in whether or not he would read them. Thus, having decided in a general way upon the construction of my novel I thought about actually rising to commence its composition; but persuaded by oriental comfort that I was nearer the Good Life engaged in meditation, I turned my mind to the deep consideration of such other matters as I deemed worthy of my attention, and, after a short while thus engaged, fell asleep.

Travelling People employed eight separate styles or conventions for nine chapters; the first and last chapters sharing one style in order to give the book cyclical unity within the motif announced by its title and epigraph. These styles included interior monologue, a letter, extracts from a journal, and a film script. This latter illustrates the method of the novel typically. The subject-matter was a gala evening at a country club, with a large number of characters involved both individually and in small groups. A film technique, cutting quickly from group to group and incidentally counterpointing the stagey artificiality of the occasion, seemed natural and apt. It is not, of course, a film; but the way it is written is intended to evoke what the reader knows as film technique.

The passage quoted above was deliberately a pastiche of eighteenth-century English, for I had found that it was necessary to return to the very beginnings of the novel in England in order to try to re-think it and re-justify it for myself. Most obvious of my debts was to the black pages of *Tristram Shandy*, but I extended the device beyond Sterne's simple use of it to indicate a character's death. The section concerned is the interior monologue of an old man prone to heart attacks; when he becomes unconscious he obviously cannot indicate this in words representing thought, but a modified form of Sterne's black pages solves the problem. First I used random-pattern grey to indicate unconsciousness after a heart attack, then a regular-pattern grey to indicate sleep or recuperative unconsciousness; and subsequently black when he dies.

Since *Travelling People* is part truth and part fiction it now embarrasses me and I will not allow it to be reprinted; though I am still pleased that its devices work. And I learnt a certain amount through it; not least that there was a lot of the writing I could do in my head without having to amass a pile of paper three feet high to see if something worked.

But I really discovered what I should be doing with *Albert Angelo* (1964) where I broke through the English disease of the objective correlative to speak truth directly if solipsistically in the novel form, and heard my own small voice. And again there were devices used to solve problems which I felt could not be dealt with in other ways. Thus a specially-designed type-character draws attention to physical descriptions which I believe tend to be skipped, do not usually penetrate. To convey what a particular lesson is like, the thoughts of a teacher are given on the right-hand side of a page in italic, with his and his pupils' speech on the left in roman, so that, though the reader obviously cannot read both at once, when he has read both he will have seen that they are simultaneous and have enacted such simultaneity for himself. When Albert finds a fortune-teller's card in the street it is further from the truth to describe it than simply to reproduce it. And when a future event must be revealed, I could (and can; can you?) think of no way nearer to the truth and more effective than to cut a section through those pages intervening so that the event may be read in its place but before the reader reaches that place.

Trawl (1966) is all interior monologue, a representation of the inside of my mind but at one stage removed; the closest one can come in writing. The only real technical problem was the representation of breaks in the mind's workings; I finally decided on a stylized scheme of 3 em, 6 em and 9 em spaces. In order not to have a break which ran-on at the end of a line looking like a paragraph, these spaces were punctuated by dots at decimal point level. I now doubt whether these dots were necessary. To make up for the absence of those paragraph breaks which give the reader's eye rest and location on the page, the line length was deliberately shortened; this gave the book a long, narrow format.

The rhythms of the language of *Trawl* attempted to parallel those of the sea, while much use was made of the trawl itself as a metaphor for the way the subconscious mind may appear to work.

With each of my novels there has always been a certain point when what has been until then just a mass of subject-matter, the material of living, of my life, comes to have a shape, a form that I recognize as a novel. This crucial interaction between the material and myself has always been reduced to a single point in time: obviously a very exciting moment for me, and a moment of great relief, too, that I am able to write another novel.

The moment at which *The Unfortunates* (1969) occurred was on the main railway station at Nottingham. I had been sent there to report a soccer match for the *Observer*, a quite routine League match, nothing special. I had hardly thought about where I was going, specifically: when you are going away to report soccer in a different city each Saturday you get the mechanics of travelling to and finding your way about in a strange place to an almost automatic state. But when I came up the stairs from the platform into the entrance hall, it hit me: I knew this city. I knew it very well. It was the city in which a very great friend of mine, one who had helped me with my work when no one else was interested, had lived until his tragic early death from cancer some two years before.

It was the first time I had been back since his death, and all the afternoon I was there the things we had done together kept coming back to me as I was going about this routine job of reporting a soccer match: the dead past and the living present interacted and transposed themselves in my mind. I realized that afternoon that I had to write a novel about this man, Tony, and his tragic and pointless death and its effect on me and the other people who knew him and whom he had left behind. The following passage from *The Unfortunates* explains his importance to me:

> To Tony, the criticism of literature was a study, a pursuit, a discipline of the highest kind in itself: to me, I told him, the only use of criticism was if it helped people to write better books. This he took as a challenge, this he accepted. Or perhaps I made the challenge, said that I would show him the novel as I wrote it, the novel I had in mind or was writing: and that he would therefore have a chance of influencing, of making better, a piece of what set out to be literature, for the sake of argument, rather than expend himself on dead men's work.

The main technical problem with *The Unfortunates* was the randomness of the material. That is, the memories of Tony and the routine football reporting, the past and the present, interwove in a completely random manner, without chronology. This is the way the mind works, my mind anyway, and for reasons given the novel was to be as nearly as possible a re-created transcript of how my mind worked during eight hours on this particular Sunday.

This randomness was directly in conflict with the technological fact of the bound book: for the bound book imposes an order, a fixed page order, on the material. I think I went some way towards solving this problem by writing the book in sections and having those sections not bound together but loose in a box. The sections are of different lengths, of course: some are only a third of a page long, others are as long as twelve pages. The longer ones were bound in themselves as sections, or signatures, as printers call them.

The point of this device was that, apart from the first and last sections which were marked as such, the other sections arrived in the reader's hands in a random order: he could read them in any order he liked. And if he imagined the printer, or some previous reader, had selected a special order, then he could shuffle them about and achieve his own random order. In this way the whole novel reflected the randomness of the material: it was itself a physical tangible metaphor for randomness and the nature of cancer.

Now I did not think then, and do not think now, that this solved the problem completely. The lengths of the sections were really arbitrary again; even separate sentences or separate words would be arbitrary in the same sense. But I continue to believe that my solution was nearer; and even if it was only marginally nearer, then it was still a better solution to the problem of conveying the mind's randomness than the imposed order of a bound book.

What matters most to me about *The Unfortunates* is that I have on recall as accurately as possible what happened, that I do not have to carry it around in my mind any more, that I have done Tony as much justice as I could at the time; that the need to communicate with myself then, and with such older selves as I might be allowed, on something about which I cared and care deeply may also mean that the novel will communicate that experience to readers, too.

I shall return shortly to readers and communicating with them. But first there are two other novels and they represent a change (again!) of direction, an elbow joint in the arm, still part of the same but perhaps going another way. Perhaps I shall come to the body, sooner or later. The ideas for both *House Mother Normal* (1971) and *Christie Malry's Own Double-Entry* (1973) came to me whilst writing *Travelling People* (indeed, I discussed them with Tony) but the subsequent three personal novels interposed themselves, demanded to be written first. I also balked at *House Mother Normal* since it seemed technically so difficult. What I wanted to do was to take an evening in an old people's home, and see a single set of events through the eyes of not less than eight old people. Due to the various deformities and deficiencies of the inmates, these events would seem to be progressively 'abnormal' to the reader. At the end, there would be the viewpoint of the House Mother, an apparently 'normal' person, and the events themselves would then be seen to be so bizarre that everything that had come before would seem 'normal' by comparison. The idea was to say something about the things we call 'normal' and 'abnormal' and the technical difficulty was to make the same thing interesting nine times over since that was the number of times the events would have to be described. By 1970 I thought that if I did not attempt the idea soon then I never would; and so sat down to it. I was relieved to find that the novel did work, on its own terms, while not asking it to do anything it clearly should not be trying to do. Each of the old people was allotted a space of twenty-one pages, and each line on each page represented the same moment in each of the other accounts; this meant an unjustified right-hand margin and led more than one reviewer to imagine the book was in verse. House Mother's account has an extra page in which she is shown to be

        the puppet or concoction of a writer (you
        always knew there was a writer behind it all?
        Ah, there's no fooling you readers!)

Nor should there be.

The reader is made very much aware that he is reading a book and being addressed by the author in *Christie Malry's Own Double-Entry*, too. The idea was that a young man who had learned the double-entry system of book-keeping started applying his knowledge to society and life; when society did him down, he did society down in order to balance the books. Form following function, the book is divided into five parts each ended by a page of accounts in which Christie attempts to draw a balance with life.

I do not really relish any more description of my work; it is there to be read, and in writing so much about technique and form I am diverting you from what the novels are about, what they are trying to say, and things like the nature of the language used, and the fact that all of them have something comic in them and three are intended to be very funny indeed. When I depart from what may mistakenly be extracted from the above as rigid principles it is invariably for the sake of the comic, for I find Sterne's reasons all-persuasive:

> ... 'tis wrote, an' please your worships, against the spleen! in order, by a more frequent and a more convulsive elevation and depression of the diaphragm, and the succussations of the inter-costal and abdominal muscles in laughter, to drive the *gall* and other *bitter juices* from the gall-bladder, liver, and sweet-bread of his majesty's subjects, with all the inimicitious passions which belong to them, down into their duodenums.

For readers it is often said that they will go on reading the novel because it enables them, unlike film or television, to exercise their imaginations, that that is one of its chief attractions for them, that they may imagine the characters and so on for themselves. Not with my novels; it follows from what I have said earlier that I want my ideas to be expressed so precisely that the very minimum of room for interpretation is left. Indeed I would go further and say that to the extent that a reader can impose his own imagination on my words, then that piece of writing is a failure. I want him to see my (vision), not something conjured out of his own imagination. How is he supposed to grow unless he will admit others' ideas? If he wants to impose his imagination, let him write his own books. That may be thought to be anti-reader; but think a little further, and what I am really doing is challenging the reader to prove his own existence as palpably as I am proving mine by the act of writing.

Language, admittedly, is an imprecise tool with which to try to achieve precision; the same word will have slightly different meanings for every person. But that is outside me; I cannot control it. I can only use words to mean something to me, and there is simply the hope (not even the expectation) that they will mean the same thing to anyone else.

Which brings us to the question of for whom I write. I am always sceptical about writers who claim to be writing for an identifiable public. How many letters and phone calls do they receive from this public that they can know it so well as to write for it? Precious few, in my experience, when I have questioned them about it. I think I (after publishing some dozen books) have personally had about five letters from 'ordinary readers', people I did not know already that is; and three of those upbraided me viciously because I had just published the book that they were going to have written.

No, apart from the disaster of *Travelling People*, I write perforce for myself, and the satisfaction has to be almost all for myself; and I can only hope there are some few people like me who will see what I am doing, and understand what I am saying, and use it for their own devious purposes.

Yet it should not have to be so. I think I do have a right to expect that most readers should be open to new work, that there should be an audience in this country willing to try to understand and be sympathetic to what those few writers not shackled by tradition are trying to do and are doing. Only when one has some contact with a continental European tradition of the avant-garde does one realize just how stultifyingly philistine is the general book culture of this country. Compared with the writers of romances, thrillers, and the bent but so-called straight novel, there are not many who are writing as though it mattered, as though they meant it, as though they meant it to matter.

Perhaps I should nod here to Samuel Beckett (of course), John Berger, Christine Brooke-Rose, Brigid Brophy, Anthony Burgess, Alan Burns, Angela Carter, Eva Figes, Giles Gordon, Wilson Harris, Rayner Heppenstall, even hasty, muddled Robert Nye, Ann Quin, Penelope Shuttle, Alan Sillitoe (for his last book only, Raw Material indeed), Stefan Themerson, and (coming) John Wheway; (stand by): and if only Heathcote Williams would write a novel . . .

Anyone who imagines himself or herself slighted by not being included above can fill in his or her name here:

. . . .

It would be a courtesy, however, to let me know his or her qualifications for so imagining.

Are we concerned with courtesy?

Nathalie Sarraute once described literature as a relay race, the baton of innovation passing from one generation to another. The vast majority of British novelists has dropped the baton, stood still, turned back, or not even realized that there is a race.

Most of what I have said has been said before, of course; none of it is new, except possibly in context and combination. What I do not understand is why British writers have not accepted it and acted upon it.

The pieces of prose (you will understand my avoidance of the term *short story*) which follow were written in the interstices of novels and poems and other work between 1960 and 1973; the dates given in the Contents are those of the year of completion. None of them seem to me like each other, though some have links and cross-references; neither can I really see either progression or retrogression. The order is that which seemed least bad late on one particular May evening; perhaps I shall regret it as soon as I see it fixed.

Make of them what you will. I offer them to you despite my experience that the incomprehension and weight of prejudice which faces anyone trying to do anything new in writing is enormous, sometimes disquieting, occasionally laughable. A national daily newspaper (admittedly one known for its reactionary opinions) returned a review copy of *Travelling People* with the complaint that it must be a faulty copy for some of the pages were black; the Australian Customs seized *Albert Angelo* (which had holes justifiably cut in some pages, you will remember) and would not release it until they had been shown the obscenities which (they were convinced) had been excised; and in one of our biggest booksellers *Trawl* was found in the Angling section . . .

DORIS LESSING

Preface to *The Golden Notebook*
(1962)

The shape of this novel is as follows:

There is a skeleton, or frame, called *Free Women*, which is a conventional short novel, about 60,000 words long, and which could stand by itself. But it is divided into five sections and separated by stages of the four Notebooks, Black, Red, Yellow and Blue. The Notebooks are kept by Anna Wulf, a central character of *Free Women*. She keeps four, and not one, because, as she recognizes, she has to separate things off from each other, out of fear of chaos, of formlessness – of breakdown. Pressures, inner and outer, end the Notebooks; a heavy black line is drawn across the page of one after another. But now that they are finished, from their fragments can come something new, *The Golden Notebook*.

Throughout the Notebooks people have discussed, theorized, dogmatized, labelled, compartmented – sometimes in voices so general and representative of the time that they are anonymous, you could put names to them like those in the old Morality Plays, Mr Dogma and Mr I-am-Free-Because-I-Belong-Nowhere, Miss I-Must-Have-Love-and-Happiness and Mrs I-Have-to-be-Good-At-Everything-I-do, Mr Where-is-a-Real-Woman? and Miss Where-is-a-Real-Man?, Mr I'm-Mad-Because-They-Say-I-Am, and Miss Life-Through-Experiencing-Everything, Mr I-Make-Revolution-and-Therefore-I-Am, and Mr and Mrs If-We-Deal-Very-Well-With-This-Small-Problem-Then-Perhaps-We-Can-Forget-We-Daren't-Look-at-The-Big-Ones. But they have also reflected each other, been aspects of each other, given birth to each other's thoughts and behaviour

– *are* each other, form wholes. In the inner Golden Notebook, things have come together, the divisions have broken down, there is formlessness with the end of fragmentation – the triumph of the second theme, which is that of unity. Anna and Saul Green the American 'break down'. They are crazy, lunatic, mad – what you will. They 'break down' into each other, into other people, break through the false patterns they have made of their pasts, the patterns and formulas they have made to shore up themselves and each other, dissolve. They hear each other's thoughts, recognize each other in themselves. Saul Green, the man who has been envious and destructive of Anna, now supports her, advises her, gives her the theme for her next book, *Free Women* – an ironical title, which begins: 'The two women were alone in the London flat.' And Anna, who has been jealous of Saul to the point of insanity, possessive and demanding, gives Saul the pretty new notebook, *The Golden Notebook*, which she has previously refused to do, gives him the theme for his next book, writing in it the first sentence: 'On a dry hillside in Algeria a soldier watched the moonlight glinting on his rifle.' In the inner Golden Notebook, which is written by both of them, you can no longer distinguish between what is Saul and what is Anna, and between them and the other people in the book.

This theme of 'breakdown', that sometimes when people 'crack up' it is a way of self-healing, of the inner self's dismissing false dichotomies and divisions, has of course been written about by other people, as well as by me, since then. But this is where, apart from the odd short story, I first wrote about it. Here it is rougher, more close to experience, before experience has shaped itself into thought and pattern – more valuable perhaps because it is rawer material.

But nobody so much as noticed this central theme, because the book was instantly belittled, by friendly reviewers as well as by hostile ones, as being about the sex war, or was claimed by women as a useful weapon in the sex war.

I have been in a false position ever since, for the last thing I have wanted to do was to refuse to support women.

To get the subject of Women's Liberation over with – I

support it, of course, because women are second-class citizens, as they are saying energetically and competently in many countries. It can be said that they are succeeding, if only to the extent they are being seriously listened to. All kinds of people previously hostile or indifferent say: 'I support their aims but I don't like their shrill voices and their nasty ill-mannered ways.' This is an inevitable and easily recognizable stage in every revolutionary movement: reformers must expect to be disowned by those who are only too happy to enjoy what has been won for them. I don't think that Women's Liberation will change much though – not because there is anything wrong with their aims, but because it is already clear that the whole world is being shaken into a new pattern by the cataclysms we are living through: probably by the time we are through, if we do get through at all, the aims of Women's Liberation will look very small and quaint.

But this novel was not a trumpet for Women's Liberation. It described many female emotions of aggression, hostility, resentment. It put them into print. Apparently what many women were thinking, feeling, experiencing, came as a great surprise. Instantly a lot of very ancient weapons were unleashed, the main ones, as usual, being on the theme of 'She is unfeminine', 'She is a man-hater'. This particular reflex seems indestructible. Men – and many women – said that the suffragettes were defeminized, masculine, brutalized. There is no record I have read of any society anywhere when women demanded more than nature offers them that does not also describe this reaction from men – and some women. A lot of women were angry about *The Golden Notebook*. What women will say to other women, grumbling in their kitchens and complaining and gossiping or what they make clear in their masochism, is often the last thing they will say aloud – a man may overhear. Women are the cowards they are because they have been semi-slaves for so long. The number of women prepared to stand up for what they really think, feel, experience with a man they are in love with is still small. Most women will still run like little dogs with stones

thrown at them when a man says: You are unfeminine, aggressive, you are unmanning me. It is my belief that any woman who
marries, or takes seriously in any way at all, a man who uses
this threat, deserves everything she gets. For such a man is a
bully, does not know anything about the world he lives in, or
about its history – men and women have taken infinite numbers
of roles in the past, and do now, in different societies. So he is
ignorant, or fearful about being out of step – a coward ... I
write all these remarks with exactly the same feeling as if I were
writing a letter to post into the distant past: I am so sure that
everything we now take for granted is going to be utterly swept
away in the next decade.

(So why write novels? Indeed, why! I suppose we have to go
on living *as if* ...)

Some books are not read in the right way because they have
skipped a stage of opinion, assume a crystallization of information in society which has not yet taken place. This book was
written as if the attitudes that have been created by the Women's
Liberation movements already existed. It came out first ten years
ago, in 1962. If it were coming out now for the first time it
might be read, and not merely reacted to: things have changed
very fast. Certain hypocrisies have gone. For instance, ten, or
even five, years ago – it has been a sexually contumacious time
– novels and plays were being plentifully written by men
furiously critical of women – particularly from the States but
also in this country – portrayed as bullies and betrayers, but
particularly as underminers and sappers. But these attitudes in
male writers were taken for granted, accepted as sound philosophical bases, as quite normal, certainly not as woman-hating,
aggressive or neurotic. It still goes on, of course – but things are
better, there is no doubt of it.

I was so immersed in writing this book, that I didn't think
about how it might be received. I was involved not merely
because it was hard to write – keeping the plan of it in my head
I wrote it from start to end, consecutively, and it was difficult –
but because of what I was learning as I wrote. Perhaps giving
oneself a tight structure, making limitations for oneself, squeezes

out new substance where you least expect it. All sorts of ideas and experiences I didn't recognize as mine emerged when writing. The actual time of writing, then, and not only the experiences that had gone into the writing, was really traumatic: it changed me. Emerging from this crystallizing process, handing the manuscript to publisher and friends, I learned that I had written a tract about the sex war, and fast discovered that nothing I said then could change that diagnosis.

Yet the essence of the book, the organization of it, everything in it, says implicitly and explicitly, that we must not divide things off, must not compartmentalize.

'Bound. Free. Good. Bad. Yes. No. Capitalism. Socialism. Sex. Love . . .' says Anna, in *Free Women*, stating a theme – shouting it, announcing a motif with drums and fanfares . . . or so I imagined. Just as I believed that in a book called *The Golden Notebook* the inner section called the Golden Notebook might be presumed to be a central point, to carry the weight of the thing, to make a statement.

But no.

Other themes went into the making of this book, which was a crucial time for me: thoughts and themes I had been holding in my mind for years came together.

One was that it was not possible to find a novel which described the intellectual and moral climate of a hundred years ago, in the middle of the last century, in Britain, in the way Tolstoy did it for Russia, Stendhal for France. (At this point it is necessary to make the obligatory disclaimers.) To read *The Red and the Black* and *Lucien Leuwen* is to know that France as if one were living there, to read *Anna Karenina* is to know that Russia. But a very useful Victorian novel never got itself written. Hardy tells us what it was like to be poor, to have an imagination larger than the possibilities of a very narrow time, to be a victim. George Eliot is good as far as she goes. But I think the penalty she paid for being a Victorian woman was that she had to be shown to be a good woman even when she wasn't according to the hypocrisies of the time – there is a great deal she does not understand because she is moral. Meredith, that astonishingly underrated writer, is perhaps nearest. Trollope tried the subject but lacked the scope. There isn't one novel that has the vigour and conflict of ideas in action that is in a good biography of William Morris.

Of course this attempt on my part assumed that the filter which is a woman's way of looking at life has the same validity as the filter which is a man's way . . . Setting that problem aside, or rather, not even considering it, I decided that to give the ideological 'feel' of our mid-century, it would have to be set among socialists and Marxists, because it has been inside the various chapters of socialism that the great debates of our time have gone on; the movements, the wars, the revolutions, have been seen by their participants as movements of various kinds of socialism, or Marxism, in advance, containment, or retreat. (I think we should at least concede the possibility that people looking back on our time may see it not at all as we do – just as we, looking back on the English, the French, or even the Russian Revolutions see them differently from the people living then.) But 'Marxism', and its various offshoots, has fermented ideas everywhere, and so fast and energetically that, once 'way out', it has already been absorbed, has become part of ordinary thinking. Ideas that were confined to the far left thirty or forty years ago had pervaded the left generally twenty years ago, and have provided the commonplaces of conventional social thought from right to left for the last ten years. Something so thoroughly absorbed is finished as a force – but it was dominant, and in a novel of the sort I was trying to do, had to be central.

Another thought that I had played with for a long time was that a main character should be some sort of an artist, but with a 'block'. This was because the theme of the artist has been dominant in art for some time – the painter, writer, musician, as exemplar. Every major writer has used it, and most minor ones. Those archetypes, the artist and his mirror-image the businessman, have straddled our culture, one shown as a boorish insensitive, the other as a creator, all excesses of sensibility and suffering and a towering egotism which has to be forgiven because of his products – in exactly the same way, of course, as the businessman has to be forgiven for the sake of his. We get used to what we have, and forget that the artist-as-exemplar is a new theme. Heroes a hundred years ago weren't often artists. They were soldiers and empire builders and explorers and clergymen and politicians – too bad about women who had scarcely succeeded in becoming Florence Nightingale yet. Only oddballs and eccentrics wanted to be artists, and had to fight for it. But to use this theme of our time, 'the artist', 'the writer', I decided it would have to be developed by giving the creature a block and discussing the reasons for the block. These would have to be linked with the disparity between the overwhelming problems of war, famine, poverty, and the tiny individual who was trying to mirror them. But what was intolerable, what really could not be borne any longer, was this monstrously isolated, monstrously narcissistic, pedestalled paragon. It seems that in their own way the young have seen this and changed it, creating a culture of their own in which hundreds and thousands of people make films, assist in making films, make newspapers of all sorts, make music, paint pictures, write books, take photographs. They have abolished that isolated, creative, sensitive figure – by copying him in hundreds of thousands. A trend has reached an extreme, its conclusion, and so there will be a reaction of some sort, as always happens.

The theme of 'the artist' had to relate to another subjectivity. When I began writing there was pressure on writers not to be 'subjective'. This pressure began inside communist movements, as a development of the social literary criticism developed in Russia in the nineteenth century, by a group of remarkable talents, of whom Belinsky was the best known, using the arts and particularly literature in the battle against Czarism and oppression. It spread fast everywhere, finding an echo as late as the fifties, in this country, with the theme of 'commitment'. It is still potent in communist countries. 'Bothering about your stupid personal concerns when Rome is burning' is how it tends to get itself expressed, on the level of ordinary life – and was hard to withstand, coming from one's nearest and dearest, and from people doing everything one respected most: like, for instance, trying to fight colour prejudice in Southern Africa. Yet all the time novels, stories, art of every sort, became more and more personal. In the Blue Notebook, Anna writes of lectures she has been giving: ' "Art during the Middle Ages was communal, unindividual; it came out of a group consciousness. It was without the driving painful individuality of the art of the bourgeois era. And one day we will leave behind the driving egotism of individual art. We will return to an art which will express not man's self-divisions and separateness from his fellows but his responsibility for his fellows and his brotherhood. Art from the West becomes more and more a shriek of torment recording pain. Pain is becoming our deepest reality . . ." I have been saying something like this. About three months ago, in the middle of this lecture, I began to stammer and couldn't finish . . .'

Anna's stammer was because she was evading something. Once a pressure or a current has started, there is no way of avoiding it: there was no way of *not* being intensely subjective: it was, if you like, the writer's task for that time. You couldn't ignore it: you couldn't write a book about the building of a bridge or a dam and not develop the mind and feelings of the people who built it. (You think this is a caricature? – Not at all. This *either/or* is at the heart of literary criticism in communist countries at this moment.) At last I understood that the way over, or through this dilemma, the unease at writing about 'petty personal problems', was to recognize that nothing is personal, in the sense that it is uniquely one's own. Writing about oneself, one is writing about others, since your problems, pains, pleasures, emotions – and your extraordinary and remarkable ideas – can't be yours alone. The way to deal with the problem of 'subjectivity', that shocking business of being preoccupied with the tiny individual who is at the same time caught up in such an explosion of terrible and marvellous possibilities, is to see him as a microcosm and in this way to break through the personal, the subjective, making the personal general, as indeed life always does, transforming a private experience – or so you think of it when still a child, '*I* am falling in love', '*I* am feeling this or that emotion, or thinking that or the other thought' – into something much larger: growing up is after all only the understanding that one's unique and incredible experience is what everyone shares.

Another idea was that if the book were shaped in the right way it would make its own comment about the conventional novel: the debate about the novel has been going on since the novel was born, and is not, as one would imagine from reading contemporary academics, something recent. To put the short novel *Free Women* as a summary and condensation of all that mass of material, was to say something about the conventional novel, another way of describing the dissatisfaction of a writer when something is finished: 'How little I have managed to say of the truth, how little I have caught of all that complexity; how can this small neat thing be true when what I experienced was so rough and apparently formless and unshaped.'

But my major aim was to shape a book which would make its own comment, a wordless statement: to talk through the way it was shaped.

As I have said, this was not noticed.

One reason for this is that the book is more in the European tradition than the English tradition of the novel. Or rather, in the English tradition as viewed at the moment. The English novel after all does include *Clarissa* and *Tristram Shandy, The Tragic Comedians* – and Joseph Conrad.

But there is no doubt that to attempt a novel of ideas is to give oneself a handicap: the parochialism of our culture is intense. For instance, decade after decade bright young men and women emerge from their universities able to say proudly: 'Of course I know nothing about German literature.' It is the mode. The Victorians knew everything about German literature, but were able with a clear conscience not to know much about the French.

As for the rest – well, it is no accident that I got intelligent criticism from people who were, or who had been, Marxists. They saw what I was trying to do. This is because Marxism looks at things as a whole and in relation to each other – or tries to, but its limitations are not the point for the moment. A person who has been influenced by Marxism takes it for granted that an event in Siberia will affect one in Botswana. I think it is possible that Marxism was the first attempt, for our time, outside the formal religions, at a worldmind, a world ethic. It went wrong, could not prevent itself from dividing and subdividing, like all the other religions, into smaller and smaller chapels, sects and creeds. But it was an attempt.

This business of seeing what I was trying to do – it brings me to the critics, and the danger of evoking a yawn. This sad bickering between writers and critics, playwrights and critics: the public have got so used to it they think, as of quarrelling children: 'Ah yes, dear little things, they are at it again.' Or: 'You writers get all that praise, or if not praise, at least all that attention – so why are you so perennially wounded?' And the public are quite right. For reasons I won't go into here, early and valuable experiences in my writing life gave me a sense of perspective about critics and reviewers; but over this novel, *The Golden Notebook*, I lost it: I thought that for the most part the criticism was too silly to be true. Recovering balance, I understood the problem. It is that writers are looking in the critics for an *alter ego*, that other self more intelligent than oneself who has seen what one is reaching for, and who judges you only by whether you have matched up to your aim or not. I have never yet met a writer who, faced at last with that rare being, a real critic, doesn't lose all paranoia and becomes gratefully attentive – he has found what he thinks he needs. But what he, the writer, is asking is impossible. Why should he expect this extraordinary being, the perfect critic (who does occasionally exist), why should there be anyone else who comprehends what he is trying to do? After all, there is only one person spinning that particular cocoon, only one person whose business it is to spin it.

It is not possible for reviewers and critics to provide what they purport to provide – and for which writers so ridiculously and childishly yearn.

This is because the critics are not educated for it; their training is in the opposite direction.

It starts when the child is as young as five or six, when he arrives at school. It starts with marks, rewards, 'places', 'streams', stars – and still, in many places, stripes. This horserace mentality, the victor and loser way of thinking, leads to 'Writer X is, is not, a few paces ahead of Writer Y. Writer Y has fallen behind. In his last book Writer Z has shown himself as better than Writer A.' From the very beginning the child is trained to think in this way: always in terms of comparison, of success, and of failure. It is a weeding-out system: the weaker get discouraged and fall out; a system designed to produce a few winners who are always in competition with each other. It is my belief – though this is not the place to develop this – that the talents every child has, regardless of his official 'IQ', could stay with him through life, to enrich him and everybody else, if these talents were not regarded as commodities with a value in the success-stakes.

The other thing taught from the start is to distrust one's own judgement. Children are taught submission to authority, how to search for other people's opinions and decisions, and how to quote and comply.

As in the political sphere, the child is taught that he is free, a democrat, with a free will and a free mind, lives in a free country, makes his own decisions. At the same time he is a prisoner of the assumptions and dogmas of his time, which he does not question, because he has never been told they exist. By the time a young person has reached the age when he has to choose (we still take it for granted that a choice is inevitable) between the arts and the sciences, he often chooses the arts because he feels that here is humanity, freedom, choice. He does not know that he is already moulded by a system: he does not know that the choice itself is the result of a false dichotomy rooted in the heart of our culture. Those who do sense this, and who don't wish to subject themselves to further moulding, tend to leave, in a half-unconscious, instinctive attempt to find work where they won't be divided against themselves. With all our institutions, from the police force to academia, from medicine to politics, we give little attention to the people who leave – that process of elimination that goes on all the time and which excludes, very early, those likely to be original and reforming, leaving those attracted to a thing because that is what they are already like. A young policeman leaves the Force saying he doesn't like what he has to do. A young teacher leaves teaching, her idealism snubbed. This social mechanism goes almost unnoticed – yet it is as powerful as any in keeping our institutions rigid and oppressive.

These children who have spent years inside the training system become critics and reviewers, and cannot give what the author, the artist, so foolishly looks for – imaginative and original judgement. What they can do, and what they do very well, is to tell the writer how the book or play accords with current patterns of feeling and thinking – the climate of opinion. They are like litmus paper. They are wind gauges – invaluable. They are the most sensitive of barometers of public opinion. You can see changes of mood and opinion here sooner than anywhere except in the political field – it is because these are people whose whole education has been just that – to look outside themselves for their opinions, to adapt themselves to authority figures, to 'received opinion' – a marvellously revealing phrase.

It may be that there is no other way of educating people. Possibly, but I don't believe it. In the meantime it would be a help at least to describe things properly, to call things by their right names. Ideally, what should be said to every child, repeatedly, throughout his or her school life is something like this:

> You are in the process of being indoctrinated. We have not yet evolved a system of education that is not a system of indoctrination. We are sorry, but it is the best we can do. What you are being taught here is an amalgam of current prejudice and the choices of this particular culture. The slightest look at history will show how impermanent these must be. You are being taught by people who have been able to accommodate themselves to a regime of thought laid down by their predecessors. It is a self-perpetuating system. Those of you who are more

robust and individual than others, will be encouraged to leave and find ways of educating yourself – educating your own judgement. Those that stay must remember, always and all the time, that they are being moulded and patterned to fit into the narrow and particular needs of this particular society.

Like every other writer I get letters all the time from young people who are about to write theses and essays about my books in various countries – but particularly in the United States. They all say: 'Please give me a list of the articles about your work, the critics who have written about you, the authorities.' They also ask for a thousand details of total irrelevance, but which they have been taught to consider important, amounting to a dossier, like an immigration department's.

These requests I answer as follows: 'Dear Student. You are mad. Why spend months and years writing thousands of words about one book, or even one writer, when there are hundreds of books waiting to be read? You don't see that you are the victim of a pernicious system. And if you have yourself chosen my work as your subject, and if you do have to write a thesis – and believe me I am very grateful that what I've written is being found useful by you – then why don't you read what I have written and make up your own mind about what you think, testing it against your own life, your own experience. Never mind about Professors White and Black.'

'Dear Writer' – they reply. 'But I have to know what the authorities say, because if I don't quote them, my professor won't give me any marks.'

This is an international system, absolutely identical from the Urals to Yugoslavia, from Minnesota to Manchester.

The point is, we are all so used to it, we no longer see how bad it is.

I am not used to it, because I left school when I was fourteen. There was a time I was sorry about this, and believed I had missed out on something valuable. Now I am grateful for a lucky escape. After the publication of *The Golden Notebook*, I made it my business to find out something about the literary machinery, to examine the process which made a critic, or a reviewer. I looked at innumerable examination papers – and couldn't believe my eyes; sat in on classes for teaching literature, and couldn't believe my ears.

You might be saying: That is an exaggerated reaction, and you have no right to it, because you say you have never been part of the system. But I think it is not at all exaggerated, and that the reaction of someone from outside is valuable simply because it is fresh and not biased by allegiance to a particular education.

But after this investigation, I had no difficulty in answering my own questions: Why are they so parochial, so personal, so small-minded? Why do they always atomize, and belittle, why are they so fascinated by detail, and uninterested in the whole? Why is their interpretation of the word *critic* always to find fault? Why are they always seeing writers as in conflict with each other, rather than complementing each other ... simple, this is how they are trained to think. That valuable person who understands what you are doing, what you are aiming for, and can give you advice and real criticism, is nearly always someone right outside the literary machine, even outside the university system; it may be a student just beginning, and still in love with literature, or perhaps it may be a thoughtful person who reads a great deal, following his own instinct.

I say to these students who have to spend a year, two years, writing theses about one book: 'There is only one way to read, which is to browse in libraries and bookshops, picking up books that attract you, reading only those, dropping them when they bore you, skipping the parts that drag – and never, never reading anything because you feel you ought, or because it is part of a trend or a movement. Remember that the book which bores you when you are twenty or thirty will open doors for you when you are forty or fifty – and vice versa. Don't read a book out of its right time for you. Remember that for all the books we have in print, are as many that have never reached print, have never been written down – even now, in this age of compulsive reverence for the written word, history, even social ethic, are taught by means of stories, and the people who have been conditioned into thinking only in terms of what is written – and unfortunately nearly all the products of our educational system can do no more than this – are missing what is before their eyes. For instance, the real history of Africa is still in the custody of black storytellers and wise men, black historians, medicine men: it is a verbal history, still kept safe from the white man and his predations. Everywhere, if you keep your mind open, you will find the truth in words *not* written down. So never let the printed page be your master. Above all, you should know that the fact that you have to spend one year, or two years, on one book, or one author, means that you are badly taught – you should have been taught to read your way from one sympathy to another, you should be learning to follow your own intuitive feeling about what you need: that is what you should have been developing, not the way to quote from other people.'

But unfortunately it is nearly always too late.

It did look for a while as if the recent student rebellions might change things, as if their impatience with the dead stuff they are taught might be strong enough to substitute something more fresh and useful. But it seems as if the rebellion is over. Sad. During the lively time in the States, I had letters with accounts of how classes of students had refused their syllabuses, and were bringing to class their own choice of books, those that they had found relevant to their lives. The classes were emotional, sometimes violent, angry, exciting, sizzling with life. Of course this only happened with teachers who were sympathetic, and prepared to stand with the students against authority – prepared for the consequences. There are teachers who know that the way they have to teach is bad and boring – luckily there are still enough, with a bit of luck, to overthrow what is wrong, even if the students themselves have lost impetus.

Meanwhile there is a country where . . .

Thirty or forty years ago, a critic made a private list of writers and poets which he, personally, considered made up what was valuable in literature, dismissing all others. This list he defended lengthily in print, for The List instantly became a subject for much debate. Millions of words were written for and against – schools and sects, for and against, came into being. The argument, all these years later, still continues . . . no one finds this state of affairs sad or ridiculous . . .

Where there are critical books of immense complexity and learning, dealing, but often at second- or third-hand, with original works – novels, plays, stories. The people who write these books form a stratum in universities across the world – they are an international phenomenon, the top layer of literary academia. Their lives are spent in criticizing, and in criticizing each other's criticism. They at least regard this activity as more important than the original work. It is possible for literary students to spend more time reading criticism and criticism of criticism than they spend reading poetry, novels, biography, stories. A great many people regard this state of affairs as quite normal, and not sad and ridiculous . . .

Where I recently read an essay about Antony and Cleopatra by a boy shortly to take A levels. It was full of originality and excitement about the play, the feeling that any real teaching about literature aims to produce. The essay was returned by the teacher like this: I cannot mark this essay, you haven't quoted from the authorities. Few teachers would regard this as sad and ridiculous . . .

Where people who consider themselves educated, and indeed as superior to and more refined than ordinary non-reading people, will come up to a writer and congratulate him or her on getting a good review somewhere – but will not consider it necessary to read the book in question, or ever to think that what they are interested in is success . . .

Where when a book comes out on a certain subject, let's say star-gazing, instantly a dozen colleges, societies, television programmes, write to the author asking him to come and speak about star-gazing. The last thing it occurs to them to do is to read the book. This behaviour is considered quite normal, and not ridiculous at all . . .

Where a young man or woman, reviewer or critic, who has

not read more of a writer's work than the book in front of him, will write patronizingly, or as if rather bored with the whole business, or as if considering how many marks to give an essay, about the writer in question – who might have written fifteen books, and have been writing for twenty or thirty years – giving the said writer instruction on what to write next, and how. No one thinks this is absurd, certainly not the young person, critic or reviewer, who has been taught to patronize and itemize everyone for years, from Shakespeare downwards.

Where a Professor of Archaeology can write of a South American tribe which has advanced knowledge of plants, and of medicine and of psychological methods: 'The astonishing thing is that these people have no written language . . .' And no one thinks him absurd.

Where, on the occasion of a centenary of Shelley, in the same week and in three different literary periodicals, three young men, of identical education, from our identical universities, can write critical pieces about Shelley, damning him with the faintest possible praise, and in identically the same tone, as if they were doing Shelley a great favour to mention him at all – and no one seems to think that such a thing can indicate that there is something seriously wrong with our literary system.

Finally . . . this novel continues to be, for its author, a most instructive experience. For instance. Ten years after I wrote it, I can get, in one week, three letters about it, from three intelligent, well-informed, concerned people, who have taken the trouble to sit down and write to me. One might be in Johannesburg, one in San Francisco, one in Budapest. And here I sit, in London, reading them, at the same time, or one after another – as always, grateful to the writers, and delighted that what I've written can stimulate, illuminate – or even annoy. But one letter is entirely about the sex war, about man's inhumanity to woman, and woman's inhumanity to man, and the writer has produced pages and pages all about nothing else, for she – but not always a she, can't see anything else in the book.

The second is about politics, probably from an old Red like

myself, and he or she writes many pages about politics, and never mentions any other theme.

These two letters used, when the book was, as it were, young, to be the most common.

The third letter, once rare but now catching up on the others, is written by a man or a woman who can see nothing in it but the theme of mental illness.

But it is the same book.

And naturally these incidents bring up again questions of what people see when they read a book, and why one person sees one pattern and nothing at all of another pattern, and how odd it is to have, as author, such a clear picture of a book, that is seen so very differently by its readers.

And from this kind of thought has emerged a new conclusion: which is that it is not only childish of a writer to want readers to see what he sees, to understand the shape and aim of a novel as he sees it – his wanting this means that he has not understood a most fundamental point. Which is that the book is alive and potent and fructifying and able to promote thought and discussion *only* when its plan and shape and intention are not understood, because that moment of seeing the shape and plan and intention is also the moment when there isn't anything more to be got out of it.

And when a book's pattern and the shape of its inner life is as plain to the reader as it is to the author – then perhaps it is time to throw the book aside, as having had its day, and start again on something new.

IAN McEWAN

An Interview with Milan Kundera

(1984)

Milan Kundera was born in Brno in 1929, the son of a famous concert pianist. He joined the Czech communist party in 1947, was expelled in 1950, reinstated in 1956 and expelled once more in 1970. He was a professor at the Prague National Film School until 1969 when he lost his post in the 'normalization' following the Russian invasion of Czechoslovakia. During the next few years the authorities made his life increasingly difficult. In 1975 the University of Rennes offered him a professorship, and since that time Kundera has made his home in France with his wife, Vera.

His first novel, *The Joke* (Faber), appeared in 1967 and was an immediate success and a major event of the 'Prague Spring'. The novel charts the calamitous life that unfolds for a young student who sends his Stalinist girlfriend a playful postcard: 'Optimism is the opium of the people! A healthy atmosphere stinks of stupidity! Long live Trotsky!' The French critic Aragon called it 'one of the greatest novels of the century'. Kundera's fine collection of stories, *Laughable Loves*, also belongs to this period. It was published by Knopf and was included in the excellent series edited by Philip Roth and published by Penguin called 'Writers from the Other Europe'.

During 'normalization', Kundera's work was banned from bookshops and libraries throughout Czechoslovakia, and since that time he has had to write for the translator. Before leaving for France he wrote two more novels, *The Farewell Party* (John Murray) and *Life is Elsewhere*. The latter won the Prix Medicis in France for the best foreign novel of 1973. It is not available in this country. Throughout the seventies Kundera's work was translated extensively. *The Book of Laughter and Forgetting* (Faber), his first novel written in exile, showed Kundera at his best. The wide range of his philosophical and political concerns and the dramas and melodramas of private life (Kundera's 'anthropology') found a new synthesis and succinctness within a more daring, or playful, structure.

His new novel, *The Unbearable Lightness of Being*, was well received in France earlier this year. Like the previous novel, it moves between comic or wistful accounts of the private lives of his characters and wry, paradoxical and sometimes anguished musings on their fates – and on all fates. The French have adopted Kundera as one of their own and he has been besieged by interviewers and profile writers. This may have contributed to his views on journalism here, and to the weariness he clearly felt at having to repeat his views. The worst is still ahead of him, however. In this country and more particularly in the United States, there are plans for a major publishing 'event'; Kundera will have to do a great deal of explaining if he is to avoid the label of 'dissident writer' which he dislikes so much.

The new novel is consistent with the earlier work in its preoccupation with the perils of systematizing human experience into dogma, especially political dogma. That Kundera can devise sexual comedies around these perils is one of his attractions. He cannot leave the Great Questions alone; but the reader is never repelled by cold abstraction. His passionate inquiries remain rooted in and nourished by the lives of his characters whom he treats with an almost parental tenderness. The abuses of power, the political control of the past, the lure of utopias, the nature of history and of existence itself – Kundera's metaphysics – are conjured with the lightest and deftest of touches out of tortuous love affairs and fickle lovers, consuming jealousies, compulsive sexual conquest, the niceties of sexual manners, the limitless comedy of arousal. His treatment of sex borders on the obsessive, and yet his achievement has been to bring both private life and political life into one comic framework and to demonstrate how both take their forms from the same source of human

inadequacies. A totalitarian government – that 'realm of uncon-
tested meaning' – generates its own abundant absurdities, its
own dark comedy, and Kundera has been both a gleeful and
pained debunker of a bureaucracy that does not dare permit its
citizens to read their countryman, Kafka.

The interview was conducted in French in an apartment near
Montparnasse where Kundera lives with his wife.

MCEWAN: Let's talk about exile first of all. Your books are
banned in Czechoslovakia and your immediate public is now
French. Is it a great loss to be cut off from your native
readership?

KUNDERA: From a general point of view, yes, it is very hard
suddenly to lose the public I'd been used to until my forties.
But personally it didn't feel all that unpleasant. My books
were banned at the time of the Russian invasion, but I
continued to live in Prague afterwards. I was fortunate in
already having a contract with the French publisher Gallimard
so I knew that what I was writing would be published. This
alleviated the situation, made it far less cruel. But I wasn't the
only one who was banned. It was really almost all of my
generation, and some of my colleagues found themselves
without any publisher at all. The idea of a French public,
though, or the public of any country other than my own, was
something abstract, something unknown. Paradoxically, this
turned out to be liberating. Your immediate public has its
demands, its tastes; it exerts an influence on you without your
being aware of it. The public annoys you too, especially in a
small country, because all of a sudden it knows you. So in the
two novels I wrote after being banned I felt very free. I was
free from censorship because I was no longer being published
in my own country, and there was no longer pressure from
the public.

MCEWAN: Was the decision to leave a difficult one, or was it
clear cut?

KUNDERA: It was a slow process. Back in '68, the people who
wanted to emigrate did so at once. At that time I was one of

the people who didn't want to leave, precisely because I thought that a writer couldn't live anywhere else except in his homeland. I remained in Czechoslovakia for seven years after the occupation. At first everything that happened was very interesting, even if sad. For a writer, especially, it was a fascinating experience to live through. But slowly it became, not just very sad, but sterile, too. And gradually it got to be enough. Even at a practical level, it wasn't possible to stay any longer. I'd had it. I'd lost my job at the university. I lost my salary. I couldn't publish any more. So there was no longer any way I could earn my living . . . I had saved a bit of money so we lasted out for a while. My wife began teaching English, but, as she didn't have permission to teach, she had to do it in secret. My awareness that I could emigrate came – I can remember it very well – in 1973. I had been awarded the Medicis Prize for *Life is Elsewhere*, and, to my surprise, the authorities gave me back my previously confiscated passport and let me go to Paris to collect the prize. We realized then that the regime was not against writers leaving, that in fact it was tacitly encouraging them. I began to think then of emigrating. A little later I was invited to teach at the University at Rennes for two years. During this time things were getting worse in Czechoslovakia, and being in France was a kind of recuperation. And I was struck by the fact that I wasn't nostalgic or homesick in the way I thought I would be. I am very happy here.

MCEWAN: Exile then is not a form of 'unbearable lightness'.

KUNDERA: Lightness, yes, perhaps, but more bearable than unbearable.

MCEWAN: Since you've been living in the West, have you found yourself enlisted in the Cold War? Have people been tempted to manipulate you or your work for their own political purposes?

KUNDERA: To be completely frank I've never felt that. But what I did feel, especially when I first arrived, was that my work was regarded in a simplistic and political way. I had the sense that people read me as a political document; everybody, whether they were on the right or the left. I was angry, and felt offended. I don't think there was any deliberate intention to manipulate me, to make me part of the Cold War. But I do think that modern society encourages journalistic thinking. That's what dominates. Journalistic thinking is fast thinking. It doesn't permit real thought, and its vision of the world is naturally very simplified. If you come from Prague or Warsaw, then automatically you are classed by journalistic non-thought as a political writer. It is not literary critics but journalists who interpret your work. And so in that sense, at first, I did suffer from their interpretations and I had to defend myself against them. And I think I succeeded. Now they seem to understand, more or less.

MCEWAN: Why exactly are you offended by a political reading of your work?

KUNDERA: Because it is a bad reading. Everything you think is important in the book you've written is ignored. Such a reading sees only one aspect: the denunciation of a communist regime. That doesn't mean I like communist regimes; I detest them. But I detest them as a citizen: as a writer I don't say what I say in order to denounce a regime. Flaubert detested bourgeois society. But if you read *Madame Bovary* as mainly a denunciation of the bourgeoisie, it would be a terrible misunderstanding of the book.

MCEWAN: In *The Unbearable Lightness of Being* your character, Tereza, takes photos of Russian tanks and soldiers in the streets of Prague at the time of the invasion. Her pictures will be published abroad. Suddenly she feels strong, fulfilled; she has a purpose. Is there a sense in which you became strong too, at that time? That your subject matter was crystallized for you at the time of the occupation?

KUNDERA: This is Tereza's affair, not mine. I didn't feel at all strong then. It is a question of private and public life. When public life becomes very intense for Tereza it frees her from her private concerns. It is a paradoxical situation: you suddenly find yourself caught up in dramatic events, threatened with death, surrounded by tragedy, and you feel very good. Why? Because you have forgotten your private sadness.

MCEWAN: In *The Book of Laughter and Forgetting* you describe two kinds of laughter. The laughter of the devil celebrates the meaninglessness of everything, while the angels' laugh, which has something of a false ring about it, rejoices in how rationally organized and well-conceived everything on earth is. I suppose you would think of Czechoslovakia as being of the Devil's party. The Czechs laugh like devils, the Russians like angels.

KUNDERA: Absolutely, yes.

MCEWAN: To belong to a small country has a profound effect on the way you see the world, then?

KUNDERA: It is very different. Consider, for instance, the national anthem. The Czech anthem begins with a simple question: 'Where is my homeland?' The homeland is understood as a question. As an eternal uncertainty. Or consider the Polish national anthem, which begins with the words: 'Poland has not yet.' And now compare this with the national anthem of the Soviet Union: 'The indissoluble union of three republics, has been joined for ever by the Great Russia.' Or the British 'Victorious, happy and glorious . . .' These are the words of a great country's anthem – glory, glorious, victorious, grandeur, pride, immortality – yes, immortality, because great nations think of themselves as immortal. You see, if you're English, you never question the immortality of your nation because you are English. Your Englishness will never be put in doubt. You may question England's politics, but not its existence.

MCEWAN: Well, once we were very big. Now we are rather small.

KUNDERA: Not all that small, though.

MCEWAN: We ask ourselves who we are, and what our position in the world is. We have an image of ourselves that was formed in another time.

KUNDERA: Yes, but you never ask yourselves what will happen when England does not exist any more. It can be asked, but it is terribly abstract. But it is a question that is constantly being asked in these small countries: what will happen when Poland no longer exists? Thirty million people live in Poland, so it is not such a small country. But the feeling is nevertheless true. I remember the opening phrase in a letter between Witold Gombrowicz and Czeslaw Milosz. Gombrowicz wrote, 'In a hundred years – if our country still exists . . .' No English, American, German or French person could ever write such a phrase.

This feeling of the frailty of existence – this sense of mortality – is linked with a vision of history. Large nations think they are making history. And if you make history you take yourself seriously; you even begin to worship yourself. People say, for instance, history will judge us. But how will it judge us? It will judge us badly. It will judge us . . .

MCEWAN: Severely?

KUNDERA: No, not severely, I wouldn't say severely. It will judge us without any authority to do so. Why think that it will judge us justly? The judgement of history is bound to be unjust, perhaps even stupid. To say that history will judge us – which is commonplace enough, everybody says it – means you automatically understand history as rational – with the right to judge, with the right to truth. It is the understanding you find among large nations who, making history, always see it as wise and positive.

If you are a small nation, though, you do not make history. You are always the object of history. History is something hostile, something you must defend yourself against. You feel, spontaneously, that history is unjust, often stupid, and you can't take it seriously. Hence our special humour: a humour capable of seeing history as grotesque.

MCEWAN: You have written a great deal about what happens when people come to believe in Utopias, when they think they have made a paradise on earth. You see them dancing in a closed circle, their hearts overflowing with an intense feeling of innocence. They are like children. Or they are on a Great March, fists raised, chanting the same syllables in unison. And yet your characters who break away from the circle are deeply cynical – sometimes attractively so. But all the same, their lives are made to seem sterile. Between this cynicism and this mindless circle-dancing you don't seem to offer us much.

KUNDERA: I'm not a priest. I can't tell people what to believe.

MCEWAN: You were in paradise yourself once. You danced in a circle after 1948, didn't you, when the communists first came into power in Czechoslovakia? When did you leave the dance? Was it another very slow process or was it decisive?

KUNDERA: The further away I get from it, the more I have the impression it was a swift process. But that is certainly the optical illusion of somebody who is already very far removed from it: it could not have been very swift.

MCEWAN: I was interested to find in the last section of your new novel, *The Unbearable Lightness of Being*, a very different attitude to paradise. Your heroine Tereza has retreated to the countryside with her husband Tomas and their dog Karenin. You write: 'Comparing Adam and Karenin leads me to the thought that in Paradise man was not yet man. Or to be more precise, man had not yet been cast out on man's path. Now we are longtime outcasts, flying through the emptiness of time in a straight line.' And just a little later you reflect on the danger of treating animals as soulless machines: 'By doing so man cuts the thread binding him to Paradise and has nothing left to hold or comfort him on his flight through the emptiness of time.' So this is a paradise worth hanging on to. What relationship does it have to that other, mindless paradise you describe so scornfully elsewhere?

KUNDERA: Tereza longs for paradise. It's a longing, ultimately, not to be man.

MCEWAN: But the man who dances in your circle, lost in mindless enthusiasm – hasn't he also ceased to be a man?

KUNDERA: Fanatical people don't cease to be human. Fanaticism is human. Fascism is human. Communism is human. Murder is human. Evil is human. This is why Tereza longs for a state in which man is not man. The paradise of political Utopia is based on the belief in man. This is why it ends in massacres. Tereza's paradise isn't based on the belief in man.

MCEWAN: Towards the end of *The Unbearable Lightness of Being*, you elaborate on the idea of kitsch. By kitsch, then, you mean more than just bad taste?

KUNDERA: Oh yes, far more. I use the word, which was first used in Munich in the nineteenth century, in its original sense. Germany and Central Europe were both Romantic in the nineteenth century – more Romantic than realist. And they really produced kitsch in enormous quantities. The nineteenth century is the first century without a style. All kinds of styles were imitated, especially in architecture: renaissance, baroque, gothic, everything all at once. Hermann Broch wrote a very fine essay called 'Comments on Kitsch' in which he asks this: wasn't the nineteenth century really the century not of Romanticism but of kitsch? By which he means a kind of absolute artistic opportunism capable of drawing on anything in order to move people emotionally. It was eclecticism with one imperative: that it must please. The great Romantics were, according to Broch, exceptions in a sea of kitsch. Broch sees Wagner as kitsch, for example, and Tchaikovsky.

MCEWAN: You have written: 'Kitsch is the aesthetic ideal of all politicians and all political parties and movements.' According to you the function of kitsch is to conceal death. Does this mean there is no conceivable politics without kitsch?

KUNDERA: In my view, politics – in the sense of political parties, elections, *modern* politics – is unthinkable without kitsch. It is inevitable. The function of the successful politician is to please. He is meant to please the largest number of people humanly possible, and to please so many you must rely on the clichés they want to hear.

MCEWAN: Do the Russians want to please?

KUNDERA: It's true they don't need to. They have power without being obliged to please people to keep it. Brezhnev didn't need to please anybody. But the party slogans, party demagogy, and all that: that's intended to please. That's kitsch on a grand scale.

MCEWAN: Ortega y Gasset said that tears and laughter are aesthetically false.

KUNDERA: Yes, I don't know that quotation, but that's right. I had a letter the other day from a Swedish reader who said: 'But do you realize that, in fact, to accept you, we cover up what disturbs us and turn you into kitsch? When *The Book of Laughter and Forgetting* was published, the reviewers talked only about the character, Tamina. It is an interesting part of the book. It's no worse than the rest. But it also has an emotional, "kitschifiable" motif – the relationship between a woman and her dead husband whom she still loves. Nobody mentioned the last part of your book which has this anti-social, anti-human quality. And the reason they didn't mention it was to kitschify you.'

MCEWAN: Let's pass on to other things. Do you think the key to all human relations is to be found in sexual relationships? Is what happens between a man and a woman a mirror for all human relationships?

KUNDERA: I don't know. It is certainly a very revealing situation, but I wouldn't like to say that everything stops there.

MCEWAN: Your starting point always seems to be a marriage, an affair . . . There seems to be an obsession with constant love-making.

KUNDERA: Yes, but it either reveals the essence of a situation or it has no place in the novel. When my characters make love, they grasp, suddenly, the truth of their life or their relationship. For example, in *The Farewell Party*: Jakob and Olga have always been secure in their relationship. All at once they sleep together, and their relationship becomes unbearable. It becomes unbearable because this feeling of pity suddenly materializes during the sexual act and it becomes something absolutely horrible: pity is an impossible foundation for love. In *The Joke*, when Ludwik makes love to Helena, we suddenly see that his sexuality is based on vengeance. The whole book is based on this single act of intercourse. When Sabina makes love with Franz, in *The Unbearable Lightness of Being*, she suddenly becomes aware that he is like a puppy feeding from her breasts, sucking. She sees him as an animal – a small animal who has come to depend on her – and this aspect of him suddenly disgusts her. At a glance, she sees the truth of their relationship.

MCEWAN: The identity of your characters is revealed through their sexuality . . .

KUNDERA: Take Tereza in *The Unbearable Lightness of Being*. Her problem is her identity, the relationship of body and soul; her soul doesn't feel comfortable in her body. It is expressed most clearly in a scene when she is making love with the engineer. She suddenly feels that her soul is completely remote during the act, watching her body making love. She becomes excited by this detachment; you see her problem, the theme on which her character is based, suddenly emerge during that act of love. In that sense, these erotic scenes serve to illuminate characters and situations.

MCEWAN: You write very well about the desire to be a victim. Being a victim, according to you, is not simply something which happens to someone, it is also something that someone, the victim, dreams.

KUNDERA: For example?

MCEWAN: Many of your characters are consumed by sexual jealousy. They inhabit their jealousy; they seem to love it, or need it. They are victims, of course, but they cultivate their own particular hell.

KUNDERA: That's an interesting idea, but to be honest I've never thought about it that way. I've got nothing much to add; you're right.

MCEWAN: You write a lot about the obsession with sexual conquest. Do you think there is any connection between that and political conquest, the conquest of one country by another?

KUNDERA: I don't know.

MCEWAN: For example, sometimes the fate of your characters is very much caught up with the fate of their country. Tamina in *The Book of Laughter and Forgetting* is strongly identified with Czechoslovakia. She is in exile, she is cut off from her own past. Can one talk of countries as victims? Some of your most victimized characters make strong identifications with the oppressors. Ruzena in *The Farewell Party*, for example, is a pathetic figure in some ways, but she sides with the mad old men who go round killing people's dogs, and she is on the side of the fat women at the swimming pool who revel in their nakedness and ugliness. There is a collusion between the oppressors and oppressed, an intimacy that is almost sexual.

KUNDERA: It is true. You're absolutely right; I was not completely conscious of it. But it is true.

MCEWAN: It would be better for me to say some things that weren't true: you could deny them eloquently . . . Novels and films where the private and the political can be resolved inside one situation are always attractive.

KUNDERA: The same things that happen at the level of high politics happen in private life. George Orwell has written of a world in which the Political Power rewrites history: decides what the truth is, what is to be remembered, what forgotten. As a novelist, though, I have different interests. I am much more interested in the fact that each of us, consciously or unconsciously, rewrites our own history. We are constantly rewriting our own biographies, constantly bringing our own sense – the sense we want – to events. We are selecting and shaping – picking out the things that reassure and flatter us, while deleting anything that might possibly detract. To rewrite history, then – to rewrite history even in Orwell's sense – is not an inhuman activity. On the contrary, it is very human. People always see the political and the personal as different worlds, as if each had its own logic, its own rules. But the very horrors that take place on the big stage of politics resemble, strangely but insistently, the small horrors of our private life.

MCEWAN: You once said you thought it was the task of the novel to expose 'anthropological scandals'. What did you mean by that?

KUNDERA: I was talking about the situation in totalitarian states. I said that for a writer everything that was going on there was not a political scandal, but an anthropological one. That is, I didn't look at it in terms of what a political regime could do, but in terms of this question: what is man capable of?

MCEWAN: But why scandal?

KUNDERA: A scandal is what shocks us; everybody talks about the shocking ways of this bureaucracy, this communist system, that has given birth to the gulags, political trials, and stalinist purges. They describe it all as a political scandal. But people forget the obvious fact that a political system can do no more than the men in it: if man wasn't capable of killing, no political system could engender a war. A system exists around the limits of what human beings can do. Nobody, for example, can spit four metres into the air, even if the system demands it. You can't do more than half a metre. Or piss that far: even if Stalin orders it, you can't do it. But you can kill. So the anthropological question – the question of what man is capable of – is always there behind the political one.

MCEWAN: I have the impression you believe the novel is capable of granting us a very special understanding of the world, of permitting insights that no other form of enquiry could equal.

KUNDERA: Yes, I believe that the novel can say something that can't be said any other way. But just what this specific thing is, it is very difficult to say. You could put it negatively. You could say, for example, that the novel's purpose is not to describe society, because there are certainly better ways of doing that. Nor does it exist to describe history, because that can be done by historiography. Novelists are not here to denounce stalinism because Solzhenitsyn can do that in his proclamations. But the novel is the only way to describe, to show, to analyse, to peel away human existence in all its aspects. I don't see any intellectual activity which could do what the novel accomplishes. Not even existential philosophy. Because the novel has an inbuilt scepticism in relation to all systems of thought. Novels naturally begin by assuming that it is essentially impossible to fit human life into any kind of system. That is why the questions you put to me a moment ago were not easy for me to answer. The questions of paradise, or power, or the relation of power to existence or to eroticism. I examine these questions only as they are expressed in the relations between different fictional characters, and that means that, in the novel, you are always aware of several possible answers to every question. The novel doesn't answer questions: it offers possibilities.

MCEWAN: A distinctive feature of your fiction is the presence of the author as a kind of chorus, questioning and commenting on the behaviour and motives of his characters. This voice seems to emerge in *The Joke* and its presence has been very strong in the last two novels. Are the techniques of the traditional novel, with its invisible author, insufficient for your purposes?

KUNDERA: Well, there are three things to say here. First, I'd already used that technique in an earlier book. You'll find this narrator in *Life is Elsewhere*. You'll find it too in my short stories. But it is true that recently I've used this voice more and more. Second, you ask if this kind of narration supersedes the traditional novel, which doesn't need any commentary. But it was really only in the nineteenth century that the narrator disappeared completely. He was always there in eighteenth-century novels. He is there in Rabelais, in Cervantes, in Sterne. My third point: I said earlier that for me the value of the novel is in the way it can examine the essence of a situation. It doesn't just represent situations – jealousy, say, or tenderness, or the taste for power – it arrests them, comes to a halt by them, looks closely at them, ponders them, interrogates them, asks questions of them, understands them as enigmas. Once you start to understand them as enigmas then you have to start thinking about them. Take jealousy, for example. It is so commonplace as to make any explanation seem unnecessary. But if you begin to pause and think about it, it is different. It's unbearable to see a woman you love making love to another man. Suddenly the commonplace becomes difficult, troubling, enigmatic. I'd even say it is the novelist's ambition to represent the enigmatic, precisely because so much in everyday life has become commonplace and trivialized. I need to hear in the novel the voice that is thinking, but not the voice of a philosopher. What does that mean? You asked me questions about my novels which already contained a great deal of knowledge, even though formulated as questions. That's very much like the novelist's method, which is to go further and further, right to the heart of the problem, without ever offering an answer.

MCEWAN: You go to great lengths to avoid giving your characters a 'psychology' – in fact your work seems quite opposed to the psychological novel. You often stop to remind us that your characters are pure artifice. And yet, paradoxically, you manage to make them seem very real. I think this is because your intrusive narrator talks about your characters in much the same way as perceptive people might talk about a close friend. Your interventions are a form of higher gossip. And that makes us think these characters really exist.

KUNDERA: Yes, that's right. I don't claim to know everything about the character. I can't, just as I can't claim to know everything about a friend. I am really writing on the level of hypothesis. It is the same with friends. Even if you are talking of your best friend – and you say everything that can be said – your observation remains a hypothesis.

MCEWAN: Was it your admiration for Kafka that caused you to write that the novel investigates life in the trap the world has become?

KUNDERA: Ah yes, the novel of today examines the trap the world has become. The history of the novel is a mirror of man's history, but something happened when Kafka arrived . . . something which is still not properly recognized. Usually Modernism in the novel is represented by the trinity of Joyce, Proust and Kafka. Whereas it has always seemed to me that Proust and Joyce are the fulfilment, the completion of a long process of evolution that goes back to Flaubert. Something quite different begins with Kafka and possibly with Broch and Musil. Until Kafka, the monster that man fought against was the monster inside him – what determined his inner life, his past, his childhood, his complexes. In Kafka, for the first time, the monster comes from the outside: the world is perceived as the trap. In Kafka, man is being determined from outside himself: the power of *The Castle*, from the power of the invisible tribunal of *The Trial*. In my books, it is history which traps the European man. What are the possibilities in a world that has become our trap? What choices do we have? What forms of life are there? Now it makes no difference, ultimately, if K. has an Oedipus complex or a father-fixation: it won't change his fate in the least. But it would change the fate of a Proust character completely. The world of Proust or Flaubert was open. History was invisible. It was something that couldn't be grasped, even. For us, history is concrete, palpable. It is war. It is a political regime. It is the end of Europe. It is absolutely graspable – *grasping* – and we're in it: caught. Hence, the trap.

MCEWAN: You have a phrase about solitude being violated in Kafka's characters.

KUNDERA: Yes. You're surrounded by a community – that was Kafka's nightmare – in which your solitude is utterly violated, massacred: it ceases to exist. Everybody can see you; you're never alone. Kafka is still interpreted in the terms of the generation that preceded him. It's like talking about Beethoven in terms of Haydn. Kafka is still seen through the romantic cliché of solitude: that man is threatened by solitude, that solitude is purely negative, that the tragedy of the intellectual is that he has lost his roots among the people. And Kafka himself is thus the author suffering from solitude, looking for community, for brotherhood, wanting to find his place in the world – even though it was precisely this very cliché which Kafka turned upside down. Kafka's world is in fact totally different. The Land Surveyor in *The Castle* is bored and fed up with the world around him. It's not brotherhood he's looking for; it's a job. But instead he's pestered by everybody. He is watched. He sleeps in the same bed as his assistants and can't sleep with Frida because they are always there, with him. In Kafka, those who find their place in society do so by renouncing their solitude and, in the long run, their personalities.

What, ultimately, does brotherhood mean? Kafka turns the notion on its head. It becomes something hateful, terrible, and threatening. Kafka challenges one of the most accepted notions about society. And this is precisely the task of all novelists: to challenge, constantly, the principal notions on which our very existence is based.

Translated from the French by Ian Patterson

ITALO CALVINO

Cybernetics and Ghosts

Lecture delivered in Turin and other Italian cities,
November 1967

I

It all begin with the first storyteller of the tribe. Men were already exchanging articulate sounds, referring to the practical needs of their daily lives. Dialogue was already in existence, and so were the rules that it was forced to follow. This was the life of the tribe, a very complex set of rules on which every action and every situation had to be based. The number of words was limited, and, faced with the multiform world and its countless things, men defended themselves by inventing a finite number of sounds, combined in various ways. Modes of behaviour, customs, and gestures too were what they were and none other, constantly repeated while harvesting coconuts or scavenging for wild roots, while hunting lions or buffalo, marrying in order to create new bonds of relationship outside the clan, or at the first moments of life, or at death. And the more limited the choices of phrase or behaviour, the more complex the rules of language or custom were forced to become in order to master an ever-increasing variety of situations. The extreme poverty of ideas about the world then available to man was matched by a detailed, all-embracing code of rules.

The storyteller began to put forth words, not because he thought others might reply with other, predictable words, but to test the extent to which words could fit with one another, could give birth to one another, in order to extract an explanation of the world from the thread of every possible spoken narrative and from the arabesque that nouns and verbs, subjects and predicates performed as they unfolded from one another. The figures available to the storyteller were very few: the jaguar, the coyote, the toucan, the piranha; or else father and son, brother-in-law and uncle, wife and mother and sister and mother-in-law. The actions these figures could perform were likewise rather limited: they could be born, die, copulate, sleep, fish, hunt, climb trees, dig burrows, eat and defecate, smoke vegetable fibres, make prohibitions, transgress them, steal or give away fruit or other things – things that were also classified in a limited catalogue. The storyteller explored the possibilities implied in his own language by combining and changing the permutations of the figures and the actions, and of the objects on which these actions could be brought to bear. What emerged were stories, straightforward constructions that always contained correspondences or contraries – the sky and the earth, fire and water, animals that flew and those that dug burrows – and each term had its array of attributes and a repertoire of its own. The telling of stories allowed certain relationships among the various elements and not others, and things could happen in a certain order and not in others: prohibition had to come before transgression, punishment after transgression, the gift of magic objects before the trial of courage. The immobile world that surrounded tribal man, strewn with signs of the fleeting correspondences between words and things, came to life in the voice of the storyteller, spun out into the flow of a spoken narrative within which each word acquired new values and transmitted them to the ideas and images they defined. Every animal, every object, every relationship took on beneficial or malign powers that came to be called magical powers but should, rather, have been called narrative powers, potentialities contained in the word, in its ability to link itself to other words on the plane of discourse.

Primitive oral narrative, like the folk tale that has been handed down almost to the present day, is modelled on fixed structures, on, we might almost say, prefabricated elements – elements, however, that allow of an enormous number of combinations.

Vladimir Propp, in the course of his studies of Russian folk tales, came to the conclusion that all such tales were like variants of a single tale and could be broken down into a limited number of narrative functions. Forty years later Claude Lévi-Strauss, working on the myths of the Indians of Brazil, saw these as a system of logical operations between permutable terms, so that they could be studied according to the mathematical processes of combinatorial analysis.

Even if the folk imagination is therefore not boundless like the ocean, there is no reason to think of it as being like a water tank of small capacity. On an equal level of civilization, the operations of narrative, like those of mathematics, cannot differ all that much from one people to another, but what can be constructed on the basis of these elementary processes can present unlimited combinations, permutations, and transformations.

Is this true only of oral narrative traditions? Or can it be maintained of literature in all its variety of forms and complexities? As early as the 1920s, the Russian Formalists began to make modern stories and novels the object of their analysis, breaking down their complex structures into functional segments. In France today the semiological school of Roland Barthes, having sharpened its knives on the structures of advertising or of women's fashion magazines, is at last turning its attention to literature; the eighth issue of the magazine *Communications* was devoted to the structural analysis of the short story. Naturally enough, the material that lends itself best to this kind of treatment is still to be found in the various forms of popular fiction. If the Russians studied the Sherlock Holmes stories, today it is James Bond who provides the structuralists with their most apt exemplars.

But this is merely the first step in the grammar and syntax of narrative fiction. The combinatorial play of narrative possibilities soon passes beyond the level of content to touch upon the relationship of the narrator to the material related and to the reader: and this brings us to the toughest set of problems facing contemporary fiction. It is no coincidence that the researches of the French structuralists go hand in hand (and sometimes co-exist in the same person) with the creative work of the 'Tel Quel' group. For the latter – and here I am paraphrasing statements by one of their authorized interpreters – writing consists no longer in narrating but in saying that one is narrating, and what one says becomes identified with the very act of saying. The psychological person is replaced by a linguistic or even a grammatical person, defined solely by his place in the discourse. These formal repercussions of a literature at the second or third degree, such as occurred in France with the *nouveau roman* of ten years ago, for which another of its exponents suggested the word 'scripturalism', can be traced back to combinations of a certain number of logico-linguistic (or better, syntactical-rhetorical) operations, in such a way as to be reducible to formulas that are the more general as they become less complex.

I will not go into technical details on which I could only be an unauthorized and rather unreliable commentator. My intention here is merely to sum up the situation, to make connections between a number of books I have recently read, and to put these in the context of a few general reflections. In the particular way today's culture looks at the world, one tendency is emerging from several directions at once. The world in its various aspects is increasingly looked upon as *discrete* rather than *continuous*. I am using the term 'discrete' in the sense it bears in mathematics, a discrete quantity being one made up of separate parts. Thought, which until the other day appeared to us as something fluid, evoking linear images such as a flowing river or an unwinding thread, or else gaseous images such as a kind of vaporous cloud – to the point where it was sometimes called 'spirit' (in the sense of 'breath') – we now tend to think of as a series of discontinuous states, of combinations of impulses acting on a finite (though enormous) number of sensory and motor organs. Electronic brains, even if they are still far from producing all the functions of the human brain, are nonetheless capable of providing us with a convincing theoretical model for the most complex processes of our memory, our mental associations, our imagination, our conscience. Shannon, Weiner, von Neumann, and Turing have radically altered our image of our mental processes. In the place of the ever-changing cloud that we carried in our heads until the other day, the condensing and dispersal of which we attempted to understand by describing impalpable psychological states and shadowy landscapes of the soul – in the place of all this we now feel the rapid passage of signals on the intricate circuits that connect the relays, the diodes, the transistors with which our skulls are crammed. Just as no chess player will ever live long enough to exhaust all the combinations of possible moves for the thirty-two pieces on the chessboard, so we know (given the fact that our minds are chessboards with hundreds of billions of pieces) that not even in a lifetime lasting as long as the universe would one ever manage to make all possible plays. But we also know that all these are implicit in the overall code of mental plays, according to the rules by which each of us, from one moment to the next, formulates his thoughts, swift or sluggish, cloudy or crystalline as they may be.

I might also say that what is finite and numerically calculable is superseding the indeterminateness of ideas that cannot be subjected to measurement and delimitation; but this formulation runs the risk of giving an oversimplified notion of how things stand. In fact, the very opposite is true: every analytical process, every division into parts, tends to provide an image of the world that is ever more complicated, just as Zeno of Elea, by refusing to accept space as continuous, ended up by separating Achilles from the tortoise by an infinite number of intermediate points. But mathematical complexity can be digested instantly by electronic brains. Their abacus of only two numerals permits them to make instantaneous calculations of a complexity unthinkable for human brains. They have only to count on two fingers to bring into play incredibly rapid matrices of astronomical sums. One of the most arduous intellectual efforts of the Middle Ages has only now become entirely real: I refer to the Catalan monk Raymond Lully and his *ars combinatoria*.

The process going on today is the triumph of discontinuity, divisibility, and combination over all that is flux, or a series of minute nuances following one upon the other. The nineteenth century, from Hegel to Darwin, saw the triumph of historical continuity and biological continuity as they healed all the fractures of dialectical antitheses and genetic mutations. Today this perspective is radically altered. In history we no longer follow the course of a spirit immanent in the events of the world, but the curves of statistical diagrams, and historical research is leaning more and more toward mathematics. And as for biology, Watson and Crick have shown us how the transmission of the characteristics of the species consists in the duplication of a certain number of spiral-shaped molecules formed from a certain number of acids and bases. In other words, the endless variety of living forms can be reduced to the combination of certain finite quantities. Here again, it is information theory that imposes its patterns. The processes that appeared most resistant to a formulation in terms of number, to a quantitative description, are not translated into mathematical patterns.

Born and raised on quite different terrain, structural linguistics tends to appear in terms of a play of contraries every bit as simple as information theory. And linguists, too, have begun to talk in terms of codes and messages, to attempt to establish the entropy of language on all levels, including that of literature.

Mankind is beginning to understand how to dismantle and reassemble the most complex and unpredictable of all its machines: language. Today's world is far richer in words and concepts and signs than the world that surrounded primitive man, and the uses of the various levels of language are a great deal more complex. Using transformational mathematical patterns, the American school led by Chomsky is exploring the deep structure of language, lying at the roots of the logical processes that may constitute no longer a historical characteristic of man, but a biological one. And extreme simplification of logical formulas, on the other hand, is used by the French school of structural semantics headed by A. J. Greimas. This school analyzes the narrative quality of all discourse, which may be reduced to a ratio between what they call *actants*.

After a gap of almost thirty years, a 'Neo-Formalist' school has been reborn in the Soviet Union, employing the results of cybernetic research and structural semiology for the analysis of literature. Headed by a mathematician, Kholmogorov, this school carries out studies of a highly academic scientific nature based on the calculation of probabilities and the quantity of information contained in poems.

A further encounter between mathematics and literature is taking place in France, under the banner of hoaxing and practical joking. This is the Ouvroir de Littérature Potentielle (Oulipo), founded by Raymond Queneau and a number of his mathematician friends. This almost clandestine group of ten people is an offshoot of the Collège de Pataphysique, the literary society founded in memory of Alfred Jarry as a kind of academy of intellectual scorn. Meanwhile, the researches of Oulipo into the mathematical structure of the sestina in the work of the Provençal troubadours and of Dante are no less austere than the studies of the Soviet cyberneticists. It should not be forgotten that Queneau is the author of a book called *Cent Mille Milliards de Poèmes*, which purports to be not so much a book as the rudimentary model of a machine for making sonnets, each one different from the last.

Having laid down these procedures and entrusted a computer with the task of carrying out these operations, will we have a machine capable of replacing the poet and the author? Just as we already have machines that can read, machines that perform a linguistic analysis of literary texts, machines that make translations and summaries, will we also have machines capable of conceiving and composing poems and novels?

The interesting thing is not so much the question whether this problem is soluble in practice – because in any case it would not be worth the trouble of constructing such a complicated machine – as the theoretical possibility of it, which would give rise to a series of unusual conjectures. And I am not now thinking of a machine capable merely of 'assembly-line' literary production, which would already be mechanical in itself. I am thinking of a writing machine that would bring to the page all those things that we are accustomed to consider as the most jealously guarded attributes of our psychological life, of our daily experience, our unpredictable changes of mood and inner elations, despairs and moments of illumination. What are these if not so many linguistic 'fields', for which we might well succeed in establishing the vocabulary, grammar, syntax, and properties of permutation?

What would be the style of a literary automaton? I believe that its true vocation would be for classicism. The test of a poetic-electronic machine would be its ability to produce traditional works, poems with closed metrical forms, novels that follow all the rules. In this sense the use so far made of machines by the literary avant-garde is still too human. Especially in Italy, the machine used in these experiments is an instrument of chance, of the destructuralization of form, of protest against every habitual logical connection. I would therefore say that it is still an entirely lyrical instrument, serving a typical human need: the production of disorder. The true literature machine will be one that itself feels the need to produce disorder, as a reaction against its preceding production of order: a machine that will produce avant-garde work to free its circuits when they are choked by too long a production of classicism. In fact, given that developments in cybernetics lean toward machines capable of learning, of changing their own programmes, of developing their own sensibilities and their own needs, nothing prevents us from foreseeing a literature machine that at a certain point feels unsatisfied with its own traditionalism and starts to propose new ways of writing, turning its own codes completely upside down. To gratify critics who look for similarities between things literary and things historical, sociological, or economic, the machine could correlate its own changes of style to the variations in certain statistical indices of production, or income, or military expenditure, or the distribution of decision-making powers. That indeed will be the literature that corresponds perfectly to a theoretical hypothesis: it will, at last, be *the* literature.

II

Now, some of you may wonder why I so gaily announce prospects that in most men of letters arouse tearful laments punctuated by cries of execration. The reason is that I have always known, more or less obscurely, that things stood this way, not the way they were commonly said to stand. Various aesthetic theories maintained that poetry was a matter of inspiration descending from I know not what lofty place, or welling up from I know not what great depths, or else pure intuition, or an otherwise not identified moment in the life of the spirit, or the Voice of the Times with which the Spirit of the World chooses to speak to the poet, or a reflection of social structures that by means of some unknown optical phenomenon is projected on the page, or a direct grasp on the psychology of the depths that enables us to ladle out images of the unconscious, both individual and collective; or at any rate something intuitive, immediate, authentic, and all-embracing that springs up who knows how, something equivalent and homologous to something else, and symbolic of it. But in these theories there always remained a void that no one knew how to fill, a zone of darkness between cause and effect: how does one arrive at the written page? By what route is the soul or history or society or the subconscious transformed into a series of black lines on a white page? Even the most outstanding theories of aesthetics were silent on this point. I felt like someone who, due to some misunderstanding, finds himself among people who are discussing business that is no business of his. Literature as I knew it was a constant series of attempts to make one word stay put after another by following certain definite rules; or, more often, rules that were neither definite nor definable, but that might be extracted from a series of examples, or rules made up for the occasion – that is to say, derived from the rules followed by other writers. And in these operations the person 'I', whether explicit or implicit, splits into a number of different figures: into an 'I' who is writing and an 'I' who is written, into an empirical 'I' who looks over the shoulder of the 'I' who is writing and into a mythical 'I' who serves as a model for the 'I' who is written. The 'I' of the author is dissolved in the writing. The so-called personality of the writer exists within the very act of writing: it is the product and the instrument of the writing process. A writing machine that has been fed an instruction appropriate to the case could also devise an exact and unmistakable 'personality' of an author, or else it could be adjusted in such a way as to evolve or change 'personality' with each work it composes. Writers, as they have always been up to now, are already writing machines; or at least they are when things are going well. What Romantic terminology called genius or talent or inspiration or intuition is nothing other than finding the right road empirically, following one's nose, taking short cuts, whereas the machine would follow a systematic and conscientious route while being extremely rapid and multiple at the same time.

Once we have dismantled and reassembled the process of literary composition, the decisive moment of literary life will be that of reading. In this sense, even though entrusted to machines, literature will continue to be a 'place' of privilege within the human consciousness, a way of exercising the potentialities contained in the system of signs belonging to all societies at all times. The work will continue to be born, to be judged, to be destroyed or constantly renewed on contact with the eye of the reader. What will vanish is the figure of the author, that personage to whom we persist in attributing functions that do not belong to him, the author as an exhibitor of his own soul in the permanent Exhibition of Souls, the author as the exploiter of sensory and interpretive organs more receptive than the average . . . The author: that anachronistic personage, the bearer of messages, the director of consciences, the giver of lectures to cultural bodies. The rite we are celebrating at this moment would be absurd if we were unable to give it the sense of a funeral service, seeing the author off to the Nether Regions and celebrating the constant resurrection of the work of literature; if we were unable to introduce into this meeting of ours something of the gaiety of those funeral feasts at which the ancients re-established their contact with living things.

And so the author vanishes – that spoiled child of ignorance – to give place to a more thoughtful person, a person who will know that the author is a machine, and will know how this machine works.

III

At this point I think I have done enough to explain why it is with a clear conscience and without regrets that I state that my place could perfectly well be occupied by a mechanical device. But I am sure that many of you will remain rather unconvinced by my explanation, finding that my attitude of oft-repeated abnegation, of renunciation of the writer's prerogatives out of the love of truth, must surely be wrong; and that under all this something else must be lurking. I already feel that you are searching for less flattering motives for my attitude. I have nothing against this sort of inquiry. Behind every idealistic position that we adopt we can find the nitty-gritty of practical interest, or, even more often, of some basic psychological motivation. Let us see what my psychological reaction is when I learn that writing is purely and simply a process of combination among given elements. Well, then, what I instinctively feel is a sense of relief, of security. The same sort of relief and sense of security that I feel every time I discover that a mess of vague and indeterminate lines turns out to be a precise geometric form; or every time I succeed in discerning a series of facts, and choices to be made out of a finite number of possibilities, in the otherwise shapeless avalanche of events. Faced with the vertigo of what is countless, unclassifiable, in a state of flux, I feel reassured by what is finite, 'discrete', and reduced to a system. Why is this? Does my attitude contain a hidden element of fear of the unknown, of the wish to set limits to my world and crawl back into my shell? Thus my stance, which was intended to be provocative and even profane, allows of the suspicion that, on the contrary, it is dictated by some kind of intellectual agoraphobia, almost a form of exorcism to defend me from the whirlwinds that literature so constantly has to face.

Let us attempt a thesis contrary to the one I have developed so far (this is always the best way to avoid getting trapped in the spiral of one's own thoughts). Did we say that literature is entirely involved with language, is merely the permutation of a restricted number of elements and functions? But is the tension in literature not continually striving to escape from this finite number? Does it not continually attempt to say something it cannot say, something that it does not know, and that no one could ever know? A thing cannot be known when the words and concepts used to say it and think it have not yet been used in that position, not yet arranged in that order, with that meaning. The struggle of literature is in fact a struggle to escape from the confines of language; it stretches out from the utmost limits of what can be said; what stirs literature is the call and attraction of what is not in the dictionary.

The storyteller of the tribe puts together phrases and images: the younger son gets lost in the forest, he sees a light in the distance, he walks and walks; the fable unwinds from sentence to sentence, and where is it leading? To the point at which something not yet said, something as yet only darkly felt by presentiment, suddenly appears and seizes us and tears us to pieces, like the fangs of a man-eating witch. Through the forest of fairy tale the vibrancy of myth passes like a shudder of wind.

Myth is the hidden part of every story, the buried part, the region that is still unexplored because there are as yet no words to enable us to get there. The narrator's voice in the daily tribal assemblies is not enough to relate the myth. One needs special times and places, exclusive meetings; the words alone are not enough, and we need a whole series of signs with many meanings, which is to say a rite. Myth is nourished by silence as well as by words. A silent myth makes its presence felt in secular narrative and everyday words; it is a language vacuum that draws words up into its vortex and bestows a form on fable.

But what is a language vacuum if not a vestige of taboo, of a ban on mentioning something, on pronouncing certain names, of a prohibition either present or ancient? Literature follows paths that flank and cross the barriers of prohibition, that lead to saying what could not be said, to an invention that is always a reinvention of words and stories that have been banished from the individual or collective memory. Therefore myth acts on fable as a repetitive force, obliging it to go back on its tracks even when it has set off in directions that appear to lead somewhere completely different.

The unconscious is the ocean of the unsayable, of what has been expelled from the land of language, removed as a result of ancient prohibitions. The unconscious speaks – in dreams, in verbal slips, in sudden associations – with borrowed words, stolen symbols, linguistic contraband, until literature redeems these territories and annexes them to the language of the waking world.

The power of modern literature lies in its willingness to give a voice to what has remained unexpressed in the social or individual unconscious: this is the gauntlet it throws down time and again. The more enlightened our houses are, the more their walls ooze ghosts. Dreams of progress and reason are haunted by nightmares. Shakespeare warns us that the triumph of the Renaissance did not lay the ghosts of the medieval world who appear on the ramparts at Dunsinane or Elsinore. At the height of the Enlightenment, Sade and the Gothic novel appear. At one stroke Edgar Allan Poe initiates the literature of aestheticism and the literature of the masses, naming and liberating the ghosts that Puritan America trails in its wake. Lautréamont explodes the syntax of the imagination, expanding the visionary world of the Gothic novel to the proportions of a Last Judgment. In automatic associations of words and images the Surrealists discover an objective rationale totally opposed to that of our intellectual logic. Is this the triumph of the irrational? Or is it the refusal to believe that the irrational exists, that anything in the world can be considered extraneous to the reason of things, even if something eludes the reasons determined by our historical condition, and also eludes limited and defensive so-called rationalism?

So here we are, carried off into an ideological landscape quite different from the one we thought we had decided to live in, there with the relays of diodes of electronic computers. But are we really all that far away?

IV

The relationship between combinatorial play and the unconscious in artistic activity lies at the heart of one of the most convincing aesthetic theories currently in circulation, a formula that draws upon both psychoanalysis and the practical experience of art and letters. We all know that in matters of literature and the arts Freud was a man of traditional tastes, and that in his writings connected with aesthetics he did not give us any pointers worthy of his genius. It was a Freudian art historian, Ernst Kris, who first put forward Freud's study of word-play as the key to a possible aesthetics of psychoanalysis. Another gifted art historian, Ernst Gombrich, developed this notion in his essay on Freud and the psychology of art.

The pleasure of puns and feeble jokes is obtained by following the possibilities of permutation and transformation implicit in language. We start from the particular pleasure given by any combinatorial play, and at a certain point, out of the countless combinations of words with similar sounds, one becomes charged with special significance, causing laughter. What has happened is that the juxtaposition of concepts that we have stumbled across by chance unexpectedly unleashes a preconscious idea, an idea, that is, half buried in or erased from our consciousness, or maybe only held at arm's length or pushed aside, but powerful enough to appear in the consciousness if suggested not by any intention on our part, but by an objective process.

The processes of poetry and art, says Gombrich, are analogous to those of a play on words. It is the childish pleasure of the combinatorial game that leads the painter to try out arrangements of lines and colours, the poet to experiment with juxtapositions of words. At a certain moment things click into place, and one of the combinations obtained – through the combinatorial mechanism itself, independently of any search for meaning or effect on any other level – becomes charged with an unexpected meaning or unforeseen effect which the conscious mind would not have arrived at deliberately: an unconscious meaning, in fact, or at least the premonition of an unconscious meaning.

So we see that the two routes followed by my argument have here come together. Literature is a combinatorial game that pursues the possibilities implicit in its own material, independent of the personality of the poet, but it is a game that at a certain point is invested with an unexpected meaning, a meaning that is not patent on the linguistic plane on which we were working but has slipped in from another level, activating something that on the second level is of great concern to the author or his society. The literature machine can perform all the permutations possible on a given material, but the poetic result will be the particular effect of one of these permutations on a man endowed with a consciousness and an unconscious, that is, an empirical and historical man. It will be the shock that occurs only if the writing machine is surrounded by the hidden ghosts of the individual and of his society.

To return to the storyteller of the tribe, he continues imperturbably to make his permutations of jaguars and toucans until the moment comes when one of his innocent little tales explodes into a terrible revelation: a myth, which must be recited in secret, and in a secret place.

V

I am aware that this conclusion of mine contradicts the most authoritative theories about the relationship between myth and fable.

Until now it has generally been said that the fable is a 'profane' story, something that comes after myth, a corruption or vulgarization or secularization of it, or that fable and myth co-exist and counterbalance each other as different functions of a single culture. The logic of my argument, however – until some more convincing new demonstration comes along to blow it sky-high – leads to the conclusion that the making of fables precedes the making of myths. Mythic significance is something one comes across only if one persists in playing around with narrative functions.

Myth tends to crystallize instantly, to fall into set patterns, to pass from the phase of myth-making into that of ritual, and hence out of the hands of the narrator into those of the tribal institutions responsible for the preservation and celebration of myths. The tribal system of signs is arranged in relation to myth; a certain number of signs become taboo, and the 'secular' storyteller can make no direct use of them. He goes on circling around them, inventing new developments in composition, until in the course of this methodical and objective labour he suddenly gets another flash of enlightenment from the unconscious and the forbidden. And this forces the tribe to change its set of signs once more.

Within this general context, the function of literature varies according to the situation. For long periods of time literature appears to work in favour of consecration, the confirmation of values, the acceptance of authority. But at a certain moment, something in the mechanism is triggered, and literature gives birth to a movement in the opposite direction, refusing to see things and say things the way they have been seen and said until now.

This is the main theme of a book called *Le due tensioni* (*The Two Tensions*), which comprises the previously unpublished notes of Elio Vittorini (Milan: Il Saggiatore, 1967). According to Vittorini, literature until now has been too much the 'accomplice of nature', that is, of the mistaken notion of an immutable nature, a Mother Nature, whereas its true value emerges only when it becomes a critic of the world and our way of looking at the world. In one chapter that may well state his definitive position, Vittorini seems to be starting from scratch on a study of the place of literature in human history. As soon as writing and books are born, he says, the human race is divided into a civilized part – the part of the race that long ago took the step into the Neolithic Age – and another part (called savage) that got stuck in the Paleolithic, and in which the Neolithics could not even recognize their ancestors: a part of humanity that thinks that things have always been the way they are, just as they think that masters and servants have always existed. Written literature is born already laden with the task of consecration, of supporting the established order of things. This is a load that it discards extremely slowly, in the course of millennia, becoming in the process a private thing, enabling poets and writers to express their own personal troubles and raise them to the level of consciousness. Literature gets to this point, I would add, by means of combinatorial games that at a certain moment become charged with preconscious subject matter, and at last find a voice for these. And it is by this road to freedom opened up by literature that men achieved the critical spirit, and transmitted it to collective thought and culture.

VI

Concerning this double aspect of literature, here, toward the end of my little talk, it is relevant to mention an essay by the German poet and critic Hans Magnus Enzensberger, 'Topological Structures in Modern Literature', which I read in the Buenos Aires magazine *Sur* (May–June 1966). He reviews the numerous instances of labyrinthine narratives from ancient times up to Borges and Robbe-Grillet, or of narratives one inside another like Chinese boxes, and he asks himself the meaning of modern literature's insistence on these themes. He evokes the image of a world in which it is easy to lose oneself, to get disoriented – a world in which the effort of regaining one's orientation acquires a particular value, almost that of a training for survival. 'Every orientation,' he writes, 'presupposes a disorientation. Only someone who has experienced bewilderment can free himself of it. But these games of orientation are in turn games of disorientation. Therein lies their fascination and their risk. The labyrinth is made so that whoever enters it will stray and get lost. But the labyrinth also poses the visitor a challenge: that he reconstruct the plan of it and dissolve its power. If he succeeds, he will have destroyed the labyrinth; for one who has passed through it, no labyrinth exists.' And Enzensberger concludes: 'The moment a topological structure appears as a metaphysical structure the game loses its dialectical balance, and literature turns into a means of demonstrating that the world is essentially impenetrable, that any communication is impossible. The labyrinth thus ceases to be a challenge to human intelligence and establishes itself as a facsimile of the world and of society.'

Enzensberger's thesis can be applied to everything in literature and culture that today – after von Neumann – we see as a combinatorial mathematical game. The game can work as a challenge to understand the world or as a dissuasion from understanding it. Literature can work in a critical vein or to confirm things as they are and as we know them to be. The boundary is not always clearly marked, and I would say that on this score the spirit in which one reads is decisive: it is up to the reader to see to it that literature exerts its critical force, and this can occur independently of the author's intentions.

I think this is the meaning one might give to my most recent story, which comes at the end of my book *t zero*. In this story we see Alexandre Dumas taking his novel *The Count of Monte Cristo* from a supernovel that contains all possible variants of the life story of Edmond Dantès. In their dungeon Edmond

Dantès and the Abbot Faria go over the plans for their escape and wonder which of the possible variants is the right one. The Abbot Faria digs tunnels to escape from the castle, but he always goes wrong and ends up in ever-deeper cells. On the basis of Faria's mistakes Dantès tries to draw a map of the castle. While Faria, by the sheer number of his attempts, comes close to achieving the perfect escape, Dantès moves toward imagining the perfect prison – the one from which no escape is possible. His reasons are explained in the passage I shall now quote:

> If I succeed in mentally constructing a fortress from which it is impossible to escape, this imagined fortress either will be the same as the real one – and in this case it is certain we shall never escape from here, but at least we will achieve the serenity of knowing we are here because we could be nowhere else – or it will be a fortress from which escape is even more impossible than from here – which would be a sign that here an opportunity of escape exists: we have only to identify the point where the imagined fortress does not coincide with the real one and then find it.

And that is the most optimistic finale that I have managed to give to my story, to my book, and also to this essay.

SELECTED BIBLIOGRAPHY

There are many studies of the contemporary novel. The following books are a selection for those who wish to follow some of the issues raised in the introduction and the essays about the nature and direction of contemporary fiction internationally. In addition, there are various useful series on individual writers, such as Warner's 'Writers of the Seventies' series, and Methuen's 'Contemporary Writers'. James Vinson's collection *Contemporary Novelists* (London and New York, 1976) gives valuable information about contemporary authors, and a useful bibliography is Irving Adelman and Rita Dworkin, *The Contemporary Novel: A Checklist of Critical Literature on the British and American Novel Since 1945* (Metuchen, New Jersey, 1972). Among the various magazines which represent or explore contemporary literature, I recommend *Granta, Contemporary Literature, Twentieth Century Literature, Modern Fiction Studies, Critique* and *The Critical Quarterly*.

Robert Alter, *Partial Magic: The Novel as a Self-Conscious Genre* (Berkeley, 1979).
John Barth, *The Friday Book: Essays and Other Nonfiction* (New York, 1984).
Jo David Bellamy, *Superfiction: Or the American Story Transformed* (New York, 1975).
Bernard Bergonzi, *The Situation of the Novel* (London, 1970).
Bernard Bergonzi (ed.), *Innovations* (London, 1968).
Malcolm Bradbury, *Possibilities: Essays on the State of the Novel* (London and New York, 1972).
Malcolm Bradbury, *No, Not Bloomsbury* (London and New York, 1987).
Christine Brooke-Rose, *A Rhetoric of the Unreal* (Cambridge, 1981).
Jerry H. Bryant, *The Open Decision: The Contemporary American Novel and Its Intellectual Background* (New York, 1970).

SELECTED BIBLIOGRAPHY

Anthony Burgess, *Homage to QWERTYUIOP* (London, 1986).
Christopher Butler, *After the Wake: An Essay on the Contemporary Avant Garde* (Oxford, 1980).
Michel Butor, *Inventory: Essays*, ed. Richard Howard (New York, 1968; London, 1970).
Italo Calvino, *The Literature Machine* (London, 1987).
Charles Caramello, *Silverless Mirrors: Book, Self and Postmodern American Fiction* (Tallahassee, 1983).
Umberto Eco, *Faith in Fakes*, trans. William Weaver (London, 1986).
Raymond Federman (ed.), *Surfiction: Fiction Now and Tomorrow* (Chicago, 1975).
John Fletcher, *Claude Simon and Fiction Now* (London, 1975).
William H. Gass, *Fiction and the Figures of Life* (New York, 1970).
James Gindin, *Postwar British Fiction: New Accents and Attitudes* (London, 1962).
Gerald Graff, *Literature Against Itself: Literary Ideas in Modern Society* (Chicago and London, 1979).
Ihab Hassan, *Radical Innocence: Studies in the Contemporary American Novel* (Princeton, 1962).
Ihab Hassan, *The Dismemberment of Orpheus: Towards a Postmodern Literature* (New York, 1971).
Ihab Hassan, *The Postmodern Turn* (Ohio, 1987).
Stephen Heath, *The Nouveau Roman: A Study in the Practice of Writing* (London, 1972).
Linda Hutcheon, *Narcissistic Narrative: The Metafictional Paradox* (Waterloo, Ontario, 1980).
Rosemary Jackson, *Fantasy: The Literature of Subversion* (London, 1981).
Gabriel Josipovici, *The World and the Book: A Study of Modern Fiction* (London, 1977).
Frederick R. Karl, *A Reader's Guide to the Contemporary English Novel* (London, rev. ed., 1965).
Steven G. Kellman, *The Self-Begetting Novel* (London, 1980).
Frank Kermode, *Modern Essays* (London, 1971).
Marcus Klein (ed.), *The American Novel Since World War II* (New York, 1967).
Jerome Klinkowitz, *Literary Disruptions: The Making of a Post-Contemporary American Fiction* (Urbana, 1975; rev. ed., 1980).

243

SELECTED BIBLIOGRAPHY

Richard Kostelanetz (ed.), *Contemporary Literature* (New York, 1964).

David Lodge, *The Novelist at the Crossroads and Other Essays on Fiction and Criticism* (London, 1971).

David Lodge, *The Modes of Modern Writing* (London, 1977).

Thomas McCormack (ed.), *Afterwords: Novelists on Their Novels* (New York, 1969).

Brian McHale, *Postmodernist Fiction* (New York and London, 1987).

Vivian Mercier, *A Reader's Guide to the New Novel, from Queneau to Pinget* (New York, 1971).

Raymond Olderman, *Beyond the Waste Land: The American Novel in the 1960s* (New Haven, 1972).

Alain Robbe-Grillet, *For a New Novel: Essays on Fiction*, trans. Richard Howard (New York and London, 1965).

Philip Roth, *Reading Myself and Others* (New York, 1975).

Nathalie Sarraute, *Tropisms and The Age of Suspicion*, trans. Maria Jolas (New York and London, 1963).

Robert Scholes, *Fabulation and Metafiction* (Urbana, Chicago, London, 1979).

Sally Sears and Georgiana W. Lord (eds.), *The Discontinuous Universe: Selected Writings in Contemporary Consciousness* (New York and London, 1972).

George Steiner, *Language and Silence* (London, 1967).

Tony Tanner, *City of Words: American Fiction 1950–1970* (London, 1971).

Gore Vidal, *Matters of Fact and Fiction: Essays 1973–76* (New York, 1977).

Patricia Waugh, *Metafiction: The Theory and Practice of Self-Conscious Fiction* (London and New York, 1984).

Mas'ud Zaverzadeh, *The Mythopoeic Reality* (Urbana, Chicago, London, 1976).

Heide Zeigler and Christopher Bigsby (eds.), *The Radical Imagination and the Liberal Tradition: Interviews with Contemporary English and American Novelists* (London, 1982).

NOTES ON AUTHORS

IRIS MURDOCH was born in Dublin in 1919 and educated at both Oxford and Cambridge. She entered the Civil Service in 1942, worked for UNRRA at the end of the war, and came under the influence of French philosophy, as she showed in her study *Sartre: Romantic Rationalist* (1953; recently revised and reissued). She then taught philosophy at St Anne's College, Oxford, before publishing, in 1954, her first novel *Under the Net*. Since then her career as one of Britain's major novelists has been as prolific as it has been distinguished. Some twenty-five novels, including *The Bell* (1958), *A Severed Head* (1961), *The Nice and the Good* (1968), *Bruno's Dream* (1969), *An Accidental Man* (1972), *The Black Prince* (1973), *Nuns and Soldiers* (1980), *The Philosopher's Pupil* (1983), and *The Book and the Brotherhood* (1987) show her extraordinary range and development. She has written several plays and philosophical studies, including *The Sovereignty of Good* (1970) and *The Fire and the Sun* (1977). Her work has won many prizes, including the Booker Prize for *The Sea, The Sea* in 1978; she is a Dame of the British Empire. The essay of 1961 reprinted here is her clearest statement on the nature of the novel.

PHILIP ROTH was born in Newark, New Jersey, in 1933 and educated at Bucknell College and the University of Chicago. One of the leading Jewish-American novelists of the postwar period, he established his career with *Goodbye, Columbus*, a novella and five stories which appeared in 1959 and won the National Book Award. Since then many novels, novellas and satires have appeared, including *Letting Go* (1962), *Portnoy's Complaint* (1969), *The Breast* (1972), *My Life as a Man* (1974), *The Professor of Desire* (1977), *The Ghost Writer* (1979), *Zuckerman Unbound* (1981), and *The Counterlife* (1986). In 1980 *A Philip Roth Reader* selected some of his most notable work, and his essays are collected in *Reading Myself and Others* (1975), which includes the essay reprinted here.

MICHEL BUTOR was born in 1926 at Mons en Barouel, France. He studied philosophy at the Sorbonne, taught in several countries, including England, and became Professor of Comparative Literature at the University of Geneva. His fiction is associated with the *nouveau roman*, and includes the novels *L'Emploi du Temps* (1957; translated as *Passing Time*), *La Modification* (*Second Thoughts*) (1957), and *Degrés* (*Degrees*) (1960). His intellectual influence as a critic is represented in his three volumes of essays *Repertoire I, II* and *III* (1960, 1964, 1968). These were part-reprinted in *Inventory: Essays* (1958), translated and edited by Richard Howard, from which the essay here is taken.

SAUL BELLOW, awarded the Nobel Prize for Literature in 1976, was born in Quebec in 1915. His immigrant Jewish family moved to Chicago, the setting of many of his novels, when he was nine. He studied at Chicago, Northwestern and Wisconsin universities, and published his first novel *Dangling Man* in 1944. Surely the leading postwar American novelist, his books include *The Victim* (1947), *The Adventures of Augie March* (1953), *Henderson the Rain King* (1959), *Herzog* (1964), *Humboldt's Gift* (1975), *The Dean's December* (1982) and *Some Die of Heartbreak* (1987). He holds honorary degrees from Harvard and Yale, and is a commander of the French Legion of Honour. He has also written several novellas, plays and short stories, and many influential essays.

JOHN BARTH was born in 1930 in Maryland and educated at Pennsylvania State University. He has taught at several American universities, including Buffalo and Johns Hopkins. An influential figure in 'postmodern' experiment in American fiction, his novels include *The Floating Opera* (1956), *The End of the Road* (1958), *The Sot-Weed Factor* (1960), *Giles Goat-Boy* (1966), *LETTERS* (1979), *Sabbatical* (1982) and *The Tidewater Tales* (1987). His *Lost in the Funhouse* (1968) offered 'fiction for print, tape, live voice', and his *Chimera* (1972), which won the National Book Award, contains three novellas going back to the origins of myth and narration. *The Friday Book* (1984) collects essays and other non-fiction, and reprints, in slightly different form, the essay here, along with Barth's comment that is often misread as a Swansong of Literature piece ('It isn't'). It can be usefully read against Barth's later (1980) piece 'The Literature of Replenishment', also in *The Friday Book*.

DAVID LODGE was born in London in 1935 and educated at University College, London. He joined the English Department of Birmingham University in 1960 and became Professor of English, retiring in 1987 to be a full-time writer (he retains the title of Honorary Professor of Modern English Literature). A prolific novelist and critic, his fiction includes *The Picturegoers* (1960), *The British Museum Is Falling Down* (1965), *Out of the Shelter* (1970), *Changing Places* (1975), *Small World* (1984) and *Nice Work* (1988). He is author of several volumes of important criticism of the novel, including *Language of Fiction* (1966), *The Novelist at the Crossroads* (1971), from which the essay here is taken, *The Modes of Modern Writing* (1977), and *Working With Structuralism* (1981).

FRANK KERMODE was formerly King Edward VII Professor of English at Cambridge University, and has taught in many universities in both Britain and the United States. A leading critic of Renaissance and modern literature, his books include *Romantic Image* (1957), *Puzzles and Epiphanies* (1963), *The Sense of an Ending* (1967), *Genesis of Secrecy* (1979), and *The Classic* (1983). He co-edited with Robert Alter *The Literary Guide to the Bible* (1987) and is editor of the Fontana Modern Masters series.

JOHN FOWLES was born in 1926 in Essex, read French and German at Oxford, and taught abroad for a time until the success of his novel *The Collector* (1963) allowed him to live by writing. Among the most powerful of postwar British novelists, he is author of *The Magus* (1965), *The French Lieutenant's Woman* (1969) which became a major film, *Daniel Martin* (1977), and *A Maggot* (1985). His stories are collected in *The Ebony Tower* (1974). He has written a good deal of criticism, especially of nineteenth-century fiction, as well as a speculative book *The Aristos* (1964). The essay here on the writing of his best-known book, *The French Lieutenant's Woman*, has been reprinted in various forms.

B. S. JOHNSON was born in 1933 in Hammersmith, went to King's College, London, and soon acquired the reputation of a striking and remarkable avant-garde novelist. His works of fiction include *Travelling People* (1963), *Albert Angelo* (1964), *The Unfortunates* (1969), a novel in a box, and *Christie Malry's Own Double-Entry*

(1973). He also wrote poetry, plays and television scripts, and directed in television. *Aren't You Rather Young to be Writing Your Memoirs?* is an experimental collection of short stories, the introduction to which is reprinted here. B. S. Johnson died suddenly in 1975.

DORIS LESSING was born in 1919 in Persia (now Iran) and when she was five moved with her family to Southern Rhodesia (now Zimbabwe) where she took an active interest in left-wing politics, and married twice. In 1949 she moved to London and published her first novel *The Grass Is Singing* (1950), beginning a remarkable fictional career. Her books include the 'Children of Violence' sequence beginning with *Martha Quest* (1952, 1954, 1958, etc.), and the remarkable *The Golden Notebook* (1962), from the reprint of which the essay here is taken. Other works include *Briefing for a Descent Into Hell* (1971), *The Memoirs of a Survivor* (1974), the 'Canopus in Argos' sequence, and *The Good Terrorist* (1985). She has written plays, verse, and many short stories, and received many literary honours.

IAN MCEWAN was born in 1948 and studied at the universities of Sussex and East Anglia, where he took an MA in Creative Writing. His first collection of short stories, *First Love, Last Rites* (1975) won the Somerset Maugham Award. A second volume, *In Between the Sheets*, appeared in 1979, and thereafter McEwan established himself as a leading figure in the younger generation of British novelists with *The Cement Garden* (1978), *The Comfort of Strangers* (1981), and *The Child in Time* (1987). He has also written television and screen plays and an oratorio.

MILAN KUNDERA was born in Brno, Czechoslovakia, in 1929. Despite struggles with the Communist Party, he became a professor at the Prague Institute for Advanced Cinematographic Studies, but lost his post after the 'Prague Spring' of 1968. In 1975 he settled in France and published *The Book of Laughter and Forgetting* (1980), a bitter, experimental satire which lost him his Czech citizenship. In 1985 Kundera published *The Unbearable Lightness of Being*, subsequently made into a remarkable film. Kundera, who is also an effective essayist, has been a potent influence on many Western writers for his teasing of historical and political certainties.

NOTES ON AUTHORS

ITALO CALVINO was born in Cuba in 1923 and grew up in San Remo, Italy. The leading Italian novelist of the postwar generation, he has been justly compared with Jorge Luis Borges and Gabriel Garcia Marquez for his discovery of innovative forms of fictional expression and his impact on the overall direction of contemporary fiction. His many works include *The Baron in the Trees* (1959), *Cosmicomics* (1965), *Invisible Cities* (1972), *The Castle of Crossed Destinies* (1973), *If On a Winter's Night a Traveller* ... (1979) and *Mr Palomar* (1983). He has published many essays, some collected in *The Literature Machine* (1987), from which the essay here is taken. Italo Calvino died in Rome in 1985.